W9-CCP-075

In this collection . . .

Benjamin Franklin stresses the importance of literacy in a piece taken from his autobiography.

Cotton Mather's firsthand record of the Salem witch trials exposes the dangers of religious fervor and fanaticism.

Gloria Steinem forwards her own inimitable brand of feminist individualism and freedom of choice.

Albert Einstein comments on education and its place in the future of human development.

Plus other commentaries and musings from some of the most important and famous figures in American history.

M. Jerry Weiss is the distinguished service professor of communications emeritus at New Jersey City University. He is the author or editor of numerous works on literature and education. **Helen S. Weiss** is a freelance author/editor. Together they have edited seven anthologies for young adult readers. They live in Upper Montclair, New Jersey.

THE SIGNET BOOK OF
AMERICAN ESSAYS

Edited by

M. Jerry Weiss
and Helen S. Weiss

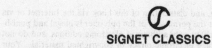

SIGNET CLASSICS

SIGNET CLASSICS
Published by New American Library, a division of
Penguin Group (USA) Inc., 375 Hudson Street,
New York, New York 10014, USA
Penguin Group (Canada), 90 Eglinton Avenue East, Suite 700, Toronto,
Ontario M4P 2Y3, Canada (a division of Pearson Penguin Canada Inc.)
Penguin Books Ltd., 80 Strand, London WC2R 0RL, England
Penguin Ireland, 25 St. Stephen's Green, Dublin 2,
Ireland (a division of Penguin Books Ltd.)
Penguin Group (Australia), 250 Camberwell Road, Camberwell, Victoria 3124,
Australia (a division of Pearson Australia Group Pty. Ltd.)
Penguin Books India Pvt. Ltd., 11 Community Centre, Panchsheel Park,
New Delhi - 110 017, India
Penguin Group (NZ), cnr Airborne and Rosedale Roads, Albany,
Auckland 1310, New Zealand (a division of Pearson New Zealand Ltd.)
Penguin Books (South Africa) (Pty.) Ltd., 24 Sturdee Avenue,
Rosebank, Johannesburg 2196, South Africa

Penguin Books Ltd., Registered Offices:
80 Strand, London WC2R 0RL, England

First published by Signet Classics, an imprint of New American Library,
a division of Penguin Group (USA) Inc.

First Printing, August 2006
10 9 8 7 6 5 4

For these creative people who have enriched many lives: Avi, T. A. Barron, Don Gallo, Paul B. Janeczko, Gordon Korman, Walter Dean Myers, and Jerry Spinelli.

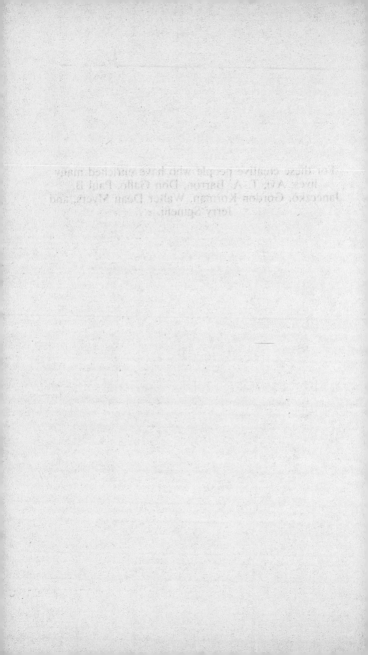

Contents

~~~

CONTENTS

Religious Fervor

Intellectual Freedom

Women Speak Out

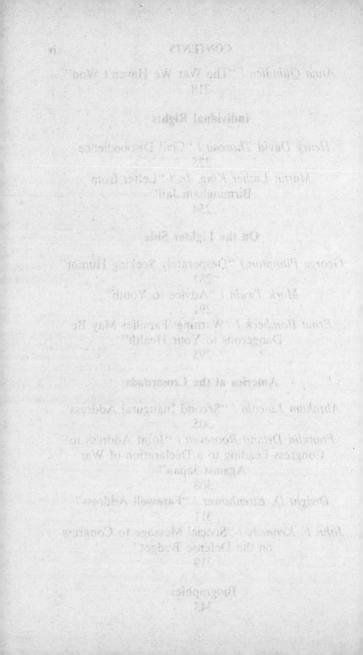

ACKNOWLEDGMENTS

With great appreciation, we give our thanks to the following for their valuable assistance:

Tracy Bernstein, our editor, who has encouraged and given us excellent advice.

The authors, editors, and agents for all of their cooperation and contributions.

Sam Rubin, archivist, John F. Kennedy Presidential Library.

Archivist at Dwight D. Eisenhower Presidential Library.

Archivist at Franklin D. Roosevelt Presidential Library.

Dan Lundy, Penguin Books (USA) Inc., for his continuous support.

Eileen B. Weiss and Sharon E. Weiss for their helpful information and services.

Introduction

In *A Handbook to Literature, Ninth Edition* (Prentice Hall, 2003), by William Harmon and Hugh Holman, the essay is defined as "a moderately brief prose description of a restricted topic." Of course, beyond that, the varieties are endless. Certain magazine and newspaper articles can be considered essays. There are technical and scholarly essays and personal narrative essays. Essays may make an argument, report facts, or discuss an issue. They vary widely in form, tone, and length.

However, as Harmon and Holman point out, essays can broadly be divided into "formal" and "informal" types. Formal essays are often written to persuade or report, and literary style may be of secondary importance. In contrast, informal essays are written primarily to entertain and tend to have a livelier and more personal style, as well as greater experimentation with form.

For this volume, we have selected a wide range of both formal and informal essays and have arranged them in the categories listed in the contents. This topical arrangement makes it easy to see that certain issues have arisen again and again in our history. If a certain topic strikes you as unimportant, consider that it may have deep significance to other readers just as it had for writers throughout the history of the United States. That is one purpose of essays, to make us think about our world. They help us to see other perspectives and to form, for better or worse, opinions. That is the power of reading. It is both personal and provocative.

We have drawn our selections from books, magazines, journals, letters, and speeches. We also asked some individuals to write original essays for us because of their positions, experiences, and knowledge of certain areas. We are extremely grateful to all the authors.

Political leaders, presidents and first ladies, teachers and activists, columnists, editors, and others—all of these writers, whether "classical" or "current," wrestle with issues relevant to us today. Our hope is that their essays provoke thought and discussion—and writing—in communities around this great country.

—M. Jerry Weiss
and Helen S. Weiss

ASPECTS OF
LITERACY

Benjamin Franklin

From THE AUTOBIOGRAPHY
(17??)

From a Child I was fond of Reading, and all the little Money that came into my Hands was ever laid out in Books. Pleas'd with the Pilgrim's Progress, my first Collection was of John Bunyan's Works, in separate little Volumes. I afterwards sold them to enable me to buy R. Burton's Historical Collections; they were small Chapmen's Books and cheap, 40 or 50 in all.—My Father's little Library consisted chiefly of Books in polemic Divinity, most of which I read, and have since often regretted, that at a time when I had such a Thirst for Knowledge, more proper Books had not fallen in my Way, since it was now resolv'd I should not be a Clergyman. Plutarch's Lives there was, in which I read abundantly, and I still think that time spent to great Advantage. There was also a Book of Defoe's called an Essay on Projects and another of Dr Mather's call'd Essays to do Good, which perhaps gave me a Turn of Thinking that had an Influence on some of the principal future Events of my Life.

This Bookish Inclination at length determin'd my Father to make me a Printer, tho' he had already one

Son, (James) of that Profession. In 1717 my Brother James return'd from England with a Press & Letters to set up his Business in Boston. I lik'd it much better than that of my Father, but still had a Hankering for the Sea.—To prevent the apprehended Effect of such an Inclination, my Father was impatient to have me bound to my Brother. I stood out some time, but at last was persuaded and signed the Indentures, when I was yet but 12 Years old.—I was to serve as an Apprentice till I was 21 Years of Age, only I was to be allow'd Journeyman's Wages during the last Year. In a little time I made great Proficiency in the Business, and became a useful Hand to my Brother. I now had Access to better Books. An Acquaintance with the Apprentices of Booksellers, enabled me sometimes to borrow a small one, which I was careful to return soon & clean. Often I sat up in my Room reading the greatest Part of the Night, when the Book was borrow'd in the Evening & to be return'd early in the Morning lest it should be miss'd or wanted.—And after some time an ingenious Tradesman* who had a pretty Collection of Books, & who frequented our Printing House, took Notice of me, invited me to his Library, & very kindly lent me such Books as I chose to read. I now took a Fancy to Poetry, and made some little Pieces. My Brother, thinking it might turn to account encourag'd me, & put me on composing two occasional Ballads. One was called the *Light House Tragedy,* & contain'd an Acc^t of the drowning of Capt. Worthilake with his Two Daughters; the other was a Sailor Song on the Taking of *Teach* or Blackbeard the Pirate. They were wretched Stuff, in the Grubstreet Ballad Stile, and when they were printed he sent me about the Town to sell them. The first sold

*Mr. Matthew Adams

wonderfully, the Event being recent, having made a great Noise. This flatter'd my Vanity. But my Father discourag'd me, by ridiculing my Performances, and telling me Verse-makers were generally Beggars; so I escap'd being a Poet, most probably a very bad one. But as Prose Writing has been a great Use to me in the Course of my Life, and was a principal Means of my Advancement, I shall tell you how in such a Situation I acquir'd what little Ability I have in that Way.

There was another Bookish Lad in the Town, John Collins by Name, with whom I was intimately acquainted. We sometimes disputed, and very fond we were of Argument, & very desirous of confuting one another. Which disputacious Turn, by the way, is apt to become a very bad Habit, making People often extreamly disagreable in Company, by the Contradiction that is necessary to bring it into Practice, & thence, besides souring & spoiling the Conversation, is productive of Disgusts & perhaps Enmities where you may have occasion for Friendship. I had caught it by reading my Father's Books of Dispute about Religion. Persons of good Sense, I have since observ'd, seldom fall into it, except Lawyers, University Men, and Men of all Sorts that have been bred at Edinborough. A Question was once some how or other started between Collins & me, of the Propriety of educating the Female Sex in Learning, & their Abilities for Study. He was of Opinion that it was improper; & that they were naturally unequal to it. I took the contrary Side, perhaps a little for Dispute sake. He was naturally more eloquent, had a ready Plenty of Words, and sometimes as I thought bore me down more by his Fluency than by the Strength of his Reasons. As we parted without settling the Point, & were not to see one another again for some time, I sat down to put my Arguments in Writing, which I copied fair &

sent to him. He answer'd & I reply'd. Three or four Letters of a Side had pass'd, when my Father happen'd to find my Papers, and read them. Without entring into the Discussion, he took occasion to talk to me about the Manner of my Writing, observ'd that tho' I had the Advantage of my Antagonist in correct Spelling & pointing (which I ow'd to the Printing House) I fell far short in elegance of Expression, in Method and in Perspicuity, of which he convinc'd me by several Instances. I saw the Justice of his Remarks, & thence grew more attentive to the *Manner* in Writing, and determin'd to endeavour at Improvement.—

About this time I met with an odd Volume of the Spectator. I had never before seen any of them. I bought it, read it over and over, and was much delighted with it. I thought the Writing excellent, & wish'd if possible to imitate it. With that View, I took some of the Papers, & making short Hints of the Sentiment in each Sentence, laid them by a few Days, and then without looking at the Book, try'd to compleat the Papers again, by expressing each hinted Sentiment at length & as fully as it had been express'd before, in any suitable Words that should come to hand.

Then I compar'd my Spectator with the Original, discover'd some of my Faults & corrected them. But I found I wanted a Stock of Words or a Readiness in recollecting & using them, which I thought I should have acquir'd before that time, if I had gone on making Verses, since the continual Occasion for Words of the same Import but of different Length, to suit the Measure, or of different Sound for the Rhyme, would have laid me under a constant Necessity of searching for Variety, and also have tended to fix that Variety in my Mind, & make me Master of it. Therefore I took some of the Tales & turn'd them into Verse:

And after a time, when I had pretty well forgotten the Prose, turn'd them back again. I also sometimes jumbled my Collections of Hints into Confusion, and after some Weeks, endeavour'd to reduce them into the best Order, before I began to form the full Sentences & compleat the Paper. This was to teach me Method in the Arrangement of Thoughts. By comparing my Work afterwards with the original, I discover'd many faults and amended them; but I sometimes had the Pleasure of Fancying that in certain Particulars of small Import, I had been lucky enough to improve the Method or the Language and this encourag'd me to think I might possibly in time come to be a tolerable English Writer, of which I was extreamly ambitious.

My Time for these Exercises & for Reading, was at Night after Work, or before Work began in the Morning; or on Sundays when I contrived to be in the Printing House alone, evading as much as I could the common Attendance on publick Worship, which my Father used to exact of me when I was under his Care:—And which indeed I still thought a Duty; tho' I could not, as it seemed to me, afford the Time to practise it.

When about 16 Years of Age, I happen'd to meet with a Book written by one Tryon, recommending a Vegetable diet. I determined to go into it. My Brother being yet unmarried, did not keep House, but boarded himself & his Apprentices in another Family. My refusing to eat Flesh occasioned an Inconveniency, and I was frequently chid for my singularity. I made my self acquainted with Tryon's Manner of preparing some of his Dishes, such as Boiling Potatoes, or Rice, making Hasty Pudding, & a few others, and then propos'd to my Brother, that if he would give me Weekly half the Money he paid for my Board, I would board my self. He instantly agreed to it, and I presently

found that I could save half what he paid me. This
was an additional Fund for buying Books: But I had
another Advantage in it. My Brother and the rest
going from the Printing House to their Meals, I remain'd there alone, and dispatching presently my light
Repast (which often was no more than a Bisket or a
Slice of Bread, a Handful of Raisins or a Tart from
the Pastry Cook's, and a Glass of Water) had the rest
of the Time till their Return, for Study, in which I
made the greater Progress from that greater Clearness
of Head & quicker Apprehension which usually attend
Temperance in Eating & Drinking. And now it was
that being on some Occasion made asham'd of my
Ignorance in Figures, which I had twice fail'd in learning when at School, I took Cocker's Book of Arithme-
tick, & went thro' the whole by my self with great
Ease.—I also read Seller's & Sturmy's Books of Navigation, & became acquainted with the little Geometry
they contain, but never proceeded far in that Science.—
And I read about this Time Locke on Human Understanding and the Art of Thinking by Messrs du Port
Royal.

While I was intent on improving my Language, I
met with an English Grammar (I think it was Green-
wood's) at the End of which there were two little
Sketches of the Arts of Rhetoric and Logic, the latter
finishing with a Specimen of a Dispute in the Socratic
Method. And soon after I procur'd Xenophon's Memorable Things of Socrates, wherein there are many
Instances of the same Method. I was charm'd with it,
adopted it, dropt my abrupt Contradiction, and positive Argumentation, and put on the humble En-
quirer & Doubter. And being then, from reading
Shaftsbury & Collins, become a real Doubter in many
Points of our Religious Doctrine, I found this Method
safest for my self & very embarrassing to those against

whom I used it, therefore I took a Delight in it, prac-
tis'd it continually & grew very artful & expert in
drawing People even of superior Knowledge into Con-
cessions the Consequences of which they did not fore-
see, entangling them in Difficulties out of which they
could not extricate themselves, and so obtaining Victo-
ries that neither my self nor my Cause always deserved.—I continu'd this Method some few Years, but
gradually left it, retaining only the Habit of expressing
my self in Terms of modest Diffidence, never using
when I advance any thing that may possibly be disputed, the Words, *Certainly, undoubtedly,* or any others that give the Air of Positiveness to an Opinion;
but rather say, *I conceive,* or *I apprehend* a Thing to
be so or so, *It appears to me,* or *I should think it so
or so for such & such Reasons,* or *I imagine* it to be
so, or *it is so* if *I am not mistaken.*—This Habit I
believe has been of great Advantage to me, when I
have had occasion to inculcate my Opinions & persuade Men into Measures that I have been from time
to time engag'd in promoting.—And as the chief Ends
of Conversation are to *inform,* or to be *informed,* to
please or to *persuade,* I wish well meaning sensible
Men would not lessen their Power of doing Good by
a Positive assuming Manner that seldom fails to disgust, tends to create Opposition, and to defeat every
one of those Purposes for which Speech was given us,
to wit, giving or receiving Information, or Pleasure:
For If you would *inform,* a positive dogmatical Manner in advancing your Sentiments, may provoke Contradiction & prevent a candid Attention. If you wish
Information & Improvement from the Knowledge of
others and yet at the same time express your self as
firmly fix'd in your present Opinions, modest sensible
Men, who do not love Disputation, will probably leave
you undisturb'd in the Possession of your Error; and

by such a Manner you can seldom hope to recommend
your self in *pleasing* your Hearers, or to persuade
those whose Concurrence you desire.—Pope says,
judiciously,

> *Men should be taught as if you taught them not,*
> *And things unknown propos'd as things forgot,—*

farther recommending it to us,

> *To speak tho' sure, with seeming Diffidence.*

And he might have coupl'd with this Line that which
he has coupled with another, I think less properly,

> *For want of Modesty is want of Sense.*

If you ask why *less properly,* I must repeat the Lines;

> "Immodest Words admit of *no* Defence;
> "*For* Want of Modesty is Want of Sense."

Now is not *Want of Sense,* (where a Man is so unfortunate as to want it) some Apology for his *Want of
Modesty*? and would not the Lines stand more justly
thus?

> Immodest Words admit *but this* Defence,
> That Want of Modesty is Want of Sense.

This however I should submit to better Judgments.—

Katherine Paterson

Why?
(1989)

There is a question that I get everywhere I go these days. The question is, Why do you write for children? Although it's a question I'm constantly being asked, it is one for which I have never had an adequate response. Perhaps, I thought, if I write a speech about it, I might figure out for myself why I write for children.

But it's not easy to begin. You see, I not only don't know why I write for children, I don't know why I became a writer at all. I never meant to be a writer. When budding young novelists of ten or eleven ask me, "When did you first know that you wanted to be a writer?" I feel rather embarrassed to admit that I was already a writer and well past my thirtieth birthday before I realized that a writer was indeed what I wanted to be when I grew up.

I wrote as a child but I certainly didn't plan to be a writer. I loved books, and I read a great deal, but I never imagined that I might write them. Actually, when I was nine, I had a dual fantasy life in which on some days I was the leader of a group of commandos

11

saving the world from Axis domination, and on others I was the benevolent queen of the United States of America. Of course, I indulged in these grandiose fantasies because I was finding the real world a tough place to inhabit.

Once, over lunch with another children's writer, we found ourselves exchanging schooldays horror stories. But, unlike me, Beth was a gutsy little kid. She fought back. She wrote to Ann Landers complaining about her sixth-grade teacher. When the teacher went into her desk, found the letter, opened the sealed and stamped envelope, and read it, Beth dragged her down to the principal's office on the charge of interfering with the U.S. mails, which eleven-year-old Beth knew to be a federal offense. And do you know what the principal said? To the teacher, mind you? "You are out of line."

I loved it. If I'd had sense enough to fantasize that scene it would have beaten out the royal pretensions and military triumphs in nothing flat.

"Why do you write children's books?" I asked her. "You don't have any childhood problems that need working out. You did it on the spot."

Well, there, I've let it slip. Yes, I probably do still have lots of childhood goblins that need exorcising. How could I ever deny the connection between James Johnson's troubled life at General Douglas MacArthur Elementary School and certain bleak days in my own past?

I worry about Mr. Dolman a lot. I, too, have been a teacher. And I know, with the rarest of exceptions, that teachers do not see with the eyes of a child. I still remember a child I taught once and wonder if he thought of me the way James thinks of Mr. Dolman. I didn't intend to humiliate him. I was just trying to jog him to be a little more responsible. It is not a memory I wish to dwell upon.

Now that I have been a parent and a writer as well as a child, I seem always to be on the child's side. But I know that children are not fair. They do not see either their teachers or their parents objectively. They only see from their own limited vision. When I write for children I try not only to be true to a child's point of view but I try as well to give hints that the world is wider than it seems to a child, and that other people may be more complex and even more understanding and compassionate than the child character sees them to be.

For a writer to succeed in this attempt, however, demands the cooperation of a careful and perceptive reader. There are those who think that a writer for children should not ask for this level of wisdom from her readers. Maybe not. But I don't seem able to write in any other way, and I have been very fortunate in the readers who choose my books. A great number of them seem not only willing to dig below the surface, they seem eager to. "I didn't catch on the first time I read it, but when I read it again . . ." is a refrain I hear surprisingly often. And, I must say, it is music to a writer's ears.

Why do you write for children? In the past year, I've begun to answer the question defensively. When someone asks "Why?" my response has been "Why not?" Because it has begun to occur to me that it is the implied objection that needs defending, not my choice of audience.

Why not write for children? If I became a writer for children more or less accidentally, I soon learned that I had stumbled into what was for me the world's best job—perhaps, as I say to my husband, the only job I'd be able to keep.

Any free-lance writer has the opportunity of choosing her own subjects and her own work methods and schedule, but I, as a writer for children, have an even more enviable situation. I know when I spend a year, two years, or more on a book, that I will be sending it to people who value books. Their first question is not, "How can we turn this manuscript into a property that will make money for us?" but, "How can we turn this manuscript into a book that children will want to read?"

I know that the book I have written will be carefully, even lovingly edited and copyedited. If a book is to have illustrations, I know that a lot of thought will be given to selecting an appropriate illustrator. Whether the book is illustrated or not, a designer will make sure that its look will be satisfying. I have had books where jacket illustration after jacket illustration was rejected because it didn't reflect what my editor felt was the heart of the story. Other houses may have different philosophies, but at the houses where I have been fortunate enough to work, it is the book itself that is of primary importance, not any subsidiary sales that it might eventually bring to the publisher.

My publishing houses have known that it takes time for a children's book to find its readers, and they are willing to keep a book in print long enough for that to happen. I have friends who write novels for adults who find their books on a remainder table in less than six months of their original publication. An adult novel is declared a best-seller before it is published by dint of advertising dollars and prepublication sales to chain bookstores and paperback and movie contracts. A child's book becomes a best-seller because it is read and loved by hundreds of thousands of children who literally wear out the originally published copies.

Still, people seem to think that a writer who is any

good at all is wasting her efforts writing exclusively for children. "No one will ever take you seriously," I'm told by speakers who do not even realize that they have just relegated to nonpersonhood not only me but all the children who read my books and take them quite seriously. But that's because in this country we refuse to take children seriously.

In 1981 I was invited to the Polish Embassy, and the ambassador awarded me a medal presented to *Bridge to Terabithia* by the Polish section of the International Board on Books for Young People in honor of Janusz Korczak.

"I need to explain to you about this man," the ambassador said. And during the informal ceremony in the embassy parlor he talked of Korczak, who was one of the first people in Europe to be concerned about the nurture, education, and psychology of children. He was a director of two orphanages in the city of Warsaw—one Jewish, the other gentile. When the Germans invaded he was given a chance to escape the country, but he chose to move into the ghetto with his Jewish orphans, and when they were taken to Treblinka, he went with them. At the train station, he took two children by the hand. The rest followed him, heads held high, into the boxcar. It is told that the guards from the ghetto saluted as he passed.

"I cannot claim," the ambassador went on, "that my father and Dr. Korczak were friends, but my father, too, taught pedagogy at the University of Warsaw, so they were colleagues. And since my father also died violently during the occupation, I always think of them together."

In November 1981, Poland was in turmoil. There were food riots in Warsaw on the same day that I was given the medal and had a leisurely lunch with the ambassador. Three weeks later, Ambassador Spasowski resigned his post and defected in order, he said, "to show my solidarity with the Polish people." I suppose that awarding that medal honoring a children's psychologist and protector to a writer of a book for children was among his last official acts.

I'll never forget that day. Nor will I forget the commentary on it made by a friend of mine. "What other country do you know of," she asked, "that has for a hero someone who gave his life for children?"

You see, we are not accustomed to taking children that seriously. That's why we call a school lunch program a frill and weapons, necessities. That's why we can mortgage our children's future with an unbelievable deficit and casually poison the environment in which they will have to live.

Can you begin to imagine the difference it would make to the present and to the future of the world if we were to begin to take children seriously? For one thing, we would respect the adults who care for and educate children. At the very least we would make sure they were carefully selected, rigorously trained, and generously compensated.

I don't need to tell you how far from the real world such fantasies are, but at least those of us who do take children seriously should stop apologizing for what we do. "I am only a teacher." "I am only a librarian." "I am only a mother." "I only write for children." We've let the rest of our society sell us cheap. And in so doing we've betrayed the children entrusted to our care and nurture.

The scientist Jacob Bronowski was one of those rare people who take children seriously. The final chapter of his book *The Ascent of Man* is titled "The Long Childhood." Bronowski argued that it is our long childhood that has made us not only unique in nature but that has allowed us to develop civilization. For most of human history, you see, there was no distinct period called childhood. In the nomad tribes of Persia, for example, the girls are already little mothers and the boys little herdsmen. What distinguishes nomadic life from what we consider civilization is the long childhood. The time and opportunity for the young to learn not only how to imitate the parent—animals do that—but a time for the child to develop strategies for life, values to live by.

Looking at the great civilizations of China, India, and Europe in the Middle Ages, Bronowski declares that by one test they all fail: "They limit the freedom of the imagination of the young."

And what of us? We have been willing to risk bankruptcy of the wealthiest nation in the world to build weapons of mass destruction, but we have pled poverty when it comes to nurturing the imaginations of our young. We don't have the money to buy books, we don't have the money for breakfasts or lunches that will fuel their brains as well as their bodies. "A mind is a terrible thing to waste," an ad for The United Negro College Fund tells us, but we continue to do so because we don't take children seriously.

But maybe it's more than that. Perhaps we are afraid of what might happen should the young truly begin to think. We've seen it in history over and over. Socrates in Athens, Sir Thomas More in England, Janusz Korczak in Warsaw, Gandhi in India, Jesus in Jerusalem, King in Memphis. They will grow up, you see, and question us. They will push back the boundaries of our knowledge, they will wonder aloud about the foundations on which we have built our power. And we can't risk that, can we?

I stopped in the middle of writing this to watch a few minutes of Oliver North's testimony before the congressional hearing. What he was saying to me was that he had to shred those documents because they might fall into enemy hands. But in his definition, you and I are the enemy. Anyone who might question the absolute rightness of what he was doing would be the enemy. Our nation, more and more, treats its citizens the way we treat our children. Those in power are the experts who cannot risk sharing with the ordinary their special knowledge—that knowledge which, if they were at liberty to share, would explain why they were above the law that they expect you and me to obey. This in the two hundredth year of the birth of the Constitution, which of all human documents regards the intelligence and judgment of ordinary people with the most respect and says that no one is above the law that governs everyone.

It's interesting how often people say to me, "Well, of course, your books aren't really for children," and think, thereby, that they have complimented me. Actually, my books are for anyone who is kind enough to read them. The great majority of those readers are, have been, and I profoundly hope will continue to be under the age of fourteen.

I got a letter once from a troubled child who poured out her anguish over her parents' divorce and her own subsequent behavior. "When I read *Gilly Hopkins*," she said, "I realized that you were the only person in the world who could understand how I feel." Poor child, I thought, not even I understand how you feel.

And as much as you and I wish to spare our children pain and so try to pretend to ourselves that they cannot feel as deeply as we, they do hurt, they do fear, they do grieve; and even when we cannot fully understand, we who care for them must take these feelings seriously.

Gerard Manley Hopkins captures what I am trying

to say in his poem "Spring and Fall: To a Young Child":

> Márgarét, are you gríeving
> Over Goldengrove unleaving?
> Leáves, like the things of man, you
> With your fresh thoughts care for, can you?
> Áh! ás the heart grows older
> It will come to such sights colder
> By and by, nor spare a sigh
> Though worlds of wanwood leafmeal lie;
> And yet you *will* weep and know why.
> Now no matter, child, the name:
> Sórrow's spríngs áre the same.
> Nor mouth had, no nor mind, expressed
> What heart heard of, ghost guessed:
> It ís the blight man was born for,
> It is Margaret you mourn for.

When the child mourns the falling of the leaves in autumn, the poet says, she is unknowingly mourning the brevity, the frailty, of her own life in the world. Now, the child cannot articulate this. She hasn't the words or the experience, but she has the feelings. She does weep without fully understanding why. "Áh! ás the heart grows older / It will come to such sights colder. . . ." Those of us who write for the young choose the passionate heart over the cold intellect every time.

Let me read you a poem written by a twelve-year-old girl in response to *Bridge to Terabithia*:

As the stubborn stream swirls and pulls out a song,
The hillside stands in the cold dark sky.
Over the hillside stands a lonely palace.

Before it shook with joy
   But now its queen is dead
So the sour sweet wind blows the tassels of the weak
   rope,
And the tree mourns and scolds the rope,
Saying "Couldn't you have held on a little longer?"

Why do I write for children? I'm practicing. Someday, if I keep working at it, I may write a book worthy of such a reader.

Eudora Welty

WRITING AND ANALYZING
A STORY
(1955)

Writers are often asked to give their own analysis of some story they have published. I never saw, as reader or writer, that a finished story stood in need of any more from the author: for better or worse, there the story is. There is also the question of whether or not the author could provide the sort of analysis asked for. Story writing and critical analysis are indeed separate gifts, like spelling and playing the flute, and the same writer proficient in both has been doubly endowed. But even he can't rise and do both at the same time.

To me as a story writer, generalizations about writing come tardily and uneasily, and I would limit them, if I were wise, by saying that any conclusions I feel confidence in are stuck to the particular story, part of the animal. The most trustworthy lesson I've learned from work so far is the simple one that the writing of each story is sure to open up a different prospect and pose a new problem; and that no past story bears recognizably on a new one or gives any promise of help, even if the writing mind had room for help and the wish that it would come. Help offered from outside the frame of the story would be itself an intrusion.

It's hard for me to believe that a writer's stories, taken in their whole, are written in any typical, predictable, systematically developing, or even chronological way—for all that a serious writer's stories are ultimately, to any reader, so clearly identifiable as his. Each story, it seems to me, thrives in the course of being written only as long as it seems to have a life of its own.

Yet it may become clear to a writer in retrospect (or so it did to me, although I may have been simply tardy to see it) that his stories have repeated themselves in shadowy ways, that they have returned and may return in future too—in variations—to certain themes. They may be following, in their own development, some pattern that's been very early laid down. Of course, such a pattern is subjective in nature; it may lie too deep to be consciously recognized until a cycle of stories and the actions of time have raised it to view. All the same, it is a pattern of which a new story is not another copy but a fresh attempt made in its own full-bodied right and out of its own impulse, with its own pressure, and its own needs of fulfillment.

It seems likely that all of one writer's stories do tend to spring from the same source within him. However they differ in theme or approach, however they vary in mood or fluctuate in their strength, their power to reach the mind or heart, all of one writer's stories carry their signature because of the one impulse most characteristic of his own gift—to praise, to love, to call up into view. But then, what countless stories by what countless authors share a common source! For the source of the short story is usually lyrical. And all writers speak from, and speak to, emotions eternally the same in all of us: love, pity, terror do not show favorites or leave any of us out.

The tracking down of a story might do well to start not in the subjective country but in the world itself. What in this world leads back most directly, makes the clearest connection to these emotions? What is the pull on the line? For some outside signal has startled or moved the story-writing mind to complicity: some certain irresistible, alarming (pleasurable or disturbing), magnetic person, place or thing. The outside world and the writer's response to it, the story's quotients, are always different, always differing in the combining; they are always—or so it seems to me—most intimately connected with each other.

This living connection is one that by its nature is not very open to generalization or discoverable by the ordinary scrutinies of analysis. Never mind; for its existence is, for any purpose but that of the working writer, of little importance to the story itself. It is of merely personal importance. But it is of extraordinary, if temporary, use to the writer for the particular story. Keeping this connection close is a writer's testing device along the way, flexible, delicate, precise, a means of guidance. I would rather submit a story to the test of its outside world, to show what it was doing and how it went about it, than to the method of critical analysis which would pick the story up by its heels (as if it had swallowed a button) to examine the writing process as analysis in reverse, as though a story—or any system of feeling—could be more accessible to understanding for being hung upside down.

It is not from criticism but from this world that stories come in the beginning; their origins are living reference plain to the writer's eye, even though to his eye alone. The writer's mind and heart, where all this exterior is continually *becoming* something—the moral, the passionate, the poetic, hence the *shaping* idea—can't be mapped and plotted. (Would this help—any more than a map hung on the wall changes the world?) It's the form it takes when it comes out the other side, of course, that gives a story something unique—its life. The story, in the way it has arrived at what it is on the page, has been something learned, by dint of the story's challenge and the work that rises to meet it—a process as uncharted for the writer as if it had never been attempted before.

Since analysis has to travel backward, the path it goes is an ever-narrowing one, whose goal is the vanishing point, beyond which only "influences" lie. But the writer of the story, bound in the opposite direction, works into the open. The choices multiply, become more complicated and with more hanging on them, as with everything else that has a life and moves. "This story promises me fear and joy and so I write it" has been the writer's beginning. The critic, coming to the end of his trail, may call out the starting point he's found, but the writer knew his starting point first and for what it was—the jumping-off place. And all along, the character of the choices—the critic's decisions and the writer's—is wholly different. I think that the writer's outbound choices were to him the *believable* ones, not necessarily defensible on other grounds; impelled, not subject to scheme but to feeling; that they came with an arrow inside them. They have been *fiction's* choices: one-way and fateful; strict as art, obliged as feeling, powerful in their authenticity.

The story and its analysis are not mirror-opposites of each other. They are not reflections, either one. Criticism indeed is an art, as a story is, but only the story is to some degree a vision; there is no explanation outside fiction for what its writer is learning to do. The simplest-appearing work may have been brought off (when it does not fail) on the sharp edge of experiment, and it was for this its writer was happy to leave behind him all he knew before, and the safety of that, when he began the new story.

I feel that our ever-changing outside world and some learnable lessons about writing fiction are always waiting side by side for us to put into connection, if we can. A writer should say this only of himself and offer an example. In a story I wrote recently called "No Place for You, My Love," the outside world—a definite place in it, of course—not only suggested how to write it but repudiated a way I had already tried. What follows has no claim to be critical analysis; it can be called a piece of hindsight from a working point of view.

What changed my story was a trip. I was invited to drive with an acquaintance, one summer day, down south of New Orleans to see that country for the first (and so far, only) time; and when I got back home, full of the landscape I'd seen, I realized that without being aware of it at the time, I had treated the story to my ride, and it had come into my head in an altogether new form. I set to work and wrote the new version from scratch.

As first written, the story told, in subjective terms, of a girl in a claustrophobic predicament: she was caught fast in the over-familiar, monotonous life of her small town, and immobilized further by a prolonged and hopeless love affair; she could see no way out. As a result of my ride, I extricated—not the girl, but the story.

This character had been well sealed inside her world, by nature and circumstance, just where I'd put her. But she was sealed in to the detriment of the story, because I'd made hers the point of view. The primary step now was getting outside her mind; on that instant I made her a girl from the Middle West. (She'd been before what I knew best, a Southerner.) I kept outside her by taking glimpses of her through the eyes of a total stranger: casting off the half-dozen familiars the first girl had around her, I invented a single new character, a man whom I brought into the story *to be* a stranger, and I was to keep out of his mind, too. I had double-locked the doors behind me.

It would have been for nothing had the original impulse behind the story not proved itself alive; it now took on new energy. That country—that once-submerged, strange land of "south from South"—which had so stamped itself upon my imagination put in an unmistakable claim now as the very image of the story's predicament. It pointed out to me at the same time where the real point of view belonged. Once I'd escaped those characters' minds, I saw it was outside them—suspended, hung in the air between two people, fished alive from the surrounding scene. As I wrote further into the story, something more real, more essential, than the characters were on their own was revealing itself. In effect, though the characters numbered only two, there had come to be a sort of third character along on the ride—the presence of a relationship between the two. It was what grew up between them meeting as strangers, went on the excursion with them, nodded back and forth from one to the other—listening, watching, persuading or denying them, enlarging or diminishing them, forgetful sometimes of why they were or what they were doing here—in its domain—and helping or betraying them along.

(Here I think it perhaps should be remembered that characters in a short story have not the size and importance and capacity for development they have in a novel, but are subservient altogether to the story as a whole.)

This third character's role was that of hypnosis—it was what a relationship *can do,* be it however brief, tentative, potential, happy or sinister, ordinary or extraordinary. I wanted to suggest that its being took shape as the strange, compulsive journey itself, was palpable as its climate and mood, the heat of the day—but was its spirit too, a spirit that held territory, that which is seen fleeting past by two vulnerable people who might seize hands on the run. There are moments in the story when I say neither "she felt" nor "he felt" but "they felt."

This is to grant that I rode out of the old story on the back of the girl and then threw away the girl; but I saved my story, for, entirely different as the second version was, it was what I wanted to tell. Now my subject was out in the open, provided at the same time with a place to happen and a way to say it was happening. All I had to do was recognize it, which I did a little late.

Anyone who has visited the actual scene of this story will possibly recognize it when he meets it here, for the story is visual and the place is out of the ordinary. The connection between a story and its setting may not always be so plain. For no matter whether the "likeness" is there for all to see or not, the place, once entered into the writer's mind in a story, is, in the course of writing the story, *functional.*

Thus I wanted to make seen and believed what was to me, in my story's grip, literally apparent—that secret and shadow are taken away in this country by the merciless light that prevails there, by the river that is like an exposed vein of ore, the road that descends as one with the heat—its nerve (these are all terms in the story), and that the heat is also a visual illusion, shimmering and dancing over the waste that stretches ahead. I was writing of a real place, but doing so in order to write about my subject. I was writing of exposure, and the shock of the world; in the end I tried to make the story's inside outside and then leave the shell behind.

The vain courting of imperviousness in the face of exposure is this little story's plot. Deliver us all from the naked in heart, the girl thinks (this is what I kept of her). "So strangeness gently steels us," I read today in a poem of Richard Wilbur's. Riding down together into strange country is danger, a play at danger, secretly poetic, and the characters, in attempting it as a mutual feat, admit nothing to each other except the wicked heat and its comical inconvenience. The only time they will yield or touch is while they are dancing in the crowd that to them is comically unlikely (hence insulating, non-conducting) or taking a kiss outside time. Nevertheless it happens that they go along aware, from moment to moment, as one: as my third character, the straining, hallucinatory eyes and ears, the roused-up sentient being of that place. Exposure begins in intuition; and the intuition comes to its end in showing the heart that has expected, while it dreads, that exposure. Writing it as I'd done before, as a story of concealment, in terms of the hermetic and the familiar, had somehow resulted in my own effective concealment of what I meant to show.

Now, the place had suggested to me that something demoniac was called for—the speed of the ride pitted against the danger of an easy or conventionally tempting sympathy, the heat that in itself drives on the driver in the face of an inimical world. Something wilder than ordinary communication between well-disposed strangers, and more ruthless and more tender, more pressing and acute, than their automatic, saving ironies and graces, I felt, and do so often feel, has to come up against a world like that.

I did my best to merge, or even to identify, the abstract with the concrete as it became possible in this story—where setting, characters, mood, and method of writing all worked as parts of the same thing and subject to related laws and conditionings. The story *had* to be self-evident, and to hold its speed to the end—a speed I think of as racing, though it may not seem so to the reader.

Above all, I had no wish to sound mystical, but I admit that I did expect to sound mysterious now and then, if I could: this was a circumstantial, realistic story in which the reality *was* mystery. The cry that rose up at the story's end was, I hope unmistakably, the cry of that doomed relationship—personal, mortal, psychic— admitted in order to be denied, a cry that the characters were first able (and prone) to listen to, and then able in part to ignore. The cry was authentic to my story: the end of a journey *can* set up a cry, the shallowest provocation to sympathy and love does hate to give up the ghost. A relationship of the most fleeting kind has the power inherent to loom like a genie—to become vocative at the last, as it has already become present and taken up room; as it has spread out as a destination however unlikely; as it has glimmered and rushed by in the dark and dust outside, showing occasional points of fire. Relationship *is* a pervading and changing mystery; it is not words that make it so in life, but words have to make it so in a story. Brutal or lovely, the mystery waits for people wherever they go, whatever extreme they run to.

I had got back at the end of the new story to suggesting what I had taken as the point of departure in the old, but there was no question in my mind which story was nearer the mark of my intention. This may not reflect very well on the brightness of the author at work; it may cause a reader to wonder how often a story has to rescue itself. I think it goes to show, all the same, that subject, method, form, style, all wait upon—indeed hang upon—a sort of double thunder-clap at the author's ears: the break of the living world upon what is already stirring inside the mind, and the answering impulse that in a moment of high conscious-ness fuses impact and image and fires them off to-gether. There never really was a sound, but the impact is always recognizable, granting the author's sensitivity and sense; and if the impulse so projected is to some degree fulfilled, it may give some pleasure in its course to the writer and reader. The living world itself re-mains just the same as it always was, and luckily enough for the story, among other things, for it can test and talk back to the story any day in the week. Between the writer and the story he writes, *there* is the undying third character.

Sam Pickering

COMPOSING A LIFE

(1985)

Last month I received a letter that began, "Are you the Samuel Pickering that went to Sewanee twenty years ago?" I did not know how to answer the letter. A boy with my name once attended college at Sewanee, and although I knew him fairly well and think I liked him, that boy had long since disappeared. Some good things happened to him at college, and I have often considered writing about them. The trouble is that I am not sure if the things I remember actually happened. Did that boy actually carry a hammer into Professor Martin's class one day, and when an old roommate Jimmy asked why he had it, did that boy really say, "For nailing hands to desks." And did he tell Jimmy to flatten his hand out on the desk if he did not believe him—whereupon, trusting a friend, Jimmy did so. Shortly afterwards when Professor Martin asked Jimmy why he had screamed, did Jimmy answer, "Pickering hit me with a hammer"? And did that boy stand up and say, "I cannot tell a lie; I hit him with my little hammer."

No, no—the person who I have become certainly

didn't do that. This person lives in a world without Jimmys, hammers, screams, and exclamation points. For fifteen years I have taught writing. For ten of these years writing has taught me, and I have labored not so much to compose sentences as to compose my life. Hours at the desk and countless erasures have brought success. I haven't committed a comma blunder in almost five years, certainly not since I married Vicki. Happily I have forgotten what participles and gerunds are, but then I have forgotten most things: books, loves, and most of my identities. At my dining room table, dangling modifiers are not mentioned, and I ignore all question marks as my days are composed, not of lurid prose and purple moments, but of calm of mind and forthright, workaday sentences.

Rarely do I use a complex sentence, and even more rarely do I live with complexity. In a simple style I write about simple people, people born before the first infinitive was split and the wrath of grammarians fell upon mankind. Occasionally I write about a small town in Virginia where I spent summers as a boy. In the center of the town was the railway station. Clustered about it were the bank and post office, Ankenbauer's Café and Horace Vickery's store. Mr. Vickery was a big man; alongside him, his wife, whom he called "Little Bitty Bird," seemed no larger than a sparrow. Mrs. Vickery spent her days in the domestic nest over the store where she delighted in rearranging furniture. One night Mr. Vickery returned home late from a meeting of the Masons; and if the truth be known, he came home a trifle "happy." Not wanting to wake Mrs. Vickery, he did not turn on the bedroom light. He undressed in the dark and after hanging his clothes up, silently slipped into his pajamas then leaned over to get into bed. Alas, the bed was not where he remembered it; Mrs. Vickery had spent the evening moving furniture, and as Mr. Vickery reached to pull back the covers, he fell to the floor in a great heap. "Oh, Little Bitty Bird," he sang out once he got his breath, "what have you done?"

By rearranging her few possessions Mrs. Vickery was able to create new worlds for herself. Distant places did not appeal to her, and when her husband took the day train to Richmond, seventeen miles away, she stayed home, content to shift a chair or dresser. As I think about Mrs. Vickery now, her life seems almost ideal. In my seven years in eastern Connecticut, I have lived simply, rarely traveling to Hartford thirty miles away. Years ago simplicity held little attraction for me, and I traveled far afield seeking the confusion of mixed metaphors and long, run-on sentences. Dashes marked my days, and I dreamed of breaking through the tried and the safe into the unknown. Once in Baku on the Caspian Sea, Soviet police dogged my footsteps, and I retreated into the twisting byways of the old town where I would suddenly disappear and then just as suddenly reappear, much to my pleasure and, as I thought, to the amazement of the police. When I began to write, I was taught to vary my style. "Use different sentence structures; be different people," teachers told me. And for a while I did that, meandering along slowly then darting forward only to turn back abruptly like the boy in Baku. Here I would insert a compound sentence, there a noun clause, here a gray man of mystery, there a colorful eccentric. For years experimenting was good, and although I didn't publish much, I had many styles and identities. Now the older and simpler me stays home, and as my car is a family station wagon—an American-made Plymouth Reliant—I have only one style, the solid, economical, fifty-thousand-mile-warranteed reliable style of the short declarative sentence.

Other kinds of sentences offend me and seem unsound and unsettling. Words, rules, and life confuse people. The simple style orders confusion, at first producing the illusion of control and then, after time, the reality. When pressure makes a person bear down so hard that he or his pencil breaks, he should struggle to write simply. By doing so one can regain composure. For years shots made me faint, and I shuddered whenever I entered a doctor's office. Then one day I found myself in a small room waiting for a blood test while another man sat on a couch outside. When the nurse appeared and saw me and the man outside, she called a companion on the telephone. "Mary," she said, "you better come down. There's two here waiting to be stuck. I'll stick the one inside, and you stick the one outside." What a wondrously insensitive thing to say, I thought, certain I would soon topple over. I was wrong; suddenly my nervousness vanished as I pondered sticking the nurse's remarks into an article I was writing. And that shot and those that have followed have passed without a tumble. Thoughts about writing never fail to contribute to my composure. Whenever I visit a doctor now, I don't walk into his office trembling in expectation of the worst sort of parsing. Instead I am ready to turn the experience into a story and thus control it. Once while in the Mideast, I picked up an exotic fungus. Although the fungus was out of sight, it grew on a part of my body that made me uneasy, and as soon as I returned to Connecticut I went to a dermatologist. "Good God," he exclaimed when I showed the fungus to him; "I have never seen anything like that." Then pausing for a moment, he added cheerfully, "All I can say is that I am glad it is on you and not on me."

I am not always successful in composing things. Sometimes words get out of hand and, carrying me beyond the full stops I plan, spill over into the tentative world of the colon and expose parts of life that ought to remain buried. Some time ago I decided to write about my summers in Virginia. The essay didn't turn out to be the hymn to golden days that I envisioned. When it appeared in print, I read it and was disturbed. None of my periods worked. "Good country people," the essay began, "scare the hell out of me. Once I liked the country and thought that the closer a person was to the soil, the nearer he was to God. I know better now. The closer a person is to the soil, the dirtier he is." The essay bothered me until I read a note a boy handed in with a story he wrote as an assignment for a course I teach in children's literature. The students were told to write cheerful stories with positive endings. "I am sorry this is such a terrible story," the boy explained, "but I just couldn't think of a good one. They all kept coming out the other way around with Evil triumphing. I am a very disobedient person by nature." All people and sentences are disobedient; and after reading the note, I realized that words, like human beings, occasionally violated the best outlines. All one could do was erase, rewrite, and hope that evil would not triumph in the final draft.

As a person has to struggle with words to make them obedient, so one has to revise life. The effort to become simple and perhaps boring is difficult, but I am succeeding. At least twice a week I tell my wife Vicki that she is fortunate to be married to such a conventional person. "Stop saying the same simple-minded things," she replies; "you are hopelessly repetitive." "Ah, ha," I think, "a few more years and my full stops will block everything unsettling." In passing, I should add that as one grows older and better able to master simple thoughts, he will, nevertheless, vio-

late many rules of grammar. I, for example, am over
forty and don't have the energy I once had. Despite
suggestions that urge me to use the active rather than
the passive voice, I am afraid I live in the passive. Let
young writers attempt to manage lively active verbs
and do all sorts of creative things to predicates. For
my part I am content to be acted upon. Occasionally
I ponder taking a forceful part in life but the fit passes.
As one grows older, material goods become less
important; as one learns the virtues of the oblique
approach, direct objects disappear from life.

Age has taught me the value of a familiar, relaxed
style and life, beyond direct objects. On weekends I
run races. My goal is never to complete a race in the
first 50 percent of the finishers. Unlike top road racers,
my performance never disappoints me. Sometimes I
am tempted to thrust ahead but I always resist. Last
weekend as I trotted down a street, a young woman
yelled, "You are so cute." To be honest, after hearing
that I hoisted my legs up a bit and pranced for a while,
but then as soon as I was around the corner and out
of sight, I settled back into a slow, comfortable rhythm
and let a crowd of younger active runners rush by,
chasing celebrity and trophies.

Age and the experience it brings lead a person to
break many grammar rules. Students in my writing
classes always confuse *its* the possessive with *it's* the
contraction. When I first began to teach, I railed
against the error, attributing ignorance about the possessive to a left-wing conspiracy that was sweeping the
nation and undermining the concept of private property. Nowadays I don't give a hoot about the possessive, in great part because I no longer have anything
that is mine and mine alone. My two little boys, aged
three and one, have converted me to socialism, something no learned text or philosopher was able to do.

What I once thought belonged to me, I now realize is theirs too. My papers are pushed aside and my desk has become a parking lot for Corgi Juniors, Hot Wheels, and Matchbox cars. At night Vicki and I don't sleep alone; we share our bed with an ever-changing group of visitors including Little Bear, Big Bear, Green Worm, and Blue Pillow.

Like a good essay, the composed life has a beginning, middle, and definite ending. Youth can dream about the future and imagine a multitude of endings, and as a result usually can't write well. After forty, dreams stop and one buys life insurance. Instead of evoking visions of idyllic pleasure, the ellipsis that looms ahead leads only to an erasure and an empty notebook. For the writer beyond forty the end is clear and nothing can change it. In contrast the past is infinitely malleable, and I often write about it, trying to give shape to fragments that cling to memory. In classes I tell students to write about the small things in the first paragraph of life and not worry about the conclusion. It will take care of itself. All writers should avoid shadowlands where things are not clear and simple. Occasionally, the complex and mysterious tempt me, and I consider writing about such things as a train journey I made on Christmas Eve, 1964, from Bucharest to Sofia. Guards with tommy guns paced up and down inside the cars while outside the train whistle blew hauntingly through the night. Near the Bulgarian border snow began to fall, and I joined a funeral party that was drinking sorrow away. At the border when guards began to pull people roughly from the train, I opened the window in my compartment and serenaded them with Christmas carols. I got through "Hark the Herald Angels Sing" and was just beginning "The First Noel" when a somber man entered the compartment and grabbing my jacket, pulled me back inside to the seat. Without saying anything, he sat next to me. The funeral party looked at him, then left, and the two of us rode all the way to Sofia in silence. I often wonder what went through the man's mind as we traveled through Christmas morning together. Yet whenever I begin to speculate, my thoughts soon turn toward summers and trains in Virginia. Men sat on the porch of Vickery's store, and as the trains passed through, said things that I remembered, simple things that now seem more important and more lasting than all the mysterious silences I have known. "She's a long one," someone would invariably say about a slow freight; "on the way to Richmond," somebody would add. Toward evening when the coal train to Fredericksburg was due, a man was sure to look at his watch and say, "About time for the coal train." "And for my dinner," someone else would say and then get up and start home.

The reading I assigned students in writing courses once created difficulty for me. Anthologies always contain a few pieces by well-known writers, people that students will hear about someday. Setting myself up as an authority when I was unknown bothered me. Even worse I knew I would always be unknown. Aside from writing an essay that would find its way into an anthology and thrust me out of anonymity, something that was impossible for a person so passive, I didn't know what to do. A little thought and some labor at revising, however, worked a change. I wrote a piece in which I celebrated anonymity and as a consequence am now wonderfully content. Oddly enough, being unknown and being satisfied with a passive, simple style has brought me attention. Not long ago the *Willimantic Chronicle,* our local newspaper, began an article on road racing by quoting me. Unfortunately, or perhaps fortunately, for fame can disrupt a simple style, the

article began with a typographical error. "Ass Sam
Pickering has noted," the paper stated—I have forgotten the rest. After such a beginning, it seems unimportant.

A problem arises after one turns life into a series
of balanced, short declarative sentences. Well-placed
modifiers and proper subordination do not lend themselves to startling essays. The run-on life, like the sentence, breaks through propriety and occasionally
stumbles into interesting constructions. I wondered if I
would be able to write once my sentences were under
control and my life simple. I should not have worried.
Almost every day the postman brings me matter for
essays. "Good going old horse," a former student
wrote after he read something of mine. "My Dear
Samuel Pickering, Jr, I have read your brilliant book
and found great satisfaction in it," a woman wrote
after reading an article of mine in a quarterly. "Our
universe is rolling on in an endless chain of miseries
and misfortunes," a man wrote from Syria; "it is the
law of our land that we all should die one day; we die
when children, money, profession, fame either, can do
us nothing. We stand alone, stripped out of everything,
in a contest, without spectators, without glamour and
hope of win or fear of loss—with much delight and
disbelief in our competitor's right and still less confidence in ours. My father died 20 days ago dreaming
in the world to come."

As transitions link fragments of life and enable one
to escape despair, that terrible sense that nothing matters and chance determines everything, so they bind
my disparate letters into articles. Many years ago, before the first sentence of my life was conceived, my
grandfather owned a dairy. Although grandfather had
several businesses, Henry Hackenbridge his herdsman
assumed the dairy was the most important. Every day

Henry came to grandfather's house and in great detail described the mood of the herd. When grandfather went out of town, Henry wrote him letters daily. Once after breakfast at the old Ritz in New York, grandfather went to fetch his letter. "Yes, sir, Mr. Ratcliffe, there is something for you," the clerk said and started to hand grandfather a letter. Suddenly a look of concern came over the clerk's face, and he said, "Oh, dear, I am so sorry." Grandfather was puzzled until he saw the letter. Under the address in big, clear letters, Henry had written, "P.S. Grandma slipped last night." Although the clerk did not know it, Grandma was not my grandfather's mother or wife. She was an old cow, and the night before she had not fallen on the stairs or in the hall, but had in the language of the dairy, lost her calf. When I search for the right transition, I often think of this story. If I can find the right word and am able to keep my life and sentences simple, chances are good that I won't slip too often.

Richard Lederer

THE MIRACLE OF LANGUAGE
(2006)

"Language is the Rubicon that divides man from beast," declared the philologist Max Muller. The boundary between human and animal—between the most primitive savage and the highest ape—is the language line. In some tribes in Africa, a baby is called a *kuntu,* a "thing," not yet a *muntu,* a "person." It is only through the gift of language that the child acquires reason, the complexity of thought that sets him or her apart from the other creatures who share this planet. The birth of language is the dawn of humanity; in our beginning was the word. We have always been endowed with language because before we had words, we were not human beings.

"The limits of my language," wrote the philosopher Ludwig Wittgenstein, "are the limits of my mind. All I know is what I have words for." Without the word we are imprisoned; possessing the word, we are set free. Listen now to the stories of four thinkers—two men, two women; two whites, two blacks—as they give eloquent testimony to the emancipating power of language.

Most of us cannot remember learning our first word,

41

but Helen Keller recalled that event in her life with a flashing vividness. She remembered because she was deaf, mute, and blind from the age of nineteen months and did not learn her first word until she was seven.

When Helen was six, an extraordinary teacher named Anne Mansfield Sullivan entered her life. Miss Sullivan was poor, ill, and nearly blind herself, but she possessed a tenacious vitality that was to force her pupil's unwilling mind from the dark, silent prison in which it lived: "Before my teacher came to me, I lived in a world that was a no-world. I cannot hope to describe adequately that unconscious yet conscious time of nothingness. I did not know that I knew aught, or that I lived or acted or desired."

In his play *The Miracle Worker,* William Gibson shows us what happened when Anne Sullivan first met Helen's mother:

MRS. KELLER: What will you teach her first?
ANNE SULLIVAN: First, last—and in between, language.
MRS. KELLER: Language.
ANNE SULLIVAN: Language is to the mind more than light is to the eye.

The miracle that Anne Sullivan worked was to give Helen Keller language, for only language could transform a small animal that looked like a child, a *kuntu,* into a human being, a *muntu.* Day after day, month after month, Anne Sullivan spelled words into Helen's hand. Finally, when Helen was seven years old and working with her teacher in the presence of water, she spoke her first word. Years later she described that moment in *The Story of My Life* (1902):

*Somehow the mystery of language was revealed
to me. I knew then that "w-a-t-e-r" meant that
wonderful cool something that was flowing over
my hand. That living word awakened my soul,
gave it light, hope, joy, set it free! . . . I left the
well-house eager to learn. Everything had a name,
and each name gave birth to a new thought.*

Not only did Helen Keller learn to speak, write, and
understand the English language. She graduated *cum
laude* from Radcliffe College and went on to become
a distinguished lecturer and writer. But perhaps the
most poignant moment in her life came when, at the
age of nine, she was able to say to Anne Sullivan, "I
am not dumb now."

Richard Wright spent his childhood in the Jim Crow
South—a prison of poverty, fear, and racism. He was born
on a farm near Natchez, Mississippi, and, when he was
five, his sharecropper father deserted the family. Richard, his mother, and his brother had to move from one
community to another throughout the South so that he
seldom remained in one school for an entire year. Yet
somehow Richard Wright escaped the prison of hunger
and hatred to become the most significant black writer
in America, the author of *Native Son* (1940) and *Black
Boy* (1945), two watershed books in American literature.

In *Black Boy,* Wright's unsparing autobiography, he
describes his liberation at the age of eighteen. Because
black people were not allowed library privileges,
Wright used the card of a friendly white man along
with a forged note that said, "Dear Madam: Will you
please let this nigger boy have some books by H. L.
Mencken." He obtained a copy of Mencken's *A Book
of Prefaces,* and all at once the sun of great literature
burst through the window of his prison:

That night in my rented room, while letting the hot water run over my pork and beans in the sink, I opened A Book of Prefaces *and began to read. I was jarred and shocked by the style, the clear, clean, sweeping sentences. Why did he write like that? And how did one write like that? . . . I stood up, trying to realize what reality lay behind the meaning of the words. Yes, this man was fighting with words. He was using words as a weapon, using them as one would use a club. . . . Then, maybe, perhaps, I could use them as a weapon. . . .*

What strange world was this? I concluded the book with the conviction that I had somehow overlooked something terribly important in life. I had once tried to write, had once reveled in feeling, had let my crude imagination roam, but the impulse to dream had been slowly beaten out of me by experience. Now it surged up again and I hungered for books, new ways of looking and seeing.

The titles of his first three works—*Uncle Tom's Children, Native Son,* and *Black Boy*—keep alive the abiding memory that Richard Wright always carried for the child who opened a book by H. L. Mencken and discovered a world, for the son who never felt himself native to the country of his birth, and for the boy who struggled out of the depths to speak for those who remained behind.

In *The Autobiography of Malcolm X* (1964), Malcolm tells how he rose from a world of thieving, pimping, and drug peddling to become one of the most articulate and dynamic leaders of the black revolution in America. Like Helen Keller and Richard Wright, Malcolm X was walled within a prison, in this instance the Norfolk Prison Colony, and, like them, it was through the gift of language that he gained his liberation.

Frustrated by his inability to express himself in writing, Malcolm borrowed a dictionary from the prison school and slowly, painstakingly, began to copy, word by word and page by page, the entire dictionary onto his tablet. "With every succeeding page, I also learned of people and places and events from history. Actually the dictionary is like a miniature encyclopedia." As his vocabulary expanded, an already powerful speaker experienced a new empowerment through literacy. He read all day and even at night, in the faint glow of a corridor light:

> Anyone who has read a great deal can imagine the new world that opened up. Let me tell you something: from then until I left that prison, in every free moment I had, if I was not reading in the library, I was reading in my bunk. You couldn't have gotten me out of books with a wedge. . . . Months passed without my even thinking about being imprisoned. In fact, up to then, I had never been so truly free in my life.

The last of our four prisoners is Anne Frank, a young Jewish girl who grew up in Amsterdam during the Nazi occupation of Holland. In July of 1942 Anne's family was forced into hiding in the upper story of an Amsterdam warehouse, where they remained for twenty-five months. The rooms became more suffocating than any prison one could imagine. The Franks, who shared the space with another family and with an elderly dentist, were unable to feel the sun's warmth, unable to breathe fresh air. While the warehouse was in operation during the day, there could be no noise of any kind—no speaking, no unnecessary movements, no running of water.

Then, in 1944, the hideout was discovered by the police. Of the eight who had been crowded into the sealed-off attic rooms, only Mr. Frank survived the ensuing horrors of the concentration camps. In March 1945, two months before the liberation of Holland and three months before her sixteenth birthday, Anne Frank perished in the camp at Bergen-Belsen. According to one witness, she "died peacefully, feeling that nothing bad was happening to her."

Anne may have been devoured by the concentration camps, but her voice was not stilled. From the pages of a small, red-checkered, cloth-covered diary book, she speaks to us across the years. The diary was the favorite gift that Anne received for her thirteenth birthday. She named it Kitty and determined to express to her new confidante her innermost thoughts, concerns, and desires. Between the covers of Kitty the young girl, Anne Frank, recorded her moving commentary on war and its impact on human beings:

> I see the eight of us with our "Secret Annexe"
> as if we were a little piece of blue heaven, surrounded by heavy black rain clouds. The round,
> clearly defined spot where we stand is still safe,
> but the clouds gather more closely about us and
> the circle which separates us from the approaching danger closes more and more tightly.
> Now we are so surrounded by danger and darkness that we bump against each other, as we
> search desperately for a means of escape. We all
> look down below, where people are fighting each
> other, we look above, where it is quiet and beautiful, and meanwhile we are cut off by the great
> dark mass, which will not let us go upwards, but

*which stands before us as an impenetrable wall;
it tries to crush us, but cannot do so yet. I can
only cry and implore: "Oh, if only the black circle
could recede and open the way for us!"*

Finally the Franks were betrayed, and on August 4, 1944, the fury of the Gestapo burst upon them. The invaders confiscated the silverware and Chanukah candlestick, but they threw the family's papers to the floor, including Anne's diary, which was recovered a year later by Mr. Frank.

The Nazis had failed in their mission. *Anne Frank: The Diary of a Young Girl* was first published in 1947 and has since been translated into tens of languages and sold millions of copies. No one has described its impact more eloquently than Anne's biographer, Ernst Schnabel: "Her voice was preserved out of the millions that were silenced, this voice no louder than a child's whisper. . . . It has outlasted the shouts of the murderers and soared above the voices of time."

What do the stories of Helen Keller, Richard Wright, Malcolm X, and Anne Frank say to us? They tell us that the world we perceive is the world we see through words. They tell us, as Wittgenstein once wrote, that "of what we cannot speak, we must be silent." They tell us that human beings grapple with the mystery of life by trying to find words to say what it is. They tell us that we must never take for granted the miracle of language.

ON EDUCATION

ON EDUCATION

Ralph Waldo Emerson

THE AMERICAN SCHOLAR
(1837)

*An Oration Delivered before the Phi Beta Kappa
Society, at Cambridge, August 31, 1837*

Mr. President and Gentlemen:
    I greet you on the recommencement of our
literary year. Our anniversary is one of hope, and,
perhaps, not enough of labor. We do not meet for
games of strength or skill, for the recitation of histories, tragedies, and odes, like the ancient Greeks; for
parliaments of love and poesy like the Troubadours;
nor for the advancement of science, like our contemporaries in the British and European capitals. Thus
far, our holiday has been simply a friendly sign of the
survival of the love of letters amongst a people too
busy to give to letters any more. As such it is precious
as the sign of an indestructible instinct. Perhaps the
time is already come when it ought to be, and will
be, something else; when the sluggard intellect of this
continent will look from under its iron lids and fill the
postponed expectation of the world with something
better than the exertions of mechanical skill. Our day

of dependence, our long apprenticeship to the learning of other lands, draws to a close. The millions that around us are rushing into life, cannot always be fed on the sere remains of foreign harvests. Events, actions arise, that must be sung, that will sing themselves. Who can doubt that poetry will revive and lead in a new age, as the star in the constellation Harp, which now flames in our zenith, astronomers announce, shall one day be the pole-star for a thousand years?

In this hope I accept the topic which not only usage but the nature of our association seem to prescribe to this day,—the AMERICAN SCHOLAR. Year by year we come up hither to read one more chapter of his biography. Let us inquire what light new days and events have thrown on his character and his hopes.

It is one of those fables which out of an unknown antiquity convey an unlooked-for wisdom, that the gods, in the beginning, divided Man into men, that he might be more helpful to himself; just as the hand was divided into fingers, the better to answer its end.

The old fable covers a doctrine ever new and sublime; that there is One Man,—present to all particular men only partially, or through one faculty; and that you must take the whole society to find the whole man. Man is not a farmer, or a professor, or an engineer, but he is all. Man is priest, and scholar, and statesman, and producer, and soldier. In the *divided* or social state these functions are parcelled out to individuals, each of whom aims to do his stint of the joint work, whilst each other performs his. The fable implies that the individual, to possess himself, must sometimes return from his own labor to embrace all the other laborers. But, unfortunately, this original unit, this fountain of power, has been so distributed to multitudes, has been so minutely subdivided and peddled out, that it is spilled into drops, and cannot be gathered. The state of society is one in which the members have suffered amputation from the trunk, and strut about so many walking monsters,—a good finger, a neck, a stomach, an elbow, but never a man.

Man is thus metamorphosed into a thing, into many things. The planter, who is Man sent out into the field to gather food, is seldom cheered by any idea of the true dignity of his ministry. He sees his bushel and his cart, and nothing beyond, and sinks into the farmer, instead of Man on the farm. The tradesman scarcely ever gives an ideal worth to his work, but is ridden by the routine of his craft, and the soul is subject to dollars. The priest becomes a form; the attorney a statute-book; the mechanic a machine; the sailor a rope of the ship.

In this distribution of functions the scholar is the delegated intellect. In the right state he is *Man Thinking*. In the degenerate state, when the victim of society, he tends to become a mere thinker, or still worse, the parrot of other men's thinking.

In this view of him, as Man Thinking, the theory of his office is contained. Him Nature solicits with all her placid, all her monitory pictures; him the past instructs; him the future invites. Is not indeed every man a student, and do not all things exist for the student's behoof? And, finally, is not the true scholar the only true master? But the old oracle said, "All things have two handles: beware of the wrong one." In life, too often, the scholar errs with mankind and forfeits his privilege. Let us see him in his school, and consider him in reference to the main influences he receives.

I. The first in time and the first in importance of the influences upon the mind is that of nature. Every day, the sun; and, after sunset, Night and her stars.

Ever the winds blow; ever the grass grows. Every day, men and women, conversing—beholding and beholden. The scholar is he of all men whom this spectacle most engages. He must settle its value in his mind. What is nature to him? There is never a beginning, there is never an end, to the inexplicable continuity of this web of God, but always circular power returning into itself. Therein it resembles his own spirit, whose beginning, whose ending, he never can find,—so entire, so boundless. Far too as her splendors shine, system on system shooting like rays, upward, downward, without centre, without circumference,—in the mass and in the particle, Nature hastens to render account of herself to the mind. Classification begins. To the young mind every thing is individual, stands by itself. By and by, it finds how to join two things and see in them one nature; then three, then three thousand; and so, tyrannized over by its own unifying instinct, it goes on tying things together, diminishing anomalies, discovering roots running under ground whereby contrary and remote things cohere and flower out from one stem. It presently learns that since the dawn of history there has been a constant accumulation and classifying of facts. But what is classification but the perceiving that these objects are not chaotic, and are not foreign, but have a law which is also a law of the human mind? The astronomer discovers that geometry, a pure abstraction of the human mind, is the measure of planetary motion. The chemist finds proportions and intelligible method throughout matter; and science is nothing but the finding of analogy, identity, in the most remote parts. The ambitious soul sits down before each refractory fact; one after another reduces all strange constitutions, all new powers, to their class and their law, and goes on forever to animate the last fibre of organization, the outskirts of nature, by insight.

Thus to him, to this schoolboy under the bending dome of day, is suggested that he and it proceed from one root; one is leaf and one is flower; relation, sympathy, stirring in every vein. And what is that root? Is not that the soul of his soul? A thought too bold; a dream too wild. Yet when this spiritual light shall have revealed the law of more earthly natures,—when he has learned to worship the soul, and to see that the natural philosophy that now is, is only the first gropings of its gigantic hand, he shall look forward to an ever expanding knowledge as to a becoming creator. He shall see that nature is the opposite of the soul, answering to it part for part. One is seal and one is print. Its beauty is the beauty of his own mind. Its laws are the laws of his own mind. Nature then becomes to him the measure of his attainments. So much of nature as he is ignorant of, so much of his own mind does he not yet possess. And, in fine, the ancient precept, "Know thyself," and the modern precept, "Study nature," become at last one maxim.

II. The next great influence into the spirit of the scholar is the mind of the Past,—in whatever form, whether of literature, of art, of institutions, that mind is inscribed. Books are the best type of the influence of the past, and perhaps we shall get at the truth,— learn the amount of this influence more conveniently,—by considering their value alone.

The theory of books is noble. The scholar of the first age received into him the world around; brooded thereon; gave it the new arrangement of his own mind, and uttered it again. It came into him life; it went out from him truth. It came to him short-lived actions; it went out from him immortal thoughts. It came to him business; it went from him poetry. It was dead fact; now, it is quick thought. It can stand, and it can go. It now endures, it now flies, it now inspires. Precisely in proportion to the depth of mind from which it issued, so high does it soar, so long does it sing.

Or, I might say, it depends on how far the process had gone, of transmuting life into truth. In proportion to the completeness of the distillation, so will the purity and imperishableness of the product be. But none is quite perfect. As no air-pump can by any means make a perfect vacuum, so neither can any artist entirely exclude the conventional, the local, the perishable from his book, or write a book of pure thought, that shall be as efficient, in all respects, to a remote posterity, as to contemporaries, or rather to the second age. Each age, it is found, must write its own books; or rather, each generation for the next succeeding. The books of an older period will not fit this.

Yet hence arises a grave mischief. The sacredness which attaches to the act of creation, the act of thought, is transferred to the record. The poet chanting was felt to be a divine man: henceforth the chant is divine also. The writer was a just and wise spirit: henceforward it is settled the book is perfect; as love of the hero corrupts into worship of his statue. Instantly the book becomes noxious: the guide is a tyrant. The sluggish and perverted mind of the multitude, slow to open to the incursions of Reason, having once so opened, having once received this book, stands upon it, and makes an outcry if it is disparaged. Colleges are built on it. Books are written on it by thinkers, not by Man Thinking; by men of talent, that is, who start wrong, who set out from accepted dogmas, not from their own sight of principles. Meek young men grow up in libraries, believing it their duty to accept the views which Cicero, which Locke, which Bacon, have given; forgetful that Cicero, Locke, and Bacon were only young men in libraries when they wrote these books.

Hence, instead of Man Thinking, we have the book-worm. Hence the book-learned class, who value books, as such; not as related to nature and the human constitution, but as making a sort of Third Estate with the world and the soul. Hence the restorers of readings, the emendators, the bibliomaniacs of all degrees.

Books are the best of things, well used; abused, among the worst. What is the right use? What is the one end which all means go to effect? They are for nothing but to inspire. I had better never see a book than to be warped by its attraction clean out of my own orbit, and made a satellite instead of a system. The one thing in the world, of value, is the active soul. This every man is entitled to; this every man contains within him, although in almost all men obstructed and as yet unborn. The soul active sees absolute truth and utters truth, or creates. In this action it is genius; not the privilege of here and there a favorite, but the sound estate of every man. In its essence it is progressive. The book, the college, the school of art, the institution of any kind, stop with some past utterance of genius. This is good, say they,—let us hold by this. They pin me down. They look backward and not forward. But genius looks forward: the eyes of man are set in his forehead, not in his hindhead: man hopes: genius creates. Whatever talents may be, if the man create not, the pure efflux of the Deity is not his;—cinders and smoke there may be, but not yet flame. There are creative manners, there are creative actions, and creative words; manners, actions, words, that is, indicative of no custom or authority, but springing spontaneous from the mind's own sense of good and fair.

On the other part, instead of being its own seer, let it receive from another mind its truth, though it were in torrents of light, without periods of solitude, inquest, and self-recovery, and a fatal disservice is done. Genius is always sufficiently the enemy of genius by over-influence. The literature of every nation bears me witness. The English dramatic poets have Shakspearized now for two hundred years.

Undoubtedly there is a right way of reading, so it be sternly subordinated. Man Thinking must not be subdued by his instruments. Books are for the scholar's idle times. When he can read God directly, the hour is too precious to be wasted in other men's transcripts of their readings. But when the intervals of darkness come, as come they must,—when the sun is hid and the stars withdraw their shining,—we repair to the lamps which were kindled by their ray, to guide our steps to the East again, where the dawn is. We hear, that we may speak. The Arabian proverb says, "A fig tree, looking on a fig tree, becometh fruitful."

It is remarkable, the character of the pleasure we derive from the best books. They impress us with the conviction the one nature wrote and the same reads. We read that verses of one of the great English poets, of Chaucer, of Marvell, of Dryden, with the most modern joy,—with a pleasure, I mean, which is in great part caused by the abstraction of all *time* from their verses. There is some awe mixed with the joy of our surprise, when this poet, who lived in some past world, two or three hundred years ago, says that which lies close to my own soul, that which I also had well-nigh thought and said. But for the evidence thence afforded to the philosophical doctrine of the identity of all minds, we should suppose some preëstablished harmony, some foresight of souls that were to be, and some preparation of stores for their future wants, like the fact observed in insects, who lay up food before death for the young grub they shall never see.

I would not be hurried by any love of system, by any exaggeration of instincts, to underrate the Book. We all know, that as the human body can be nourished on any food, though it were boiled grass and the broth of shoes, so the human mind can be fed by any knowledge. And great and heroic men have existed who had almost no other information than by the printed page. I only would say that it needs a strong head to bear that diet. One must be an inventor to read well. As the proverb says, "He that would bring home the wealth of the Indies, must carry out the wealth of the Indies." There is then creative reading as well as creative writing. When the mind is braced by labor and invention, the page of whatever book we read becomes luminous with manifold allusion. Every sentence is doubly significant, and the sense of our author is as broad as the world. We then see, what is always true, that as the seer's hour of vision is short and rare among heavy days and months, so is its record, perchance, the least part of his volume. The discerning will read, in his Plato or Shakspeare, only that least part,—only the authentic utterances of the oracle;—all the rest he rejects, were it never so many times Plato's and Shakspeare's.

Of course there is a portion of reading quite indispensable to a wise man. History and exact science he must learn by laborious reading. Colleges, in like manner, have their indispensable office,—to teach elements. But they can only highly serve us when they aim not to drill, but to create; when they gather from far every ray of various genius to their hospitable halls, and by the concentrated fires, set the hearts of their youth on flame. Thought and knowledge are natures in which apparatus and pretension avail nothing.

Gowns and pecuniary foundations, though of towns of gold, can never countervail the least sentence or syllable of wit. Forget this, and our American colleges will recede in their public importance, whilst they grow richer every year.

III. There goes in the world a notion that the scholar should be a recluse, a valetudinarian,—as unfit for any handiwork or public labor as a penknife for an axe. The so-called "practical men" sneer at speculative men, as if, because they speculate or *see,* they could do nothing. I have heard it said that the clergy,—who are always, more universally than any other class, the scholars of their day,—are addressed as women; that the rough, spontaneous conversation of men they do not hear, but only a mincing and diluted speech. They are often virtually disfranchised; and indeed there are advocates for their celibacy. As far as this is true of the studious classes, it is not just and wise. Action is with the scholar subordinate, but it is essential. Without it he is not yet man. Without it thought can never ripen into truth. Whilst the world hangs before the eye as a cloud of beauty, we cannot even see its beauty. Inaction is cowardice, but there can be no scholar without the heroic mind. The preamble of thought, the transition through which it passes from the unconscious to the conscious, is action. Only so much do I know, as I have lived. Instantly we know whose words are loaded with life, and whose not.

The world,—this shadow of the soul, or *other me,*—lies wide around. Its attractions are the keys which unlock my thoughts and make me acquainted with myself. I run eagerly into this resounding tumult. I grasp the hands of those next me, and take my place in the ring to suffer and to work, taught by an instinct that so shall the dumb abyss be vocal with speech. I pierce its order; I dissipate its fear; I dispose of it within the circuit of my expanding life. So much only of life as I know by experience, so much of the wilderness have I vanquished and planted, or so far have I extended my being, my dominion. I do not see how any man can afford, for the sake of his nerves and his nap, to spare any action in which he can partake. It is pearls and rubies to his discourse. Drudgery, calamity, exasperation, want, are instructors in eloquence and wisdom. The true scholar grudges every opportunity of action past by, as a loss of power. It is the raw material out of which the intellect moulds her splendid products. A strange process too, this by which experience is converted into thought, as a mulberry leaf is converted into satin. The manufacture goes forward at all hours.

The actions and events of our childhood and youth are now matters of calmest observation. They lie like fair pictures in the air. Not so with our recent actions,—with the business which we now have in hand. On this we are quite unable to speculate. Our affections as yet circulate through it. We no more feel or know it than we feel the feet, or the hand, or the brain of our body. The new deed is yet a part of life,—remains for a time immersed in our unconscious life. In some contemplative hour it detaches itself from the life like a ripe fruit, to become a thought of the mind. Instantly it is raised, transfigured; the corruptible has put on incorruption. Henceforth it is an object of beauty, however base its origin and neighborhood. Observe too the impossibility of antedating this act. In its grub state, it cannot fly, it cannot shine, it is a dull grub. But suddenly, without observation, the selfsame thing unfurls beautiful wings, and is an angel of wisdom. So is there no fact, no event, in our private history, which shall not, sooner or later, lose its adhesive, inert form, and astonish us by soaring from our body into the empyrean. Cradle and infancy, school and playground, the fear of boys, and dogs, and ferules, the love of little maids and berries, and many another fact that once filled the whole sky, are gone already; friend and relative, profession and party, town and country, nation and world, must also soar and sing.

Of course, he who has put forth his total strength in fit actions has the richest return of wisdom. I will not shut myself out of this globe of action, and transplant an oak into a flowerpot, there to hunger and pine; nor trust the revenue of some single faculty, and exhaust one vein of thought, much like those Savoyards, who, getting their livelihood by carving shepherds, shepherdesses, and smoking Dutchmen, for all Europe, went out one day to the mountain to find stock, and discovered that they had whittled up the last of their pine trees. Authors we have, in numbers, who have written out their vein, and who, moved by a commendable prudence, sail for Greece or Palestine, follow the trapper into the prairie, or ramble round Algiers, to replenish their merchantable stock.

If it were only for a vocabulary, the scholar would be covetous of action. Life is our dictionary. Years are well spent in country labors; in town; in the insight into trades and manufactures; in frank intercourse with many men and women; in science; in art; to the one end of mastering in all their facts a language by which to illustrate and embody our perceptions. I learn immediately from any speaker how much he has already lived, through the poverty or the splendor of his speech. Life lies behind us as the quarry from whence we get tiles and copestones for the masonry of to-day. This is the way to learn grammar. Colleges and books only copy the language which the field and the work-yard made.

But the final value of action, like that of books, and better than books, is that it is a resource. That great principle of Undulation in nature, that shows itself in the inspiring and expiring of the breath; in desire and satiety; in the ebb and flow of the sea; in day and night; in heat and cold; and, as yet more deeply ingrained in every atom and every fluid, is known to us under the name of Polarity,—these "fits of easy transmission and reflection," as Newton called them, are the law of nature because they are the law of spirit.

The mind now thinks, now acts, and each fit reproduces the other. When the artist has exhausted his materials, when the fancy no longer paints, when thoughts are no longer apprehended and books are a weariness,—he has always the resource *to live*. Character is higher than intellect. Thinking is the function. Living is the functionary. The stream retreats to its source. A great soul will be strong to live, as well as strong to think. Does he lack organ or medium to impart his truths? He can still fall back on this elemental force of living them. This is a total act. Thinking is a partial act. Let the grandeur of justice shine in his affairs. Let the beauty of affection cheer his lowly roof. Those "far from fame," who dwell and act with him, will feel the force of his constitution in the doings and passages of the day better than it can be measured by any public and designed display. Time shall teach him that the scholar loses no hour which the man lives. Herein he unfolds the sacred germ of his instinct, screened from influence. What is lost in seemliness is gained in strength. Not out of those on whom systems of education have exhausted their culture, comes the helpful giant to destroy the old or to build the new, but out of unhandselled savage nature; out of terrible Druids and Berserkers come at last Alfred and Shakspeare.

I hear therefore with joy whatever is beginning to be said of the dignity and necessity of labor to every citizen. There is virtue yet in the hoe and the spade, for learned as well as for unlearned hands. And labor is everywhere welcome; always we are invited to work; only be this limitation observed, that a man shall not for the sake of wider activity sacrifice any opinion to the popular judgments and modes of action.

I have now spoken of the education of the scholar by nature, by books, and by action. It remains to say somewhat of his duties.

They are such as become Man Thinking. They may all be comprised in self-trust. The office of the scholar is to cheer, to raise, and to guide men by showing them facts amidst appearances. He plies the slow, unhonored, and unpaid task of observation. Flamsteed and Herschel, in their glazed observatories, may catalogue the stars with the praise of all men, and the results being splendid and useful, honor is sure. But he, in his private observatory, cataloguing obscure and nebulous stars of the human mind, which as yet no man has thought of as such,—watching days and months sometimes for a few facts; correcting still his old records;—must relinquish display and immediate fame. In the long period of his preparation he must betray often an ignorance and shiftlessness in popular arts, incurring the disdain of the able who shoulder him aside. Long he must stammer in his speech; often forego the living for the dead. Worse yet, he must accept—how often!—poverty and solitude. For the ease and pleasure of treading the old road, accepting the fashions, the education, the religion of society, he takes the cross of making his own, and, of course, the self-accusation, the faint heart, the frequent uncertainty and loss of time, which are the nettles and tangling vines in the way of the self-relying and self-directed; and the state of virtual hostility in which he seems to stand to society, and especially to educated society. For all this loss and scorn, what off-set? He is to find consolation in exercising the highest functions of human nature. He is one who raises himself from private considerations and breathes and lives on public and illustrious thoughts. He is the world's eye. He is the world's heart. He is to resist the vulgar prosperity that retrogrades ever to barbarism, by preserving and communicating heroic sentiments, noble biographies, melodious verse, and the conclusions of history. Whatsoever oracles the human heart, in all emergencies, in all solemn hours, has uttered as its commentary on the world of actions,—these he shall receive and impart. And whatsoever new verdict Reason from her inviolable seat pronounces on the passing men and events of to-day,—this he shall hear and promulgate.

These being his functions, it becomes him to feel all confidence in himself, and to defer never to the popular cry. He and he only knows the world. The world of any moment is the merest appearance. Some great decorum, some fetish of a government, some ephemeral trade, or war, or man, is cried up by half mankind and cried down by the other half, as if all depended on this particular up or down. The odds are that the whole question is not worth the poorest thought which the scholar has lost in listening to the controversy. Let him not quit his belief that a popgun is a popgun, though the ancient and honorable of the earth affirm it to be the crack of doom. In silence, in steadiness, in severe abstraction, let him hold by himself; add observation to observation, patient of neglect, patient of reproach, and bide his own time,—happy enough if he can satisfy himself alone that this day he has seen something truly. Success treads on every right step. For the instinct is sure, that prompts him to tell his brother what he thinks. He then learns that in going down into the secrets of his own mind he has descended into the secrets of all minds. He learns that he who has mastered any law in his private thoughts, is master to that extent of all men whose language he speaks, and of all into whose language his own can be translated. The poet, in utter solitude remembering his spontaneous thoughts and recording them, is found to have recorded that which men in crowded cities find true for them also. The orator distrusts at first the fitness of his frank confessions, his want of knowledge of the persons he addresses, until he finds that he is the complement of his hearers;—that they drink his words because he fulfils for them their own nature; the deeper he dives into his privatest, secretest presentiment, to his wonder he finds this is the most acceptable, most public, and universally true. The people delight in it; the better part of every man feels, This is my music; this is myself.

In self-trust all the virtues are comprehended. Free should the scholar be,—free and brave. Free even to the definition of freedom, "without any hindrance that does not arise out of his own constitution." Brave; for fear is a thing which a scholar by his very function puts behind him. Fear always springs from ignorance. It is a shame to him if his tranquillity, amid dangerous times, arise from the presumption that like children and women his is a protected class; or if he seek a temporary peace by the diversion of his thoughts from politics or vexed questions, hiding his head like an ostrich in the flowering bushes, peeping into microscopes, and turning rhymes, as a boy whistles to keep his courage up. So is the danger a danger still; so is the fear worse. Manlike let him turn and face it. Let him look into its eye and search its nature, inspect its origin,—see the whelping of this lion,—which lies no great way back; he will then find in himself a perfect comprehension of its nature and extent; he will have made his hands meet on the other side, and can henceforth defy it and pass on superior. The world is his who can see through its pretension. What deafness, what stone-blind custom, what overgrown error you behold is there only by sufferance,—by your sufferance. See it to be a lie, and you have already dealt it its mortal blow.

Yes, we are the cowed,—we the trustless. It is a mischievous notion that we are come late into nature; that the world was finished a long time ago. As the world was plastic and fluid in the hands of God, so it is ever to so much of his attributes as we bring to it. To ignorance and sin, it is flint. They adapt themselves to it as they may; but in proportion as a man has any thing in him divine, the firmament flows before him and takes his signet and form. Not he is great who can alter matter, but he who can alter my state of mind. They are the kings of the world who give the color of their present thought to all nature and all art, and persuade men by the cheerful serenity of their carrying the matter, that this thing which they do is the apple which the ages have desired to pluck, now at last ripe, and inviting nations to the harvest. The great man makes the great thing. Wherever Macdonald sits, there is the head of the table. Linnæus makes botany the most alluring of studies, and wins it from the farmer and the herb-woman; Davy, chemistry; and Cuvier, fossils. The day is always his who works in it with serenity and great aims. The unstable estimates of men crowd to him whose mind is filled with a truth, as the heaped waves of the Atlantic follow the moon.

For this self-trust, the reason is deeper than can be fathomed,—darker than can be enlightened. I might not carry with me the feeling of my audience in stating my own belief. But I have already shown the ground of my hope, in adverting to the doctrine that man is one. I believe man has been wronged; he has wronged himself. He has almost lost the light that can lead him back to his prerogatives. Men are become of no account. Men in history, men in the world of to-day, are bugs, are spawn, and are called "the mass" and "the herd." In a century, in a millennium, one or two men; that is to say, one or two approximations to the right state of every man. All the rest behold in the hero or the poet their own green and crude being,—ripened; yes, and are content to be less, so *that* may attain to its full stature. What a testimony, full of grandeur, full of pity, is borne to the demands of his own nature, by the poor clansman, the poor partisan, who rejoices in the glory of his chief. The poor and the low find some amends to their immense moral capacity, for their acquiescence in a political and social inferiority. They are content to be brushed like flies from the path of a great person, so that justice shall be done by him to that common nature which it is the dearest desire of all to see enlarged and glorified. They sun themselves in the great man's light, and feel it to be their own element. They cast the dignity of man from their downtrod selves upon the shoulders of a hero, and will perish to add one drop of blood to make that great heart beat, those giant sinews combat and conquer. He lives for us, and we live in him.

Men, such as they are, very naturally seek money or power; and power because it is as good as money,—the "spoils," so called, "of office." And why not? for they aspire to the highest, and this, in their sleep-walking, they dream is highest. Wake them and they shall quit the false good and leap to the true, and leave governments to clerks and desks. This revolution is to be wrought by the gradual domestication of the idea of Culture. The main enterprise of the world for splendor, for extent, is the upbuilding of a man. Here are the materials strewn along the ground. The private life of one man shall be a more illustrious monarchy, more formidable to its enemy, more sweet and serene in its influence to its friend, than any kingdom in history. For a man, rightly viewed, comprehendeth the particular natures of all men. Each philosopher, each bard, each actor has only done for me, as by a delegate, what one day I can do for myself. The books which once we valued more than the apple of the eye, we have quite exhausted. What is that but saying that we have come up with the point of view which the universal mind took through the eyes of one scribe; we have been that man, and have passed on. First, one, then another, we drain all cisterns, and waxing greater by all these supplies, we crave a better and more abundant food. The man has never lived that can feed us ever. The human mind cannot be enshrined in a person who shall set a barrier on any one side to this unbounded, unboundable empire. It is one central fire, which, flaming now out of the lips of Etna, lightens the capes of Sicily, and now out of the throat of Vesuvius, illuminates the towers and vineyards of Naples. It is one light which beams out of a thousand stars. It is one soul which animates all men.

But I have dwelt perhaps tediously upon this abstraction of the Scholar. I ought not to delay longer to add what I have to say of nearer reference to the time and to this country.

Historically, there is thought to be a difference in the ideas which predominate over successive epochs, and there are data for marking the genius of the Classic, of the Romantic, and now of the Reflective or Philosophical age. With the views I have intimated of the oneness or the identity of the mind through all individuals, I do not much dwell on these differences. In fact, I believe each individual passes through all three. The boy is a Greek; the youth, romantic; the adult, reflective. I deny not, however, that a revolution in the leading idea may be distinctly enough traced.

Our age is bewailed as the age of Introversion. Must that needs be evil? We, it seems, are critical; we are embarrassed with second thoughts; we cannot enjoy any thing for hankering to know whereof the pleasure consists; we are lined with eyes; we see with our feet; the time is infected with Hamlet's unhappiness,—

"Sicklied o'er with the pale cast of thought."

It is so bad then? Sight is the last thing to be pitied. Would we be blind? Do we fear lest we should outsee nature and God, and drink truth dry? I look upon the discontent of the literary class as a mere announcement of the fact that they find themselves not in the state of mind of their fathers, and regret the coming state as untried; as a boy dreads the water before he has learned that he can swim. If there is any period one would desire to be born in, is it not the age of Revolution; when the old and the new stand side by side and admit of being compared; when the energies of all men are searched by fear and by hope; when the historic glories of the old can be compensated by the rich possibilities of the new era? This time, like all times, is a very good one, if we but know what to do with it.

I read with some joy of the auspicious signs of the coming days, as they glimmer already through poetry and art, through philosophy and science, through church and state.

One of these signs is the fact that the same movement which effected the elevation of what was called the lowest class in the state, assumed in literature a very marked and as benign an aspect. Instead of the sublime and beautiful, the near, the low, the common, was explored and poetized. That which had been negligently trodden under foot by those who were harnessing and provisioning themselves for long journeys into far countries, is suddenly found to be richer than all foreign parts. The literature of the poor, the feelings of the child, the philosophy of the street, the meaning of household life, are the topics of the time. It is a great stride. It is a sign—is it not?—of new vigor when the extremities are made active, when currents of warm life run into the hands and the feet. I ask not for the great, the remote, the romantic; what is doing in Italy or Arabia; what is Greek art, or Provençal minstrelsy; I embrace the common, I explore and sit at the feet of the familiar, the low. Give me insight into to-day, and you may have the antique and future worlds. What would we really know the meaning of? The meal in the firkin; the milk in the pan; the ballad in the street; the news of the boat; the glance of the eye; the form and the gait of the body;— show me the ultimate reason of these matters; show me the sublime presence of the highest spiritual cause lurking, as always it does lurk, in these suburbs and extremities of nature; let me see every trifle bristling with the polarity that ranges it instantly on an eternal law; and the shop, the plough, and the ledger referred to the like cause by which light undulates and poets sing;—and the world lies no longer a dull miscellany and lumber-room, but has form and order; there is no trifle, there is no puzzle, but one design unites and animates the farthest pinnacle and the lowest trench.

This idea has inspired the genius of Goldsmith, Burns, Cowper, and, in a newer time, of Goethe, Wordsworth, and Carlyle. This idea they have differently followed and with various success. In contrast with their writing, the style of Pope, of Johnson, of Gibbon, looks cold and pedantic. This writing is blood-warm. Man is surprised to find that things near are not less beautiful and wondrous than things remote. The near explains the far. The drop is a small ocean. A man is related to all nature. This perception of the worth of the vulgar is fruitful in discoveries. Goethe, in this very thing the most modern of the moderns, has shown us, as none ever did, the genius of the ancients.

There is one man of genius who has done much for this philosophy of life, whose literary value has never yet been rightly estimated;—I mean Emanuel Swedenborg. The most imaginative of men, yet writing with the precision of a mathematician, he endeavored to engraft a purely philosophical Ethics on the popular Christianity of his time. Such an attempt of course must have difficulty which no genius could surmount. But he saw and showed the connection between nature and the affections of the soul. He pierced the emblematic or spiritual character of the visible, audible, tangible world. Especially did his shade-loving muse hover over and interpret the lower parts of nature; he showed the mysterious bond that allies moral evil to the foul material forms, and has given in epical parables a theory of insanity, of beasts, of unclean and fearful things.

Another sign of our times, also marked by an analogous political movement, is the new importance given to the single person. Every thing that tends to insulate the individual,—to surround him with barriers of natural respect, so that each man shall feel the world is his, and man shall treat with man as a sovereign state with a sovereign state,—tends to true union as well as greatness. "I learned," said the melancholy Pestalozzi, "that no man in God's wide earth is either willing or able to help any other man." Help must come from the bosom alone. The scholar is that man who must take up into himself all the ability of the time, all the contributions of the past, all the hopes of the future. He must be an university of knowledges. If there be one lesson more than another which should pierce his ear, it is, The world is nothing, the man is all; in yourself is the law of all nature, and you know not yet how a globule of sap ascends; in yourself slumbers the whole of Reason; it is for you to know all; it is for you to dare all. Mr. President and Gentlemen, this confidence in the unsearched might of man belongs, by all motives, by all prophecy, by all preparation, to the American Scholar. We have listened too long to the courtly muses of Europe. The spirit of the American freeman is already suspected to be timid, imitative, tame. Public and private avarice make the air we breathe thick and fat. The scholar is decent, indolent, complaisant. See already the tragic consequence. The mind of this country, taught to aim at low objects, eats upon itself. There is no work for any but the decorous and the complaisant. Young men of the fairest promise, who begin life upon our shores, inflated by the mountain winds, shined upon by all the stars of God, find the earth below not in unison with these, but are hindered from action by the disgust which the principles on which business is managed inspire, and turn drudges, or die of disgust, some of them suicides. What is the remedy? They did not yet see, and thousands of young men as hopeful now crowding to the barriers for the career do not yet see, that if the single man plant himself indomitably on his instincts, and there abide, the huge world will come round to him. Patience,—patience; with the shades of all the good and great for company; and for solace the perspective of your own infinite life; and for work the study and the communication of principles, the making those instincts prevalent, the conversion of the world. Is it not the chief disgrace in the world, not to be an unit;—not to be reckoned one character;—not to yield that peculiar fruit which each man was created to bear, but to be reckoned in the gross, in the hundred, or the thousand, of the party, the section, to which we belong; and our opinion predicted geographically, as the north, or the south? Not so, brothers and friends—please God, ours shall not be so. We will walk on our own feet; we will work with our own hands; we will speak our own minds. The study of letters shall be no longer a name for pity, for doubt, and for sensual indulgence. The dread of man and the love of man shall be a wall of defence and a wreath of joy around all. A nation of men will for the first time exist, because each believes himself inspired by the Divine Soul which also inspires all men.

W.E.B. Du Bois

OF THE COMING OF JOHN

(1903)

What bring they 'neath the midnight,
　Beside the River-sea?
They bring the human heart wherein
　No nightly calm can be;
That droppeth never with the wind,
　Nor drieth with the dew;
O calm it, God; thy calm is broad
　To cover spirits too.
　　The river floweth on.

Mrs. Browning

Carlisle Street runs westward from the centre of Johnstown, across a great black bridge, down a hill and up again, by little shops and meat-markets, past single-storied homes, until suddenly it stops against a wide green lawn. It is a broad, restful place,

with two large buildings outlined against the west.
When at evening the winds come swelling from the
east, and the great pall of the city's smoke hangs wearily above the valley, then the red west glows like a
dreamland down Carlisle Street, and, at the tolling of
the supper-bell, throws the passing forms of students
in dark silhouette against the sky. Tall and black, they
move slowly by, and seem in the sinister light to flit
before the city like dim warning ghosts. Perhaps they
are; for this is Wells Institute, and these black students
have few dealings with the white city below.

And if you will notice, night after night, there is
one dark form that ever hurries last and late toward
the twinkling lights of Swain Hall,—for Jones is never
on time. A long, straggling fellow he is, brown and
hard-haired, who seems to be growing straight out of
his clothes, and walks with a half-apologetic roll. He
used perpetually to set the quiet dining-room into
waves of merriment, as he stole to his place after the
bell had tapped for prayers; he seemed so perfectly
awkward. And yet one glance at his face made one
forgive him much,—that broad, good-natured smile in
which lay no bit of art or artifice, but seemed just
bubbling good-nature and genuine satisfaction with
the world.

He came to us from Altamaha, away down there
beneath the gnarled oaks of Southeastern Georgia,
where the sea croons to the sands and the sands listen
till they sink half drowned beneath the waters, rising
only here and there in long, low islands. The white
folk of Altamaha voted John a good boy,—fine
plough-hand, good in the rice-fields, handy everywhere, and always good-natured and respectful. But
they shook their heads when his mother wanted to
send him off to school. "It'll spoil him,—ruin him,"
they said; and they talked as though they knew. But

full half the black folk followed him proudly to the station, and carried his queer little trunk and many bundles. And there they shook and shook hands, and the girls kissed him shyly and the boys clapped him on the back. So the train came, and he pinched his little sister lovingly, and put his great arms about his mother's neck, and then was away with a puff and a roar into the great yellow world that flamed and flared about the doubtful pilgrim. Up the coast they hurried, past the squares and palmettos of Savannah, through the cotton-fields and through the weary night, to Millville, and came with the morning to the noise and bustle of Johnstown.

And they that stood behind, that morning in Altamaha, and watched the train as it noisily bore playmate and brother and son away to the world, had thereafter one ever-recurring word,—"When John comes." Then what parties were to be, and what speakings in the churches; what new furniture in the front room,—perhaps even a new front room; and there would be a new schoolhouse, with John as teacher; and then perhaps a big wedding; all this and more—when John comes. But the white people shook their heads.

At first he was coming at Christmas-time,—but the vacation proved too short; and then, the next summer,—but times were hard and schooling costly, and so, instead, he worked in Johnstown. And so it drifted to the next summer, and the next,—till playmates scattered, and mother grew gray, and sister went up to the Judge's kitchen to work. And still the legend lingered,—"When John comes."

Up at the Judge's they rather liked this refrain; for they too had a John—a fair-haired, smooth-faced boy, who had played many a summer's day to its close with his darker namesake. "Yes, sir! John is at

Princeton, sir," said the broad-shouldered gray-haired Judge every morning as he marched down to the post-office. "Showing the Yankees what a Southern gentleman can do," he added; and strode home again with his letters and papers. Up at the great pillared house they lingered long over the Princeton letter,—the Judge and his frail wife, his sister and growing daughters. "It'll make a man of him," said the Judge, "college is the place." And then he asked the shy little waitress, "Well, Jennie, how's your John?" and added reflectively, "Too bad, too bad your mother sent him off,—it will spoil him." And the waitress wondered.

Thus in the far-away Southern village the world lay waiting, half consciously, the coming of two young men, and dreamed in an inarticulate way of new things that would be done and new thoughts that all would think. And yet it was singular that few thought of two Johns,—for the black folk thought of one John, and he was black; and the white folk thought of another John, and he was white. And neither world thought the other world's thought, save with a vague unrest.

Up in Johnstown, at the Institute, we were long puzzled at the case of John Jones. For a long time the clay seemed unfit for any sort of moulding. He was loud and boisterous, always laughing and singing, and never able to work consecutively at anything. He did not know how to study; he had no idea of thoroughness; and with his tardiness, carelessness, and appalling good-humor, we were sore perplexed. One night we sat in faculty-meeting, worried and serious; for Jones was in trouble again. This last escapade was too much, and so we solemnly voted "that Jones, on account of repeated disorder and inattention to work, be suspended for the rest of the term."

It seemed to us that the first time life ever struck Jones as a really serious thing was when the Dean told him he must leave school. He stared at the gray-haired man blankly, with great eyes. "Why,—why," he faltered, "but—I haven't graduated!" Then the Dean slowly and clearly explained, reminding him of the tardiness and the carelessness, of the poor lessons and neglected work, of the noise and disorder, until the fellow hung his head in confusion. Then he said quickly, "But you won't tell mammy and sister,—you won't write mammy, now will you? For if you won't I'll go out into the city and work, and come back next term and show you something." So the Dean promised faithfully, and John shouldered his little trunk, giving neither word nor look to the giggling boys, and walked down Carlisle Street to the great city, with sober eyes and a set and serious face.

Perhaps we imagined it, but someway it seemed to us that the serious look that crept over his boyish face that afternoon never left it again. When he came back to us he went to work with all his rugged strength. It was a hard struggle, for things did not come easily to him,—few crowding memories of early life and teaching came to help him on his new way; but all the world toward which he strove was of his own building, and he builded slow and hard. As the light dawned lingeringly on his new creations, he sat rapt and silent before the vision, or wandered alone over the green campus peering through and beyond the world of men into a world of thought. And the thoughts at times puzzled him sorely; he could not see just why the circle was not square, and carried it out fifty-six decimal places one midnight,—would have gone further, indeed, had not the matron rapped for lights out. He caught terrible colds lying on his back in the meadows of nights, trying to think out the solar system; he had grave doubts as to the ethics of the Fall of Rome, and strongly suspected the Germans of being thieves and rascals, despite his text-books; he pondered long over every new Greek word, and wondered why this meant that and why it couldn't mean something else, and how it must have felt to think all things in Greek. So he thought and puzzled along for himself,—pausing perplexed where others skipped merrily, and walking steadily through the difficulties where the rest stopped and surrendered.

Thus he grew in body and soul, and with him his clothes seemed to grow and arrange themselves; coat sleeves got longer, cuffs appeared, and collars got less soiled. Now and then his boots shone, and a new dignity crept into his walk. And we who saw daily a new thoughtfulness growing in his eyes began to expect something of this plodding boy. Thus he passed out of the preparatory school into college, and we who watched him felt four more years of change, which almost transformed the tall, grave man who bowed to us commencement morning. He had left his queer thought-world and come back to a world of motion and of men. He looked now for the first time sharply about him, and wondered he had seen so little before. He grew slowly to feel almost for the first time the Veil that lay between him and the white world; he first noticed now the oppression that had not seemed oppression before, differences that erstwhile seemed natural, restraints and slights that in his boyhood days had gone unnoticed or been greeted with a laugh. He felt angry now when men did not call him "Mister," he clenched his hands at the "Jim Crow" cars, and chafed at the color-line that hemmed in him and his. A tinge of sarcasm crept into his speech, and a vague bitterness into his life; and he sat long hours wondering and planning a way around these crooked things. Daily he found himself shrinking from the choked and narrow life of his native town. And yet he always planned to go back to Altamaha,—always planned to work there. Still, more and more as the day approached he hesitated with a nameless dread; and even the day after graduation he seized with eagerness the offer of the Dean to send him North with the quartette during the summer vacation, to sing for the Institute. A breath of air before the plunge, he said to himself in half apology.

It was a bright September afternoon, and the streets of New York were brilliant with moving men. They reminded John of the sea, as he sat in the square and watched them, so changelessly changing, so bright and dark, so grave and gay. He scanned their rich and faultless clothes, the way they carried their hands, the shape of their hats; he peered into the hurrying carriages. Then, leaning back with a sigh, he said, "This is the World." The notion suddenly seized him to see where the world was going; since many of the richer and brighter seemed hurrying all one way. So when a tall, light-haired young man and a little talkative lady came by, he rose half hesitatingly and followed them. Up the street they went, past stores and gay shops, across a broad square, until with a hundred others they entered the high portal of a great building.

He was pushed toward the ticket-office with the others, and felt in his pocket for the new five-dollar bill he had hoarded. There seemed really no time for hesitation, so he drew it bravely out, passed it to the busy clerk, and received simply a ticket but no change. When at last he realized that he had paid five dollars to enter he knew not what, he stood stock-still amazed. "Be careful," said a low voice behind him; "you must not lynch the colored gentleman simply because he's in your way," and a girl looked up roguishly into the eyes of her fair-haired escort. A shade of annoyance passed over the escort's face. "You *will* not understand us at the South," he said half impatiently, as if continuing an argument. "With all your professions, one never sees in the North so cordial and intimate relations between white and black as are everyday occurrences with us. Why, I remember my closest playfellow in boyhood was a little Negro named after me, and surely no two,—*well!*" The man stopped short and flushed to the roots of his hair, for there directly beside his reserved orchestra chairs sat the Negro he had stumbled over in the hallway. He hesitated and grew pale with anger, called the usher and gave him his card, with a few peremptory words, and slowly sat down. The lady deftly changed the subject.

All this John did not see, for he sat in a half-maze minding the scene about him; the delicate beauty of the hall, the faint perfume, the moving myriad of men, the rich clothing and low hum of talking seemed all a part of a world so different from his, so strangely more beautiful than anything he had known, that he sat in dreamland, and started when, after a hush, rose high and clear the music of Lohengrin's swan. The infinite beauty of the wail lingered and swept through every muscle of his frame, and put it all a-tune. He closed his eyes and grasped the elbows of the chair, touching unwittingly the lady's arm. And the lady drew away. A deep longing swelled in all his heart to rise with that clear music out of the dirt and dust of that low life that held him prisoned and befouled. If he could only live up in the free air where birds sang and setting suns had no touch of blood! Who had called him to be the slave and butt of all? And if he had called, what right had he to call when a world like this lay open before men?

Then the movement changed, and fuller, mightier harmony swelled away. He looked thoughtfully across the hall, and wondered why the beautiful gray-haired woman looked so listless, and what the little man could be whispering about. He would not like to be listless and idle, he thought, for he felt with the music the movement of power within him. If he but had some master-work, some life-service, hard,—aye, bitter hard, but without the cringing and sickening servility, without the cruel hurt that hardened his heart and soul. When at last a soft sorrow crept across the violins, there came to him the vision of a far-off home,—the great eyes of his sister, and the dark drawn face of his mother. And his heart sank below the waters, even as the sea-sand sinks by the shores of Altamaha, only to be lifted aloft again with that last ethereal wail of the swan that quivered and faded away into the sky.

It left John sitting so silent and rapt that he did not for some time notice the usher tapping him lightly on the shoulder and saying politely, "Will you step this way, please, sir?" A little surprised, he arose quickly at the last tap, and, turning to leave his seat, looked full into the face of the fair-haired young man. For the first time the young man recognized his dark boyhood playmate, and John knew that it was the Judge's son. The white John started, lifted his hand, and then froze into his chair; the black John smiled lightly, then grimly, and followed the usher down the aisle. The manager was sorry, very, very sorry,—but he explained that some mistake had been made in selling the gentleman a seat already disposed of; he would refund the money, of course,—and indeed felt the matter keenly, and so forth, and—before he had finished John was gone, walking hurriedly across the square and down the broad streets, and as he passed the park he buttoned his coat and said, "John Jones, you're a natural-born fool." Then he went to his lodgings and wrote a letter, and tore it up; he wrote an-

other, and threw it in the fire. Then he seized a scrap
of paper and wrote: "Dear Mother and Sister—I am
coming—John."

"Perhaps," said John, as he settled himself on the
train, "perhaps I am to blame myself in struggling
against my manifest destiny simply because it looks
hard and unpleasant. Here is my duty to Altamaha
plain before me; perhaps they'll let me help settle the
Negro problems there,—perhaps they won't. 'I will go
in to the King, which is not according to the law; and
if I perish, I perish.'" And then he mused and
dreamed, and planned a life-work; and the train flew
south.

Down in Altamaha, after seven long years, all the
world knew John was coming. The homes were
scrubbed and scoured,—above all, one; the gardens
and yards had an unwonted trimness, and Jennie
bought a new gingham. With some finesse and negotiation, all the dark Methodists and Presbyterians were
induced to join in a monster welcome at the Baptist
Church; and as the day drew near, warm discussions
arose on every corner as to the exact extent and nature of John's accomplishments. It was noontide on a
gray and cloudy day when he came. The black town
flocked to the depot, with a little of the white at the
edges,—a happy throng, with "Good-mawnings" and
"Howdys" and laughing and joking and jostling.
Mother sat yonder in the window watching; but sister
Jennie stood on the platform, nervously fingering her
dress,—tall and lithe, with soft brown skin and loving
eyes peering from out a tangled wilderness of hair.
John rose gloomily as the train stopped, for he was
thinking of the "Jim Crow" car; he stepped to the
platform, and paused: a little dingy station, a black
crowd gaudy and dirty, a half-mile of dilapidated shan-
ties along a straggling ditch of mud. An overwhelming

sense of the sordidness and narrowness of it all seized
him; he looked in vain for his mother, kissed coldly
the tall, strange girl who called him brother, spoke a
short, dry word here and there; then, lingering neither
for hand-shaking nor gossip, started silently up the
street, raising his hat merely to the last eager old
aunty, to her open-mouthed astonishment. The people
were distinctly bewildered. This silent, cold man,—was
this John? Where was his smile and hearty hand-
grasp? " 'Peared kind o' down in the mouf," said the
Methodist preacher thoughtfully. "Seemed monstus
stuck up," complained a Baptist sister. But the white
postmaster from the edge of the crowd expressed the
opinion of his folks plainly. "That damn Nigger," said
he, as he shouldered the mail and arranged his to-
bacco, "has gone North and got plum full o' fool notions; but they won't work in Altamaha." And the
crowd melted away.

The meeting of welcome at the Baptist Church was
a failure. Rain spoiled the barbecue, and thunder
turned the milk in the ice-cream. When the speaking
came at night, the house was crowded to overflowing.
The three preachers had especially prepared themselves, but somehow John's manner seemed to throw
a blanket over everything,—he seemed so cold and
preoccupied, and had so strange an air of restraint
that the Methodist brother could not warm up to his
theme and elicited not a single "Amen"; the Presbyte-
rian prayer was but feebly responded to, and even the
Baptist preacher, though he wakened faint enthusi-
asm, got so mixed up in his favorite sentence that he
had to close it by stopping fully fifteen minutes sooner
than he meant. The people moved uneasily in their
seats as John rose to reply. He spoke slowly and me-
thodically. The age, he said, demanded new ideas; we
were far different from those men of the seventeenth

and eighteenth centuries,—with broader ideas of human brotherhood and destiny. Then he spoke of the rise of charity and popular education, and particularly of the spread of wealth and work. The question was, then, he added reflectively, looking at the low discolored ceiling, what part the Negroes of this land would take in the striving of the new century. He sketched in vague outline the new Industrial School that might rise among these pines, he spoke in detail of the charitable and philanthropic work that might be organized, of money that might be saved for banks and business. Finally he urged unity, and deprecated especially religious and denominational bickering. "To-day," he said, with a smile, "the world cares little whether a man be Baptist or Methodist, or indeed a churchman at all, so long as he is good and true. What difference does it make whether a man be baptized in river or wash-bowl, or not at all? Let's leave all that littleness, and look higher." Then, thinking of nothing else, he slowly sat down. A painful hush seized that crowded mass. Little had they understood of what he said, for he spoke an unknown tongue, save the last word about baptism; that they knew, and they sat very still while the clock ticked. Then at last a low suppressed snarl came from the Amen corner, and an old bent man arose, walked over the seats, and climbed straight up into the pulpit. He was wrinkled and black, with scant gray and tufted hair; his voice and hands shook as with palsy; but on his face lay the intense rapt look of the religious fanatic. He seized the Bible with his rough, huge hands; twice he raised it inarticulate, and then fairly burst into the words, with rude and awful eloquence. He quivered, swayed, and bent; then rose aloft in perfect majesty, till the people moaned and wept, wailed and shouted, and a wild shrieking arose from the corners where all the pent-up feeling of the hour gathered itself and rushed into the air. John never knew clearly what the old man said; he only felt himself held up to scorn and scathing denunciation for trampling on the true Religion, and he realized with amazement that all unknowingly he had put rough, rude hands on something this little world held sacred. He arose silently, and passed out into the night. Down toward the sea he went, in the fitful starlight, half conscious of the girl who followed timidly after him. When at last he stood upon the bluff, he turned to his little sister and looked upon her sorrowfully, remembering with sudden pain how little thought he had given her. He put his arm about her and let her passion of tears spend itself on his shoulder.

Long they stood together, peering over the gray unresting water.

"John," she said, "does it make every one—unhappy when they study and learn lots of things?"

He paused and smiled. "I am afraid it does," he said.

"And, John, are you glad you studied?"

"Yes," came the answer, slowly but positively.

She watched the flickering lights upon the sea, and said thoughtfully, "I wish I was unhappy,—and—and," putting both arms about his neck, "I think I am, a little, John."

It was several days later that John walked up to the Judge's house to ask for the privilege of teaching the Negro school. The Judge himself met him at the front door, stared a little hard at him, and said brusquely, "Go 'round to the kitchen door, John, and wait." Sitting on the kitchen steps, John stared at the corn, thoroughly perplexed. What on earth had come over him? Every step he made offended someone. He had come to save his people, and before he left the depot he had hurt them. He sought to teach them at the church, and had outraged their deepest feelings. He had schooled himself to be respectful to the Judge, and then blundered into his front door. And all the time he had meant right,—and yet, and yet, somehow he found it so hard and strange to fit his old surroundings again, to find his place in the world about him. He could not remember that he used to have any difficulty in the past, when life was glad and gay. The world seemed smooth and easy then. Perhaps,—but his sister came to the kitchen door just then and said the Judge awaited him.

The Judge sat in the dining-room amid his morning's mail, and he did not ask John to sit down. He plunged squarely into the business. "You've come for the school, I suppose. Well, John, I want to speak to you plainly. You know I'm a friend to your people. I've helped you and your family, and would have done more if you hadn't got the notion of going off. Now I like the colored people, and sympathize with all their reasonable aspirations; but you and I both know, John, that in this country the Negro must remain subordinate, and can never expect to be the equal of white men. In their place, your people can be honest and respectful; and God knows, I'll do what I can to help them. But when they want to reverse nature, and rule white men, and marry white women, and sit in my parlor, then, by God! we'll hold them under if we have to lynch every Nigger in the land. Now, John, the question is, are you, with your education and Northern notions, going to accept the situation and teach the darkies to be faithful servants and laborers as your fathers were,—I knew your father, John, he belonged to my brother, and he was a good Nigger. Well—well, are you going to be like him, or are you going to try to put fool ideas of rising and equality into these folks' heads, and make them discontented and unhappy?''

"I am going to accept the situation, Judge Henderson," answered John, with a brevity that did not escape the keen old man. He hesitated a moment, and then said shortly, "Very well,—we'll try you awhile. Good-morning."

It was a full month after the opening of the Negro school that the other John came home, tall, gay, and headstrong. The mother wept, the sisters sang. The whole white town was glad. A proud man was the Judge, and it was a goodly sight to see the two swinging down Main Street together. And yet all did not go smoothly between them, for the younger man could not and did not veil his contempt for the little town, and plainly had his heart set on New York. Now the one cherished ambition of the Judge was to see his son mayor of Altamaha, representative to the legislature, and—who could say?—governor of Georgia. So the argument often waxed hot between them. "Good heavens, father," the younger man would say after dinner, as he lighted a cigar and stood by the fireplace, "you surely don't expect a young fellow like me to settle down permanently in this—this God-forgotten town with nothing but mud and Negroes?" "*I* did," the Judge would answer laconically; and on this particular day it seemed from the gathering scowl that he was about to add something more emphatic, but neighbors had already begun to drop in to admire his son, and the conversation drifted.

"Heah that John is livenin' things up at the darky school," volunteered the postmaster, after a pause.

"What now?" asked the Judge, sharply.

"Oh, nothin' in particulah,—just his almighty air and uppish ways. B'lieve I did heah somethin' about his givin' talks on the French Revolution, equality, and such like. He's what I call a dangerous Nigger."

"Have you heard him say anything out of the way?"

"Why, no—but Sally, our girl, told my wife a lot of rot. Then, too, I don't need to heah: a Nigger what won't say 'sir' to a white man, or—"

"Who is this John?" interrupted the son.

"Why, it's little black John, Peggy's son,—your old playfellow."

The young man's face flushed angrily, and then he laughed.

"Oh" said he, "it's the darky that tried to force himself into a seat beside the lady I was escorting—"

But Judge Henderson waited to hear no more. He had been nettled all day, and now at this he rose with a half-smothered oath, took his hat and cane, and walked straight to the schoolhouse.

For John, it had been a long, hard pull to get things started in the rickety old shanty that sheltered his school. The Negroes were rent into factions for and against him, the parents were careless, the children irregular and dirty, and books, pencils, and slates largely missing. Nevertheless, he struggled hopefully on, and seemed to see at last some glimmering of dawn. The attendance was larger and the children were a shade cleaner this week. Even the booby class in reading showed a little comforting progress. So John settled himself with renewed patience this afternoon.

"Now, Mandy," he said cheerfully, "that's better; but you mustn't chop your words up so: 'If—the—man—goes.' Why, your little brother even wouldn't tell a story that way, now would he?"

"Naw, suh, he cain't talk."

"All right; now let's try again: 'If the man—'"

"John!"

The whole school started in surprise, and the teacher half arose, as the red, angry face of the Judge appeared in the open doorway.

"John, this school is closed. You children can go home and get to work. The white people of Altamaha are not spending their money on black folks to have their heads crammed with impudence and lies. Clear out! I'll lock the door myself."

Up at the great pillared house the tall young son wandered aimlessly about after his father's abrupt departure. In the house there was little to interest him; the books were old and stale, the local newspaper flat, and the women had retired with headaches and sewing. He tried a nap, but it was too warm. So he sauntered out into the fields, complaining disconsolately, "Good Lord! how long will this imprisonment last!" He was not a bad fellow,—just a little spoiled and self-indulgent, and as headstrong as his proud father. He seemed a young man pleasant to look upon, as he sat on the great black stump at the edge of the pines idly swinging his legs and smoking. "Why, there isn't even a girl worth getting up a respectable flirtation with," he growled. Just then his eye caught a tall, willowy figure hurrying toward him on the narrow path. He looked with interest at first, and then burst into a laugh as he said, "Well, I declare, if it isn't Jennie, the little brown kitchen-maid! Why, I never noticed before what a trim little body she is. Hello, Jennie! Why, you haven't kissed me since I came home," he said gaily. The young girl stared at him in surprise and confusion,—faltered something inarticulate, and attempted to pass. But a wilful mood had seized the young idler, and he caught at her arm. Frightened, she slipped by; and half mischievously he turned and ran after her through the tall pines.

Yonder, toward the sea, at the end of the path,

came John slowly, with his head down. He had turned wearily homeward from the schoolhouse; then, thinking to shield his mother from the blow, started to meet his sister as she came from work and break the news of his dismissal to her. "I'll go away," he said slowly; "I'll go away and find work, and send for them. I cannot live here longer." And then the fierce, buried anger surged up into his throat. He waved his arms and hurried wildly up the path.

The great brown sea lay silent. The air scarce breathed. The dying day bathed the twisted oaks and mighty pines black and gold. There came from the wind no warning, not a whisper from the cloudless sky. There was only a black man hurrying on with an ache in his heart, seeing neither sun nor sea, but starting as from a dream at the frightened cry that woke the pines, to see his dark sister struggling in the arms of a tall and fair-haired man.

He said not a word, but, seizing a fallen limb, struck him with all the pent-up hatred of his great black arm; and the body lay white and still beneath the pines, all bathed in sunshine and in blood. John looked at it dreamily, then walked back to the house briskly, and said in a soft voice, "Mammy, I'm going away,—I'm going to be free."

She gazed at him dimly and faltered, "No'th, honey, is yo' gwine No'th agin?"

He looked out where the North Star glistened pale above the waters, and said, "Yes, mammy, I'm going—North."

Then, without another word, he went out into the narrow lane, up by the straight pines, to the same winding path, and seated himself on the great black stump, looking at the blood where the body had lain. Yonder in the gray past he had played with that dead boy, romping together under the solemn trees. The night deepened; he thought of the boys at Johnstown. He wondered how Brown had turned out, and Carey? And Jones,—Jones? Why, *he* was Jones, and he wondered what they would all say when they knew, when they knew, in that great long dining-room with its hundreds of merry eyes. Then as the sheen of the starlight stole over him, he thought of the gilded ceiling of that vast concert hall, and heard stealing toward him the faint sweet music of the swan. Hark! was it music, or the hurry and shouting of men? Yes, surely! Clear and high the faint sweet melody rose and fluttered like a living thing, so that the very earth trembled as with the tramp of horses and murmur of angry men.

He leaned back and smiled toward the sea, whence rose the strange melody, away from the dark shadows where lay the noise of horses galloping, galloping on. With an effort he roused himself, bent forward, and looked steadily down the pathway, softly humming the "Song of the Bride,"—

"Freudig geführt, ziehet dahin."
["Joyfully led, drawn onward."]

Amid the trees in the dim morning twilight he watched their shadows dancing and heard their horses thundering toward him, until at last they came sweeping like a storm, and he saw in front that haggard white-haired man, whose eyes flashed red with fury. Oh, how he pitied him,— pitied him,—and wondered if he had the coiling twisted rope. Then, as the storm burst round him, he rose slowly to his feet and turned his closed eyes toward the Sea.

And the world whistled in his ears.

Albert Einstein

ON EDUCATION
(1936)

From an address at Albany, N.Y., on the occasion of the celebration of the tercentenary of higher education in America, October 15, 1936. Translated by Lina Arronet.

A day of celebration generally is in the first place dedicated to retrospect, especially to the memory of personages who have gained special distinction for the development of the cultural life. This friendly service for our predecessors must indeed not be neglected, particularly as such a memory of the best of the past is proper to stimulate the well-disposed of today to a courageous effort. But this should be done by someone who, from his youth, has been connected with this State and is familiar with its past, not by one who like a gypsy has wandered about and gathered his experiences in all kinds of countries.

Thus, there is nothing else left for me but to speak about such questions as, independently of space and time, always have been and will be connected with educational matters. In this attempt I cannot lay any claim to being an authority, especially as intelligent and well-meaning men of all times have dealt with educational problems and have certainly repeatedly expressed their views clearly about these matters. From what source shall I, as a partial layman in the realm of pedagogy, derive courage to expound opinions with no foundations except personal experience and personal conviction? If it were really a scientific matter, one would probably be tempted to silence by such considerations.

However, with the affairs of active human beings it is different. Here knowledge of truth alone does not suffice; on the contrary this knowledge must continually be renewed by ceaseless effort, if it is not to be lost. It resembles a statue of marble which stands in the desert and is continuously threatened with burial by the shifting sand. The hands of service must ever be at work, in order that the marble continue lastingly to shine in the sun. To these serving hands mine also shall belong.

The school has always been the most important means of transferring the wealth of tradition from one generation to the next. This applies today in an even higher degree than in former times, for through modern development of the economic life, the family as bearer of tradition and education has been weakened. The continuance and health of human society is therefore in a still higher degree dependent on the school than formerly.

Sometimes one sees in the school simply the instrument for transferring a certain maximum quantity of knowledge to the growing generation. But that is not right. Knowledge is dead; the school, however, serves the living. It should develop in the young individuals those qualities and capabilities which are of value for the welfare of the commonwealth. But that does not mean that individuality should be destroyed and the individual become a mere tool of the community, like a bee or an ant. For a community of standardized individuals without personal originality and personal aims would be a poor community without possibilities for development. On the contrary, the aim must be the training of independently acting and thinking individuals, who, however, see in the service of the community their highest life problem. So far as I can judge, the English school system comes nearest to the realization of this ideal.

But how shall one try to attain this ideal? Should one perhaps try to realize this aim by moralizing? Not at all. Words are and remain an empty sound, and the road to perdition has ever been accompanied by lip service to an ideal. But personalities are not formed by what is heard and said, but by labor and activity.

The most important method of education accordingly always has consisted of that in which the pupil was urged to actual performance. This applies as well to the first attempts at writing of the primary boy as to the doctor's thesis on graduation from the university, or as to the mere memorizing of a poem, the writing of a composition, the interpretation and translation of a text, the solving of a mathematical problem or the practice of physical sport.

But behind every achievement exists the motivation which is at the foundation of it and which in turn is strengthened and nourished by the accomplishment of the undertaking. Here there are the greatest differences and they are of greatest importance to the educational value of the school. The same work may owe its origin to fear and compulsion, ambitious desire for authority and distinction, or loving interest in the object and a desire for truth and understanding, and thus to that divine curiosity which every healthy child possesses, but which so often is weakened early. The educational influence which is exercised upon the pupil by the accomplishment of one and the same work may be widely different, depending upon whether fear of hurt, egoistic passion, or desire for pleasure and satisfaction is at the bottom of this work. And nobody will maintain that the administration of the school and the attitude of the teachers do not have an influence upon the molding of the psychological foundation for pupils.

To me the worst thing seems to be for a school principally to work with methods of fear, force, and artificial authority. Such treatment destroys the sound sentiments, the sincerity, and the self-confidence of the pupil. It produces the submissive subject. It is no wonder that such schools are the rule in Germany and Russia. I know that the schools in this country are free from this worst evil; this also is so in Switzerland and probably in all democratically governed countries. It is comparatively simple to keep the school free from this worst of all evils. Give into the power of the teacher the fewest possible coercive measures, so that the only source of the pupil's respect for the teacher is the human and intellectual qualities of the latter.

The second-named motive, ambition or, in milder terms, the aiming at recognition and consideration, lies firmly fixed in human nature. With absence of mental stimulus of this kind, human cooperation would be entirely impossible; the desire for the approval of one's fellow-man certainly is one of the most important binding powers of society. In this complex of feelings, constructive and destructive forces lie closely together. Desire for approval and recognition is a healthy motive; but the desire to be acknowledged as better, stronger, or more intelligent than a fellow being or fellow scholar easily leads to an excessively egoistic psychological adjustment, which may become injurious for the individual and for the community. Therefore the school and the teacher must guard against employing the easy method of creating individual ambition, in order to induce the pupils to diligent work.

Darwin's theory of the struggle for existence and the selectivity connected with it has by many people been cited as authorization of the encouragement of the spirit of competition. Some people also in such a way have tried to prove pseudo-scientifically the necessity of the destructive economic struggle of competition between individuals. But this is wrong, because man owes his strength in the struggle for existence to the fact that he is a socially living animal. As little as a battle between single ants of an ant hill is essential for survival, just so little is this the case with the individual members of a human community.

Therefore one should guard against preaching to the young man success in the customary sense as the aim of life. For a successful man is he who receives a great deal from his fellow-men, usually incomparably more than corresponds to his service to them. The value of a man, however, should be seen in what he gives and not in what he is able to receive.

The most important motive for work in the school and in life is the pleasure in work, pleasure in its result, and the knowledge of the value of the result to the community. In the awakening and strengthening of these psychological forces in the young man, I see the most important task given by the school. Such a psychological foundation alone leads to a joyous desire for the highest possessions of men, knowledge and artist-like workmanship.

The awakening of these productive psychological powers is certainly less easy than the practice of force or the awakening of individual ambition but is the more valuable for it. The point is to develop the child-like inclination for play and the childlike desire for recognition and to guide the child over to important fields for society; it is that education which in the main is founded upon the desire for successful activity and acknowledgment. If the school succeeds in working successfully from such points of view, it will be highly honored by the rising generation and the tasks given by the school will be submitted to as a sort of gift. I have known children who preferred school-time to vacation.

Such a school demands from the teacher that he be a kind of artist in his province. What can be done that this spirit be gained in the school? For this there is just as little a universal remedy as there is for an individual to remain well. But there are certain necessary conditions which can be met. First, teachers should grow up in such schools. Second, the teacher should be given extensive liberty in the selection of the material to be taught and the methods of teaching employed by him. For it is true also of him that pleasure in the shaping of his work is killed by force and exterior pressure.

If you have followed attentively my meditations up to this point, you will probably wonder about one thing. I have spoken fully about in what spirit, according to my opinion, youth should be instructed. But I have said nothing yet about the choice of subjects for instruction, nor about the method of teaching. Should language predominate or technical education in science?

To this I answer: in my opinion all this is of secondary importance. If a young man has trained his muscles and physical endurance by gymnastics and walking, he will later be fitted for every physical work. This is also analogous to the training of the mind and the exercising of the mental and manual skill. Thus the wit was not wrong who defined education in this way: "Education is that which remains, if one has forgotten everything he learned in school." For this reason I am not at all anxious to take sides in the struggle between the followers of the classical philologic-historical education and the education more devoted to natural science.

On the other hand, I want to oppose the idea that the school has to teach directly that special knowledge and those accomplishments which one has to use later directly in life. The demands of life are much too manifold to let such a specialized training in school appear possible. Apart from that, it seems to me, moreover, objectionable to treat the individual like a dead tool. The school should always have as its aim that the young man leave it as a harmonious personality, not as a specialist. This in my opinion is true in a certain sense even for technical schools, whose students will devote themselves to a quite definite profession. The development of general ability for independent thinking and judgment should always be placed foremost, not the acquisition of special knowledge. If a person masters the fundamentals of his subject and has learned to think and work independently, he will surely find his way and besides will better be able to adapt himself to progress and changes than the person whose training principally consists in the acquiring of detailed knowledge.

Finally, I wish to emphasize once more that what has been said here in a somewhat categorical form does not claim to mean more than the personal opinion of a man, which is founded upon *nothing but* his own personal experience, which he has gathered as a student and as a teacher.

RELIGIOUS
FERVOR

Cotton Mather

THE TRYAL OF *BRIDGET BISHOP, ALIAS OLIVER,* AT THE COURT OF *OYER* AND *TERMINER,* HELD AT SALEM

(1692)

I. She was Indicted for Bewitching of several Persons in the Neighbourhood, the Indictment being drawn up, according to the *Form* in such Cases usual. And pleading, *Not Guilty,* there were brought in several persons, who had long undergone many kinds of Miseries, which were preternaturally inflicted, and generally ascribed unto an *horrible Witchcraft.* There was little occasion to prove the *Witchcraft,* it being evident and notorious to all beholders. Now to fix the *Witchcraft* on the Prisoner at the bar, the first thing used, was the Testimony of the *Bewitched*; whereof several testifi'd, That the *Shape* of the Prisoner did oftentimes very grievously Pinch them, Choke them, Bite them, and Afflict them; urging them to write their Names in a *Book,* which said Spectre called, *Ours.* One of them did further testifie, that it was the *Shape* of this Prisoner, with another, which one day took her from her Wheel, and carrying her to River-side, threatened there to Drown her, if she did not Sign to the *Book*

103

mentioned: which yet she refused. Others of them did also testifie, that the Said *Shape*, did in her Threats brag to them, that she had been the Death of Sundry Persons, then by her named; that she had *Ridden* a Man, then likewise named. Another testifi'd, the Apparition of *Ghosts* unto the Spectre of *Bishop*, crying out, *You murdered us!* About the Truth whereof, there was in the Matter of Fact but too much Suspicion.

II. It was testifi'd, That at the Examination of the Prisoner before the Magistrates, the Bewitched were extremely tortured. If she did but cast her Eyes on them, they were presently struck down; and this in such a manner that there could be no Collusion in the Business. But upon the Touch of her Hand upon them, when they lay in their Swoons, they would immediately Revive; and not upon the Touch of any ones else. Moreover, Upon some Special Actions of her Body, as the shaking of her Head, or the turning of her Eyes, they presently and painfully fell into the like postures. And many of the like Accidents now fell out, while she was at the Bar. One at the same time testifying, That she said, *She could not be troubled to see the afflicted thus tormented.*

III. There was Testimony likewise brought in, that a Man striking once at the place, where a bewitched person said, the *Shape* of this *Bishop* stood, the bewitched cried out, *That he had tore her coat,* in the place then particularly specifi'd; and the Woman's Coat was found to be Torn in that very place.

IV. One *Deliverance Hobbs,* who had confessed her being a Witch, was now tormented by the Spectres, for her Confession. And she now testifi'd, That this

Bishop tempted her to Sign the *Book* again, and to deny what she had confessed. She affirm'd, That it was the Shape of the Prisoner, which whipped her with Iron Rods, to compel her thereunto. And she affirmed, that this *Bishop* was at the General Meeting of the Witches, in a Field at *Salem*-Village, and there partook of a Diabolical Sacrament in Bread and Wine then administred.

V. To render it further unquestionable, That the Prisoner at the Bar, was the Person truly charged in THIS *Witchcraft,* there were produced many Evidences of OTHER *Witchcrafts,* by her perpetrated. For Instance, *John Cook* testifi'd, That about five or six Years ago, one Morning, about Sunrise, he was in Chamber assaulted by the *Shape* of this Prisoner: which look'd on him, grinn'd at him, and very much hurt him with a Blow on the side of the Head: and that on the same day, about Noon, the same *Shape* walked in the Room where he was, and an Apple strangely flew out of his Hand, into the Lap of his Mother, six or eight Foot from him.

VI. *Samuel Gray* testifi'd, That about fourteen Years ago, he wak'd on a Night, and saw the Room where he lay full of Light; and that he then saw plainly a Woman between the cradle, and the Bed-side, which look'd upon him. He rose, and it vanished; tho' he found the doors all fast. Looking out at the Entry-door, he saw the same Woman, in the same Garb again; and said, *In God's Name, what do you come for?* He went to Bed, and had the same Woman again assaulting him. The Child in the Cradle gave a great Screech, and the Woman disappeared. It was long before the Child could be quieted; and tho' it were a very likely thriving Child, yet from this time it pined away, and, and, after divers Months, died in a sad Condition. He knew not *Bishop,* nor her Name; but when he saw her after this, he knew by her Countenance and Apparel, and all Circumstances, that it was the Apparition of this *Bishop,* which had thus troubled him.

VII. *John Bly* and his Wife testifi'd, That he bought a Sow of *Edward Bishop,* the Husband of the Prisoner; and was to pay the Price agreed, unto another person. This Prisoner being angry that she was thus hindred from fingring the Mony, quarrell'd with *Bly.* Soon after which, the Sow was taken with strange Fits; Jumping, Leaping, and Knocking her Head against the Fence; she seemed Blind and Deaf, and would neither Eat nor be Suck'd. Whereupon a Neighbour said, she believed the Creature was *Over-looked*; and sundry other Circumstances concurred, which made the Deponents believe that *Bishop* had witched it.

VIII. *Richard Coman* testifi'd, That eight Years ago, as he lay awake in his Bed, with a Light burning in the Room, he was annoy'd with the Apparition of this *Bishop,* and of two more that were strangers to him, who came and oppressed him so, that he could neither stir himself, nor wake anyone else, and that he was the Night after, molested in the like manner; the said *Bishop,* taking him by the Throat, and pulling him almost out of the Bed. His Kinsman offered for this cause to lodge with him; and that Night, as they were awake, discoursing together, this *Coman* was once more visited by the Guests which had formerly been so troublesome; his Kinsman being at the same time struck speechless, and unable to move Hand or Foot. He had laid his Sword by him, which these unhappy Spectres did strive much to wrest from him; only he held too fast for them. He then grew able to call the People of his House; but altho' they heard him, yet they had not power to speak or stir; until at last, one of the People crying out, *What's the matter?* The Spectres all vanished.

IX. *Samuel Shattock* testify'd, That in the Year, 1680. this *Bridget Bishop,* often came to his House upon such frivolous and foolish Errands, That they suspected she came indeed with a purpose of mischief. Presently, whereupon, his eldest Child, which was of as promising Health and Sense, as any Child of its Age, began to droop exceedingly; and the oftner that Bishop came to the House, the worse grew the Child. As the Child would be standing at the Door, he would be thrown and bruised against the Stones, by an invisible Hand, and in like Sort knock his Face against the sides of the House, and bruise it after a miserable manner. Afterwards this Bishop would bring him things to Dye, whereof he can not imagine any use; and when she paid him a piece of Mony, the Purse and Mony were unaccountably conveyed out of a lock'd Box, and never seen anymore. The Child was immediately, hereupon, taken with terrible fits, whereof his friends thought he would have dyed: Indeed he did almost nothing but Cry and Sleep for several Months together; and at length his Understanding was utterly taken away. Among other Symptoms of and Inchantment upon him, one was, That there was a Board in the Garden, whereon he would walk; and all the Invitations in the World could not fetch him off. About 17 or 18 years after, there came a stranger to *Shattock's* House, who seeing the Child, said, *This poor Child is bewitched; and you have a Neighbour living not far off, who is a Witch.* He added, *Your Neighbour has had a falling out with your Wife;*

and she said, in her heart, your Wife is a proud Woman, and she would bring down her pride in this Child. He then remembered, that Bishop had parted from his Wife in muttering and menacing Terms, a little before the Child was taken ill. The abovesaid Stranger would needs carry the bewitched Boy with him, to Bishop's House, on pretense of buying a pot of Cyder. The Woman entertained him in furious manner; and flew also upon the Boy, scratching his Face till the Blood came, and saying, *Thou Rogue, what dost thou bring this fellow here to plague me?* Now it seems the Man had said, before he went, That he would fetch Blood of *her*. Ever after the Boy was follow'd with grievous Fits, which the Doctors themselves generally ascribed unto *Witchcraft*; and wherein he would be thrown still into the *Fire* or the *Water*, if he were not constantly look'd after; and it was verily believed that *Bishop* was the cause of it.

X. *John Louder* testify'd, That upon some little controversy with *Bishop* about her Fowls, going well to Bed, he did awake in the Night by Moonlight, and did see clearly the likeness of this Woman grievously oppressing him; in which miserable condition she held him, unable to help himself, till near Day. He told *Bishop* of this, but she deny'd it and threatened him very much. Quickly after this, being at home on a Lord's day, with the doors shut about him, he saw a black Pig approach him; at which, he going to kick, it vanished away. Immediately after, sitting down, he saw a black Thing jump in at the Window, and come and stand before him. The Body was like that of a Monkey, the Feet like a Cocks, but the Face much like a Mans. He being so extremely affrighted, That he could not speak; this Monster spoke to him, and said, *I am a messenger sent unto you, for I understand that you are in some trouble of Mind, and if you will be ruled by me, you shall want for nothing in this World.* Whereupon he endeavored to clap his hands upon it; but he could feel no substance; and it jumped out of the Window again; but immediately came in by the Porch, tho' the Doors were shut, and said, *You had better take my counsel!* He then struck at it with a stick, but struck only the Ground-sel, and broke the Stick: The Arm with which he struck was presently Disenabled, and it vanished away. He presently went out at the Back-door, and spied this *Bishop,* in her Orchard, going toward her House, but he had not power to set one foot forward unto her. Whereupon, returning into the House, he was immediately accosted by the same Monster he had seen before; which Goblin was now going to fly at him; whereat he cry'd out, *The whole Armour of God be between me and you!* So it sprang back, and flew over the Apple-tree; shaking many Apples off the tree, in its flying over. At its leap, it flung dirt with its Feet against the Stomack of the Man; whereon he was then struck Dumb, and so continued for three Days together. Upon the producing of this Testimony, *Bishop* deny'd that she knew this Deponent: Yet their two Orchards joined; and they had often had their little Quarrels for some years together.

XI. *William Stacy* testify'd, That receiving Mony of this *Bishop,* for work done by him; he was gone but a matter of three rods from her, and looking for his Mony, found it unaccountably gone from him. Some time after, *Bishop* asked him, whether her Father would grind her Grist for her? He demanded why? She reply'd, *Because folks count me a Witch.* He answered, *No question but he will grind it for you.* Being then gone about six rods from her, with a small Load in his Cart, suddenly the Off-wheel stump'd, and sunk down into an hole, upon plain Ground; so that the Deponent was forced to get help for recovering of the Wheel: But stepping back to look for the hole, which might give him this Disaster, there was none at all to be found. Some time after, he was waked in the Night; but it seem'd as light as day; and he perfectly saw the shape of this *Bishop* in the room, troubling of him; but upon her going out, all was dark again. He charg'd *Bishop* afterwards with it, and she deny'd it not; but was very angry. Quickly after, this Deponent having been threatened by *Bishop,* as he was in a dark Night going to the Barn, he was very suddenly taken or lifted from the Ground, and thrown against a Stone-wall: After that, he was again hoisted up and thrown down a bank, at the end of his House. After this again, passing by this *Bishop,* his Horse with a small Load, striving to draw, all his gears flew to pieces, and the Cart fell down; and this Deponent going then to lift a Bag of Corn, of about two Bushels, could not budge it with all his Might.

Many other Pranks of this *Bishop's* this Deponent was ready to testify. He also testify'd, that he verily believ'd, the said *Bishop,* was the Instrument of his Daughter *Prisailla's* Death; of which suspicion, pregnant Reasons were assigned.

XII. To crown all, *John Bly* and *William Bly* testify'd, That being employ'd by *Bridget Bishop,* to help to take down the Cellar wall of the old House wherein she formerly lived, they did in holes of the said old Wall, find several *Poppets,* made up of Rags and Hogs-bristles, with headless Pins in them, the Points being outward; whereof she could not give no Account unto the Court, That was reasonable or tolerable.

XIII. One thing that made against the Prisoner was, her being evidently convicted of *gross Lying* in the Court, several times, while she was making her Plea; but besides this, a Jury of Women found a preternatural Teat upon her Body; but upon a second search, within 3 or 4 hours, there was no such thing to be seen. There was also an Account of other People whom this Woman had afflicted; and there might have been many more, if they had been enquired for; but there was no need of them.

XIV. There was one very strange thing more, with which the Court was newly entertained. As this woman was under a Guard, passing by the great and spacious Meeting House of *Salem,* she gave a look towards the House: And immediately a *Demon* invisibly entring the Meeting house, tore down a part of it; so that tho' there was no Person to be seen there, yet the People, at the noise, running in, found a Board, which was strongly fastened with several nails, transported unto another quarter of the House.

Abraham Joshua Heschel

THE MEANING OF
THIS HOUR

(1943)

Emblazoned over the gates of the world in which we live is the escutcheon of the demons. The mark of Cain in the face of man has come to overshadow the likeness of God. There has never been so much guilt and distress, agony, and terror. At no time has the earth been so soaked with blood. Fellowmen turned out to be evil ghosts, monstrous and weird. Ashamed and dismayed, we ask: Who is responsible?

History is a pyramid of efforts and errors; yet at times it is the Holy Mountain on which God holds judgment over the nations. Few are privileged to discern God's judgment in history. But all may be guided by the words of the Baal Shem: If a man has beheld evil, he may know that it was shown to him in order that he learn his own guilt and repent; for what is shown to him is also within him.

We have trifled with the name of God. We have taken the ideals in vain. We have called for the Lord. He came. And was ignored. We have preached but eluded Him. We have praised but defied Him. Now we reap the fruits of our failure. Through centuries

His voice cried in the wilderness. How skillfully it was trapped and imprisoned in the temples! How often it was drowned or distorted! Now we behold how it gradually withdraws, abandoning one people after another, departing from their souls, despising their wisdom. The taste for the good has all but gone from the earth. Men heap spite upon cruelty, malice upon atrocity.

The horrors of our time fill our souls with reproach and everlasting shame. We have profaned the word of God, and we have given the wealth of our land, the ingenuity of our minds and the dear lives of our youth to tragedy and perdition. There has never been more reason for man to be ashamed than now. Silence hovers mercilessly over many dreadful lands. The day of the Lord is a day without the Lord. Where is God? Why didst Thou not halt the trains loaded with Jews being led to slaughter? It is so hard to rear a child, to nourish and to educate. Why dost Thou make it so easy to kill? Like Moses, we hide our face; for we are afraid to look upon *Elohim,* upon His power of judgment. Indeed, where were we when men learned to hate in the days of starvation? When raving madmen were sowing wrath in the hearts of the unemployed?

Let modern dictatorship not serve as an alibi for our conscience. We have failed to fight *for* right, *for* justice, *for* goodness; as a result we must fight *against* wrong, *against* injustice, *against* evil. We have failed to offer sacrifices on the altar of peace; thus we offered sacrifices on the altar of war. A tale is told of a band of inexperienced mountain climbers. Without guides, they struck recklessly into the wilderness. Suddenly a rocky ledge gave way beneath their feet and they tumbled headlong into a dismal pit. In the darkness of the pit they recovered from their shock only to find themselves set upon by a swarm of angry snakes. Every crevice became alive with fanged, hissing things. For each snake the desperate men slew, ten more seemed to lash out in its place. Strangely enough, one man seemed to stand aside from the fight. When indignant voices of his struggling companions reproached him for not fighting, he called back: If we remain here, we shall be dead before the snakes. I am searching for a way of escape from the pit for all of us.

Our world seems not unlike a pit of snakes. We did not sink into the pit in 1939, or even in 1933. We had descended into it generations ago, and the snakes have sent their venom into the bloodstream of humanity, gradually paralyzing us, numbing nerve after nerve, dulling our minds, darkening our vision. Good and evil, that were once as real as day and night, have become a blurred mist. In our every-day life we worshiped force, despised compassion, and obeyed no law but our unappeasable appetite. The vision of the sacred has all but died in the soul of man. And when greed, envy and the reckless will to power came to maturity, the serpents cherished in the bosom of our civilization broke out of their dens to fall upon the helpless nations.

The outbreak of war was no surprise. It came as a long expected sequel to a spiritual disaster. Instilled with the gospel that truth is mere advantage and reverence weakness, people succumbed to the bigger advantage of a lie—"the Jew is our misfortune"—and to the power of arrogance—"tomorrow the whole world shall be ours," "the peoples' democracies must depend upon force." The roar of bombers over Rotterdam, Warsaw, London, was but the echo of thoughts bred for years by individual brains, and later applauded by entire nations. It was through our failure that people started to suspect that science is a device for exploitation; parliaments pulpits for hypocrisy, and religion a pretext for a bad conscience. In the tantalized souls of those who had faith in ideals, suspicion became a dogma and contempt the only solace. Mistaking the abortions of their conscience for intellectual heroism, many thinkers employ clever pens to scold and to scorn the reverence for life, the awe for truth, the loyalty to justice. Man, about to hang himself, discovers it is easier to hang others.

The conscience of the world was destroyed by those who were wont to blame others rather than themselves. Let us remember. We revered the instincts but distrusted the prophets. We labored to perfect engines and let our inner life go to wreck. We ridiculed superstition until we lost our ability to believe. We have helped to extinguish the light our fathers had kindled. We have bartered holiness for convenience, loyalty for success, love for power, wisdom for information, tradition for fashion.

We cannot dwell at ease under the sun of our civilization as our ancestors thought we could. What was in the minds of our martyred brothers in their last hours? They died with disdain and scorn for a civilization in which the killing of civilians could become a carnival of fun, for a civilization which gave us mastery over the forces of nature but lost control over the forces of our self.

Tanks and planes cannot redeem humanity, nor the discovery of guilt by association nor suspicion. A man with a gun is like a beast without a gun. The killing of snakes will save us for the moment but not forever. The war has outlasted the victory of arms as we failed to conquer the infamy of the soul: the indifference to crime, when committed against others. For evil is indivisible. It is the same in thought and in speech, in private and in social life. The greatest task of our time is to take the souls of men out of the pit. The world has experienced that God is involved. Let us forever remember that the sense for the sacred is as vital to us as the light of the sun. There can be no nature without spirit, no world without the Torah, no brotherhood without a father, no humanity without attachment to God.

God will return to us when we shall be willing to let Him in—into our banks and factories, into our Congress and clubs, into our courts and investigating committees, into our homes and theaters. For God is everywhere or nowhere, the Father of all men or no man, concerned about everything or nothing. Only in His presence shall we learn that the glory of man is not in his will to power, but in his power of compassion. Man reflects either the image of His presence or that of a beast.

Soldiers in the horror of battle offer solemn testimony that life is not a hunt for pleasure, but an engagement for service; that there are things more valuable than life; that the world is not a vacuum. Either we make it an altar for God or it is invaded by demons. There can be no neutrality. Either we are ministers of the sacred or slaves of evil. Let the blasphemy of our time not become an eternal scandal. Let future generations not loathe us for having failed to preserve what prophets and saints, martyrs and scholars have created in thousands of years. The apostles of force have shown that they are great in evil. Let us reveal that we can be as great in goodness. We will survive if we shall be as fine and sacrificial in our homes and offices, in our Congress and clubs as our soldiers are on the fields of battle.

There is a divine dream which the prophets and rabbis have cherished and which fills our prayers, and permeates the acts of true piety. It is the dream of a world, rid of evil by the grace of God as well as by the efforts of man, by his dedication to the task of establishing the kingship of God in the world. God is waiting for us to redeem the world. We should not spend our life hunting for trivial satisfactions while God is waiting constantly and keenly for our effort and devotion.

The Almighty has not created the universe that we may have opportunities to satisfy our greed, envy and ambition. We have not survived that we may waste our years in vulgar vanities. The martyrdom of millions demands that we consecrate ourselves to the fulfillment of God's dream of salvation. Israel did not accept the Torah of their own free will. When Israel approached Sinai, God lifted up the mountain and held it over their heads, saying: "Either you accept the Torah or be crushed beneath the mountain."

The mountain of history is over our heads again. Shall we renew the covenant with God?

Neal Osherow

MAKING SENSE OF THE NONSENSICAL: AN ANALYSIS OF JONESTOWN

(1981)

Those who do not remember the past are condemned to repeat it.

—quotation on placard over Jim Jones's rostrum at Jonestown

Close to one thousand people died at Jonestown. The members of the Peoples Temple settlement in Guyana, under the direction of the Reverend Jim Jones, fed a poison-laced drink to their children, administered the potion to their infants, and drank it themselves. Their bodies were found lying together, arm in arm; over 900 perished.

How could such a tragedy occur? The image of an entire community destroying itself, of parents killing their own children, appears incredible. The media stories about the event and full-color pictures of the scene documented some of its horror but did little to illuminate the causes or to explain the processes that led to the deaths. Even a year afterwards, a CBS Evening News broadcast asserted that "it was widely assumed that time would offer some explanation for the ritualistic suicide/murder of over 900 people. . . . One year later, it does not appear that any lessons have been uncovered" (CBS News, 1979).

The story of the Peoples Temple is not enshrouded in mystery, however. Jim Jones had founded his church over twenty years before, in Indiana. His preaching stressed the need for racial brotherhood and integration, and his group helped feed the poor and find them jobs. As his congregation grew, Jim Jones gradually increased the discipline and dedication that he required from the members. In 1965, he moved to northern California; about 100 of his faithful relocated with him. The membership began to multiply, new congregations were formed, and the headquarters was established in San Francisco.

Behind his public image as a beloved leader espousing interracial harmony, "Father," as Jones was called, assumed a messiah-like presence in the Peoples Temple. Increasingly, he became the personal object of the members' devotion, and he used their numbers and obedience to gain political influence and power. Within the Temple, Jones demanded absolute loyalty, enforced a taxing regimen, and delivered sermons forecasting nuclear holocaust and an apocalyptic destruction of the world, promising his followers that they alone would emerge as survivors. Many of his harangues attacked racism and capitalism, but his most vehement anger focused on the "enemies" of the Peoples Temple—its detractors and especially its defectors. In mid-1977, publication of unfavorable magazine articles, coupled with the impending custody battle over a six-year-old Jones claimed as a "son," prompted emigration of the bulk of Temple membership to a jungle outpost in Guyana.

In November, 1978, Congressman Leo Ryan responded to charges that the Peoples Temple was holding people against their will at Jonestown. He organized a trip to the South American settlement; a small party of journalists and "Concerned Relatives" of Peoples Temple members accompanied him on his investigation. They were in Jonestown for one evening and part of the following day. They heard most residents praise the settlement, expressing their joy at being there and indicating their desire to stay. Two families, however, slipped messages to Ryan that they wanted to leave with him. After the visit, as Ryan's party and these defectors tried to board planes to depart, the group was ambushed and fired upon by Temple gunmen—five people, including Ryan, were murdered.

As the shootings were taking place at the jungle airstrip, Jim Jones gathered the community at Jonestown. He informed them that the Congressman's party would be killed and then initiated the final ritual: the "revolutionary suicide" that the membership had rehearsed on prior occasions. The poison was brought out. It was taken.

Jonestown's remoteness caused reports of the event to reach the public in stages. First came bulletins announcing the assassination of Congressman Ryan along with several members of his party. Then came rumors of mass deaths at Jonestown, then confirmations. The initial estimates put the number of dead near 400, bringing the hope that substantial numbers of people had escaped into the jungle. But as the bodies were counted, many smaller victims were discovered under the corpses of larger ones—virtually none of the inhabitants of Jonestown survived. The public was shocked, then horrified, then incredulous.

Amid the early stories about the tragedy, along with the lurid descriptions and sensational photographs, came some attempts at analysis. Most discussed the charisma of Jim Jones and the power of "cults." Jones was described as "a character Joseph Conrad might have dreamt up" (Krause, 1978), a "self-appointed messiah" whose "lust for dominion" led hundreds of "fanatic" followers to their demise (Special Report: The Cult of Death, *Newsweek*, 1978a).

While a description in terms of the personality of the perpetrator and the vulnerability of the victims provides some explanation, it relegates the event to the category of being an aberration, a product of unique forces and dispositions. Assuming such a perspective distances us from the phenomenon. This might be comforting, but I believe that it limits our understanding and is potentially dangerous. My aim in this analysis is not to blunt the emotional impact of a tragedy of this magnitude by subjecting it to academic examination. At the same time, applying social psychological theory and research makes it more conceivable and comprehensible, thus bringing it closer (in kind rather than in degree) to processes each of us encounters. Social psychological concepts can facilitate our understanding: The killings themselves, and many of the occurrences leading up to them, can be viewed in terms of obedience and compliance. The processes that induced people to join and to believe in the Peoples Temple made use of strategies involved in propaganda and persuasion. In grappling with the most perplexing questions—Why didn't more people leave the Temple? How could they actually kill their children and themselves?—the psychology of self-justification provides some insight.

CONFORMITY

The character of a church . . . can be seen in its attitude toward its detractors.

—Hugh Prather, *Notes to Myself*

At one level, the deaths at Jonestown can be viewed as the product of obedience, of people complying with the orders of a leader and reacting to the threat of force. In the Peoples Temple, whatever Jim Jones commanded, the members did. When he gathered the community at the pavilion and the poison was brought out, the populace was surrounded by armed guards who were trusted lieutenants of Jones. There are reports that some people did not drink voluntarily but had the poison forced down their throats or injected (Winfrey, 1979). While there were isolated acts of resistance and suggestions of opposition to the suicides, excerpts from a tape, recorded as the final ritual was being enacted, reveal that such dissent was quickly dismissed or shouted down:

JONES: I've tried my best to give you a good life. In spite of all I've tried, a handful of people, with their lies, have made our life impossible. If we can't live in peace then let's die in peace. (Applause) . . . We have been so terribly betrayed. . . .

What's going to happen here in the matter of a few minutes is that one of the people on that plane is going to shoot the pilot—I know that. I didn't plan it, but I know it's going to happen. . . . So my opinion is that you be kind to children, and be kind to seniors, and take the potion like they used to in ancient Greece, and step over quietly, because we are not committing suicide—it's a revolutionary act. . . . We can't go back. They're now going back to tell more lies. . . .

FIRST WOMAN: I feel like that as long as there's life, there's hope.

JONES: Well, someday everybody dies.

CROWD: That's right, that's right!

JONES: What those people gone and done, and

what they get through will make our lives worse than hell. . . . But to me, death is not a fearful thing. It's living that's cursed. . . . Not worth living like this.

FIRST WOMAN: But I'm afraid to die.

JONES: I don't think you are. I don't think you are.

FIRST WOMAN: I think there were too few who left for 1,200 people to give them their lives for those people who left. . . . I look at all the babies and I think they deserve to live.

JONES: But don't they deserve much more—they deserve peace. The best testimony we can give is to leave this goddam world. (Applause)

FIRST MAN: It's over, sister. . . . We've made a beautiful day. (Applause)

SECOND MAN: If you tell us we have to give our lives now, we're ready. (Applause)

[*Baltimore Sun*, 1979].

Above the cries of babies wailing, the tape continues, with Jones insisting upon the need for suicide and urging the people to complete the act:

JONES: Please get some medication. Simple. It's simple. There's no convulsions with it. . . . Don't be afraid to die. You'll see people land out here. They'll torture our people. . . .

SECOND WOMAN: There's nothing to worry about. Everybody keep calm and try to keep your children calm. . . . They're not crying from pain; it's just a little bitter tasting . . .

THIRD WOMAN: This is nothing to cry about. This is something we could all rejoice about. (Applause)

JONES: Please, for God's sake, let's get on with

it. . . . This is a revolutionary suicide. This is not a self-destructive suicide. (Voices praise "Dad." Applause)

THIRD MAN: Dad has brought us this far. My vote is to go with Dad. . . .

JONES: We must die with dignity. Hurry, hurry, hurry. We must hurry. . . . Stop this hysterics. Death is a million times more preferable to spending more days in this life. . . . If you knew what was ahead, you'd be glad to be stepping over tonight . . .

FOURTH WOMAN: It's been a pleasure walking with all of you in this revolutionary struggle. . . . No other way I would rather go than to give my life for socialism. Communism, and I thank Dad very much.

JONES: Take our life from us. . . . We didn't commit suicide. We committed an act of revolutionary suicide protesting against the conditions of an inhuman world [*Newsweek*, 1978b, 1979].

If you hold a gun at someone's head, you can get that person to do just about anything. As many accounts have attested,* by the early 1970s the members of the Peoples Temple lived in constant fear of severe punishment—brutal beatings coupled with public humiliation—for committing trivial or even inadvertent offenses. But the power of an authority need not be so explicitly threatening in order to induce compliance with its demands, as demonstrated by social psycho-

*The reports of ex–Peoples Temple members who defected create a very consistent picture of the tactics Jim Jones employed in his church. Jeanne Mills (1979) provides the most comprehensive personal account, and there are affidavits about the Peoples Temple sworn to by Deborah Blakey (May 12, 1978 and June 15, 1978) and Yolanda Crawford (April 10, 1978). Media stories about the Peoples Temple, which usually rely on interviews with defectors, and about Jonestown, which are based on interviews with survivors, also corroborate one another. (See especially Kilduff and Tracy [1977], *Newsweek* [1978a], Lifton [1979], and Cahill [1979].)

logical research. In Milgram's experiments (1963), a surprisingly high proportion of subjects obeyed the instructions of an experimenter to administer what they thought were very strong electric shocks to another person. Nor does the consensus of a group need be so blatantly coercive to induce agreement with its opinion, as Asch's experiments (1955) on conformity to the incorrect judgments of a majority indicate.

Jim Jones utilized the threat of severe punishment to impose the strict discipline and absolute devotion that he demanded, and he also took measures to eliminate those factors that might encourage resistance or rebellion among his followers. Research showed that the presence of a "disobedient" partner greatly reduced the extent to which most subjects in the Milgram situation (1965) obeyed the instructions to shock the person designated the "learner." Similarly, by including just one confederate who expressed an opinion different from the majority's, Asch (1955) showed that the subject would also agree far less, even when the "other dissenter's" judgment was also incorrect and differed from the subject's. In the Peoples Temple, Jones tolerated no dissent, made sure that members had no allegiance more powerful than to himself, and tried to make the alternative of leaving the Temple an unthinkable option.

Jeanne Mills, who spent six years as a high-ranking member before becoming one of the few who left the Peoples Temple, writes: "There was an unwritten but perfectly understood law in the church that was very important: 'No one is to criticize Father, his wife, or his children'" (Mills, 1979). Deborah Blakey, another longtime member who managed to defect, testified:

Any disagreement with [Jim Jones's] dictates came to be regarded as "treason." . . . Although

I felt terrible about what was happening, I was afraid to say anything because I knew that anyone with a differing opinion gained the wrath of Jones and other members. [Blakey, June 15, 1978.]

Conditions in the Peoples Temple became so oppressive, the discrepancy between Jim Jones's stated aims and his practices so pronounced, that it is almost inconceivable that members failed to entertain questions about the church. But these doubts went unreinforced. There were no allies to support one's disobedience of the leader's commands and no fellow dissenters to encourage the expression of disagreement with the majority. Public disobedience or dissent was quickly punished. Questioning Jones's word, even in the company of family or friends, was dangerous—informers and "counselors" were quick to report indiscretions, even by relatives.

The use of informers went further than to stifle dissent; it also diminished the solidarity and loyalty that individuals felt toward their families and friends. While Jones preached that a spirit of brotherhood should pervade his church, he made it clear that each member's personal dedication should be directed to "Father." Families were split: First, children were seated away from parents during services; then, many were assigned to another member's care as they grew up; and ultimately, parents were forced to sign documents surrendering custody rights. "Families are part of the enemy system," Jones stated, because they hurt one's total dedication to the "Cause" (Mills, 1979). Thus, a person called before the membership to be punished could expect his or her family to be among the first and most forceful critics (Cahill, 1979).

Besides splitting parent and child, Jones sought to

loosen the bonds between wife and husband. He forced spouses into extramarital sexual relations, which were often of a homosexual or humiliating nature, or with Jones himself. Sexual partnerships and activities not under his direction and control were discouraged and publicly ridiculed.

Thus, expressing any doubts or criticism of Jones—even to a friend, child, or partner—became risky for the individual. As a consequence, such thoughts were kept to oneself, and with the resulting impression that nobody else shared them. In addition to limiting one's access to information, this "fallacy of uniqueness" precluded the sharing of support. It is interesting that among the few who successfully defected from the Peoples Temple were couples such as Jeanne and Al Mills, who kept together, shared their doubts, and gave each other support.

Why didn't more people leave? Once inside the Peoples Temple, getting out was discouraged; defectors were hated. Nothing upset Jim Jones so much; people who left became the targets of his most vitriolic attacks and were blamed for any problems that occurred. One member recalled that after several teenage members left the Temple, "We hated those eight with such a passion because we knew any day they were going to try bombing us. I mean Jim Jones had us totally convinced of this" (Winfrey, 1979).

Defectors were threatened: Immediately after she left, Grace Stoen headed for the beach at Lake Tahoe, where she found herself looking over her shoulder, checking to make sure that she hadn't been tracked down (Kilduff and Tracy, 1977). Jeanne Mills reports that she and her family were followed by men in cars, their home was burglarized, and they were threatened with the use of confessions they had signed while still members. When a friend from the Temple paid a visit, she quickly examined Mills' ears—Jim Jones had vowed to have one of them cut off (Mills, 1979). He had made ominous predictions concerning other defectors a well: Indeed, several ex-members suffered puzzling deaths or committed very questionable "suicides" shortly after leaving the Peoples Temple (Reiterman, 1977; Tracy, 1978).

Defecting became quite a risky enterprise, and, for most members, the potential benefits were very uncertain. They had little to hope for outside of the Peoples Temple; what they had, they had committed to the church. Jim Jones had vilified previous defectors as "the enemy" and had instilled the fear that, once outside of the Peoples Temple, members' stories would not be believed by the "racist, fascist" society, and they would be subjected to torture, concentration camps, and execution. Finally, in Guyana, Jonestown was surrounded by dense jungle, the few trails patrolled by armed security guards (Cahill, 1979). Escape was not a viable option. Resistance was too costly. With no other alternatives apparent, compliance became the most reasonable course of action.

The power that Jim Jones wielded kept the membership of the Peoples Temple in line, and the difficulty of defecting helped to keep them in. But what attracted them to join Jones's church in the first place?

PERSUASION

Nothing is so unbelievable that oratory cannot make it acceptable.

—Cicero

Jim Jones was a charismatic figure, adept at oratory. He sought people for his church who would be receptive to his messages and vulnerable to his promises, and he carefully honed his presentation to appeal to each specific audience.

The bulk of the Peoples Temple membership was comprised of society's needy and neglected: the urban poor, the black, the elderly, and a sprinkling of ex-addicts and ex-convicts (Winfrey, 1979). To attract new members, Jones held public services in various cities. Leaflets would be distributed:

> PASTOR JIM JONES . . . Incredible! . . . . Miraculous! . . . Amazing! . . . The Most Unique Prophetic Healing Service You've Ever Witnessed! Behold the Word Made Incarnate In Your Midst!
>
> God works as tumorous masses are passed in every service. . . . Before your eyes, the crippled walk, the blind see! [Kilduff and Javers, 1978.]

Potential members first confronted an almost idyllic scene of blacks and whites living, working, and worshipping together. Guests were greeted and treated most warmly and were invited to share in the group's meal. As advertised, Jim Jones also gave them miracles. A number of members would recount how Jones had cured them of cancer or other dread diseases; during the service Jones or one of his nurses would reach into the member's throat and emerge with a vile mass of tissue—the "cancer" that had been passed as the person gagged. Sometimes Jim Jones would make predictions that would occur with uncanny frequency. He also received revelations about members or visitors that nobody but those individuals could know— what they had eaten for dinner the night before, for instance, or news about a far-off relative. Occasionally, he performed miracles similar to more well-established religious figures:

> There were more people than usual at the Sunday service, and for some reason the church members hadn't brought enough food to feed everyone. It became apparent that the last fifty people in line weren't going to get any meat. Jim announced, "Even though there isn't enough food to feed this multitude, I am blessing the food that we have and multiplying it—just as Jesus did in biblical times."
>
> Sure enough, a few minutes after he made this startling announcement, Eva Pugh came out of the kitchen beaming, carrying two platters filled with fried chicken. A big cheer came from the people assembled in the room, especially from the people who were at the end of the line.
>
> The "blessed chicken" was extraordinarily delicious, and several of the people mentioned that Jim had produced the best-tasting chicken they had ever eaten. [Mills, 1979.]

These demonstrations were dramatic and impressive; most members were convinced of their authenticity and believed in Jones's "powers." They didn't know that the "cancers" were actually rancid chicken gizzards, that the occurrences Jones "forecast" were staged, or that sending people to sift through a person's garbage could reveal packages of certain foods or letters of out-of-town relatives to serve as grist for Jones's "revelations" (Kilduff and Tracy, 1977; Mills, 1979). Members were motivated to believe in Jones; they appreciated the racial harmony, sense of purpose, and relief from feelings of worthlessness that the Peoples Temple provided them (Winfrey, 1979; Lifton,

1979). Even when suspecting that something was wrong, they learned that it was unwise to voice their doubts:

> One of the men, Chuck Beikman . . . jokingly mentioned to a few people standing near him that he had seen Eva drive up a few moments earlier with buckets from the Kentucky Fried Chicken stand. He smiled as he said, "The person that blessed this chicken was Colonel Sanders."
>
> During the evening meeting Jim mentioned the fact that Chuck had made fun of his gift. "He lied to some of the members here, telling them that the chicken had come from a local shop," Jim stormed. "But the Spirit of Justice has prevailed. Because of his lie Chuck is in the men's room right now, wishing that he was dead. He is vomiting and has diarrhea so bad he can't talk!"
>
> An hour later a pale and shaken Chuck Beikman walked out of the men's room and up to the front, being supported by one of the guards. Jim asked him, "Do you have anything you'd like to say?"
>
> Chuck looked up weakly and answered, "Jim, I apologize for what I said. Please forgive me."
>
> As we looked at Chuck, we vowed in our hearts that we would never question any of Jim's "miracles"—at least not out loud. Years later, we learned that Jim had put a mild poison in a piece of cake and given it to Chuck. [Mills, 1979.]

While most members responded to presentations that were emotional, one-sided, and almost sensational in tone, those who eventually assumed positions of responsibility in the upper echelons of the Peoples Temple were attracted by different considerations. Most of these people were white and came from upper-middle-class backgrounds—they included lawyers, a medical student, nurses, and people representing other occupations that demanded education and reflected a strong social consciousness. Jones lured these members by stressing the social and political aspects of the church, its potential as an idealistic experiment with integration and socialism. Tim Stoen, who was the Temple's lawyer, stated later, "I wanted utopia so damn bad I could die" (Winfrey, 1979). These members had the information and intelligence to see through many of Jones's ploys, but, as Jeanne Mills explains repeatedly in her book, they dismissed their qualms and dismissed Jones's deception as being necessary to achieve a more important aim—furthering the Cause: "For the thousandth time, I rationalized my doubts. 'If Jim feels it's necessary for the Cause, who am I to question his wisdom?' " (Mills, 1979).

It turned out to be remarkably easy to overcome their hesitancy and calm their doubts. Mills recalls that she and her husband initially were skeptical about Jones and the Peoples Temple. After attending their first meeting, they remained unimpressed by the many members who proclaimed that Jones had healed their cancers or cured their drug habits. They were annoyed by Jones's arrogance, and they were bored by most of the long service. But in the weeks following their visit, they received numerous letters containing testimonials and gifts from the Peoples Temple, they had dreams about Jones, and they were attracted by the friendship and love they had felt from both the black and the white members. When they went back for their second visit, they took their children with them. After the long drive, the Millses were greeted warmly by many members and by Jones himself. "This time . . . my mind was open to hear his message because my own beliefs had become very shaky" (Mills, 1979). As they were driving home afterwards, the children begged their parents to join the church:

> We had to admit that we enjoyed the service more this time and we told the children that we'd think it over. Somehow, though, we knew that it was only a matter of time before we were going to become members of the Peoples Temple. [Mills, 1979.]

Jim Jones skillfully manipulated the impression that his church would convey to newcomers. He carefully managed its public image. He used the letter-writing and political clout of hundreds of members to praise and impress the politicians and press that supported the Peoples Temple, as well as to criticize and intimidate its opponents (Kasindorf, 1978). Most importantly, Jones severely restricted the information that was available to the members. In addition to indoctrinating members into his own belief system through extensive sermons and lectures, he inculcated a distrust of any contradictory messages, labeling them the product of enemies. By destroying the credibility of their sources, he inoculated the membership against being persuaded by outside criticism. Similarly, any contradictory thoughts that might arise within each member were to be discredited. Instead of seeing them as having any basis in reality, members interpreted them as indications of their own shortcomings or lack of faith. Members learned to attribute the apparent discrepancies between Jones's lofty pronouncements and the rigors of life in the Peoples Temple to their personal inadequacies rather than blaming them on any fault of Jones. As ex-member Neva Sly was quoted: "We always blamed ourselves for things that didn't seem right" (Winfrey, 1979). A unique and distorting language developed within the church, in which "the Cause" became anything that Jim Jones said (Mills, 1979). It was spoken at Jonestown, where a guard tower was called the "playground" (Cahill, 1979). Ultimately, through the clever use of oratory, deception, and language, Jones could speak of death as "stepping over," thereby camouflaging a hopeless act of self-destruction as a noble and brave act of "revolutionary suicide," and the members accepted his words.

SELF-JUSTIFICATION

> Both salvation and punishment for man lie in the fact
> that if he lives wrongly he can befog himself so as not
> to see the misery of his position.
>
> —Tolstoy, "The Kreutzer Sonata"

Analyzing Jonestown in terms of obedience and the power of the situation can help to explain why the people *acted* as they did. Once the Peoples Temple had moved to Jonestown, there was little the members could do other than follow Jim Jones's dictates. They were comforted by an authority of absolute power. They were left with few options, being surrounded by armed guards and by the jungle, having given their passports and various documents and confessions to Jones, and believing that conditions in the outside world were even more threatening. The members' poor diet, heavy workload, lack of sleep, and constant exposure to Jones's diatribes exacerbated the coerciveness of their predicament; tremendous pressures encouraged them to obey.

By the time of the final ritual, opposition or escape had become almost impossible for most of the members. Yet even then, it is doubtful that many *wanted* to resist or to leave. Most had come to believe in Jones—one woman's body was found with a message scribbled on her arm during the final hours: "Jim Jones is the only one" (Cahill, 1979). They seemed to have accepted the necessity, and even the beauty, of dying—just before the ritual began, a guard approached Charles Garry, one of the Temple's hired attorneys, and exclaimed, "It's a great moment . . . we all die" (Lifton, 1979). A survivor of Jonestown, who happened to be away at the dentist, was interviewed a year following the deaths:

> If I had been there, I would have been the first one to stand in that line and take that poison and I would have been proud to take it. The thing I'm sad about is this; that I missed the ending. [Gallagher, 1979.]

It is this aspect of Jonestown that is perhaps the most troubling. To the end, and even beyond, the vast majority of the Peoples Temple members *believed* in Jim Jones. External forces, in the form of power or persuasion, can exact compliance. But one must examine a different set of processes to account for the members' internalizing those beliefs.

Although Jones's statements were often inconsistent and his methods cruel, most members maintained their faith in his leadership. Once they were isolated at Jonestown, there was little opportunity or motivation to think otherwise—resistance or escape was out of the question. In such a situation, the individual is motivated to rationalize his or her predicament; a person confronted with the inevitable tends to regard it more positively. For example, social psychological research has shown that when children believe that they will be served more of a vegetable they dislike, they will convince themselves that it is not so noxious (Brehm, 1959), and when a person thinks that she will be inter- acting with someone, she tends to judge a description of that individual more favorably (Darley and Ber- scheid, 1967).

A member's involvement in the Temple did not begin at Jonestown—it started much earlier, closer to home, and less dramatically. At first, the potential member would attend meetings voluntarily and might put in a few hours each week working for the church. Though the established members would urge the re- cruit to join, he or she felt free to choose whether to stay or to leave. Upon deciding to join, a member expended more effort and became more committed to the Peoples Temple. In small increments, Jones in- creased the demands made on the member, and only after a long sequence did he escalate the oppres- siveness of his rule and the desperation of his message. Little by little, the individual's alternatives became more limited. Step by step, the person was motivated to rationalize his or her commitment and to justify his or her behavior.

Jeanne Mills, who managed to defect two years be- fore the Temple relocated in Guyana, begins her ac- count, *Six Years with God* (1979), by writing: "Every time I tell someone about the six years we spent as members of the Peoples Temple, I am faced with an unanswerable question: 'If the church was so bad, why did you and your family stay in for so long?'" Several classic studies from social psychological research in- vestigating processes of self-justification and the theory of cognitive dissonance (see Aronson, 1980, chapter 4; Aronson, 1969) can point to explanations for such seemingly irrational behavior.

According to dissonance theory, when a person commits an act or holds a cognition that is psychologically inconsistent with his or her self-concept, the inconsistency arouses an unpleasant state of tension. The individual tries to reduce this "dissonance," usually by altering his or her attitudes to bring them more into line with the previously discrepant action or belief. A number of occurrences in the Peoples Temple can be illuminated by viewing them in light of this process. The horrifying events of Jonestown were not due merely to the threat of force, nor did they erupt instantaneously. That is, it was *not* the case that something "snapped" in people's minds, suddenly causing them to behave in bizarre ways. Rather, as the theory of cognitive dissonance spells out, people seek to *justify* their choices and commitments.

Just as a towering waterfall can begin as a trickle, so too can the impetus for doing extreme or calamitous actions be provided by the consequences of agreeing to do seemingly trivial ones. In the Peoples Temple, the process started with the effects of undergoing a severe initiation to join the church, was reinforced by the tendency to justify one's commitments, and was strengthened by the need to rationalize one's behavior.

Consider the prospective member's initial visit to the Peoples Temple, for example. When a person undergoes a severe initiation in order to gain entrance into a group, he or she is apt to judge that group as being more attractive, in order to justify expending the effort or enduring the pain. Aronson and Mills (1959) demonstrated that students who suffered greater embarrassment as a prerequisite for being allowed to participate in a discussion group rated its conversation (which actually was quite boring) to be significantly more interesting than did those students who experienced little or no embarrassment in order to be admitted. Not only is there a tendency to justify undergoing the experience by raising one's estimation of the goal—in some circumstances, choosing to experience a hardship can go so far as to affect a person's perception of the discomfort or pain he or she felt. Zimbardo (1969) and his colleagues showed that when subjects volunteered for a procedure that involves their being given electric shocks, those thinking that they had more choice in the matter reported feeling less pain from the shocks. More specifically, those who experienced greater dissonance, having little external justification to account for their choosing to endure the pain, described it as being less intense. This extended beyond their impressions and verbal reports; their performance on a task was hindered less, and they even recorded somewhat lower readings on a physiological instrument measuring galvanic skin responses. Thus the dissonance-reducing process can be double-edged: Under proper guidance, a person who voluntarily experiences a severe initiation not only comes to regard its ends more positively, but may also begin to see the means as less aversive: "We began to appreciate the long meetings, because we were told that spiritual growth comes from self-sacrifice" (Mills, 1979).

Once involved, a member found ever-increasing portions of his or her time and energy devoted to the Peoples Temple. The services and meetings occupied weekends and several evenings each week. Working on Temple projects and writing the required letters to politicians and the press took much of one's "spare" time. Expected monetary contributions changed from "voluntary" donations (though they were recorded) to the required contribution of a quarter of one's income. Eventually, a member was supposed to sign over all personal property, savings, social security checks, and the like to the Peoples Temple. Before entering the meeting room for each service, a member stopped at a table and wrote self-incriminating letters or signed blank documents that were turned over to the church. If anyone objected, the refusal was interpreted as denoting a "lack of faith" in Jones. Finally, members were asked to live at Temple facilities to save money and to be able to work more efficiently, and many of their children were raised under the care of other families. Acceding to each new demand had two repercussions: In practical terms, it enmeshed the person further into the Peoples Temple web and made leaving more difficult; on an attitudinal level, it set the aforementioned processes of self-justification into motion. As Mills (1979) describes:

> We had to face painful reality. Our life savings were gone. Jim had demanded that we sell the life insurance policy and turn the equity over to the church, so that was gone. Our property had all been taken from us. Our dream of going to an overseas mission was gone. We thought that we had alienated our parents when we told them we were leaving the country. Even the children whom we had left in the care of Carol and Bill were openly hostile toward us. Jim had accomplished all this in such a short time! All we had left now was Jim and the Cause, so we decided to buckle under and give our energies to these two.

Ultimately, Jim Jones and the Cause would require
the members to give their lives.

What could cause people to kill their children and
themselves? From a detached perspective, the image
seems unbelievable. In fact, at first glance, so does the
idea of so many individuals committing so much of
their time, giving all of their money, and even sacrific-
ing the control of their children to the Peoples Temple. Jones took advantage of rationalization processes
that allow people to justify their commitments by raising their estimations of the goal and minimizing its
costs. Much as he gradually increased his demands,
Jones carefully orchestrated the members' exposure to
the concept of a "final ritual." He utilized the leverage
provided by their previous commitments to push them
closer and closer to its enactment. Gaining a "foot in
the door" by getting a person to agree to a moderate
request makes it more probable that he or she will
agree to do a much larger deed later, as social psychol-
ogists—and salespeople—have found (Freedman and
Fraser, 1966). Doing the initial task causes something
that might have seemed unreasonable at first appear
less extreme in comparison, and it also motivates a
person to make his or her behavior appear more consistent by consenting to the larger request as well.

After indoctrinating the members with the workings
of the Peoples Temple itself, Jones began to focus
on broader and more basic attitudes. He started by
undermining the members' belief that death was to be
fought and feared and set the stage by introducing the
possibility of a cataclysmic ending for the church. As
several accounts corroborate (see Mills, 1979; Lifton,
1979; Cahill, 1979), Jones directed several "fake" suicide drills, first with the elite Planning Commission of
the Peoples Temple and later with the general membership. He would give them wine and then announce

that it had been poisoned and that they would soon die. These became tests of faith, of the members' willingness to follow Jones even to death. Jones would ask people if they were ready to die and on occasion would have the membership "decide" its own fate by voting whether to carry out his wishes. An ex-member recounted that one time, after a while

Jones smiled and said, "Well, it was a good lesson. I see you're not dead." He made it sound like we needed the 30 minutes to do very strong, introspective type of thinking. We all felt strongly dedicated, proud of ourselves. . . . [Jones] taught that it was a privilege to die for what you believed in, which is exactly what I would have been doing. [Winfrey, 1979.]

After the Temple moved to Jonestown, the "White Nights," as the suicide drills were called, occurred repeatedly. An exercise that appears crazy to the observer was a regular, justifiable occurrence for the Peoples Temple participant. The reader might ask whether this caused the members to think that the actual suicides were merely another practice, but there were many indications that they knew that the poison was truly deadly on that final occasion. The Ryan visit had been climactic, there were several new defectors, the cooks—who had been excused from the prior drills in order to prepare the upcoming meal—were included, Jones had been growing increasingly angry, desperate, and unpredictable, and, finally, everyone could see the first babies die. The membership was manipulated, but they were not unaware that this time the ritual was for real.

A dramatic example of the impact of self-justification concerns the physical punishment that was meted out in the Peoples Temple. As discussed earlier, the threat of being beaten or humiliated forced the member to comply with Jones's orders: A person will obey as long as he or she is being threatened and supervised. To affect a person's *attitudes,* however, a mild threat has been demonstrated to be more effective than a severe threat (Aronson and Carlsmith, 1963) and its influence has been shown to be far longer lasting (Freedman, 1965). Under a mild threat, the individual has more difficulty attributing his or her behavior to such a minor external restraint, forcing the person to alter his or her attitudes in order to justify the action. Severe threats elicit compliance, but, imposed from the outside, they usually fail to cause the behavior to be internalized. Quite a different dynamic ensues when it is not so clear that the action is being imposed upon the person. When an individual feels that he or she played an active role in carrying out an action that hurts someone, there comes a motivation to justify one's part in the cruelty by rationalizing it as necessary or by derogating the victim by thinking that the punishment was deserved (Davis and Jones, 1960).

Let's step back for a moment. The processes going on at Jonestown obviously were not as simple as those in a well-controlled laboratory experiment; several themes were going on simultaneously. For example, Jim Jones had the power to impose any punishments that he wished in the Peoples Temple, and, especially towards the end, brutality and terror at Jonestown were rampant. But Jones carefully controlled how the punishments were carried out. He often called upon the members themselves to agree to the imposition of beatings. They were instructed to testify against fellow members, bigger members told to beat up smaller ones, wives or lovers forced to sexually humiliate their partners, and parents asked to consent to and assist in the beatings of their children (Mills, 1979; Kilduff and Javers, 1978). The punishments grew more and more sadistic, the beatings so severe as to knock the victim unconscious and cause bruises that lasted for weeks. As Donald Lunde, a psychiatrist who has investigated acts of extreme violence, explains:

> Once you've done something that major, it's very hard to admit even to yourself that you've made a mistake, and subconsciously you will go to great lengths to rationalize what you did. It's a very tricky defense mechanism exploited to the hilt by the charismatic leader. [*Newsweek*, 1978a.]

A more personal account of the impact of this process is provided by Jeanne Mills. At one meeting, she and her husband were forced to consent to the beating of their daughter as punishment for a very minor transgression. She relates the effect this had on her daughter, the victim, as well as on herself, one of the perpetrators:

> As we drove home, everyone in the car was silent. We were all afraid that our words would be considered treasonous. The only sounds came from Linda, sobbing quietly in the back seat. When we got into our house, Al and I sat down to talk with Linda. She was in too much pain to sit. She stood quietly while we talked with her. "How do you feel about what happened tonight?" Al asked her.
> "Father was right to have me whipped," Linda answered. "I've been so rebellious lately, and I've done a lot of things that were wrong. . . .

I'm sure Father knew about those things, and that's why he had me hit so many times."

As we kissed our daughter goodnight, our heads were spinning. It was hard to think clearly when things were so confusing. Linda had been the victim, and yet we were the only people angry about it. She should have been hostile and angry. Instead, she said that Jim had actually helped her. We knew Jim had done a cruel thing, and yet everyone acted as if he were doing a loving thing in whipping our disobedient child. Unlike a cruel person hurting a child, Jim had seemed calm, almost loving, as he observed the beating and counted off the whacks. Our minds were not able to comprehend the atrocity of the situation because none of the feedback we were receiving was accurate. [Mills, 1979.]

The feedback one received from the outside was limited, and the feedback from inside the Temple member was distorted. By justifying the previous actions and commitments, the groundwork for accepting the ultimate commitment was established.

CONCLUSION

Only months after we defected from Temple did we realize the full extent of the cocoon in which we'd lived. And only then did we understand the fraud, sadism, and emotional blackmail of the master manipulator.

—Jeanne Mills, *Six Years with God*

Immediately following the Jonestown tragedy, there came a proliferation of articles about "cults" and calls for their investigation and control. From Synanon to Transcendental Meditation, groups and practices were examined by the press, which had a difficult time determining what constituted a "cult" or differentiating between those that might be safe and beneficial and those that could be dangerous. The Peoples Temple and the events at Jonestown make such a definition all the more problematic. A few hours before his murder, Congressman Ryan addressed the membership: "I can tell you right now that by the few conversations I've had with some of the folks . . . there are some people who believe this is the best thing that ever happened in their whole lives" (Krause, 1978). The acquiescence of so many and the letters they left behind indicate that this feeling was widely shared—or at least expressed—by the members.

Many "untraditional"—to mainstream American culture—groups or practices, such as Eastern religions or meditation techniques, have proven valuable for the people who experience them but may be seen as very strange and frightening to others. How can people determine whether they are being exposed to a potentially useful alternative way of living their lives or if they are being drawn to a dangerous one?

The distinction is a difficult one. Three questions suggested by the previous analysis, however, can provide important clues: Are alternatives being provided or taken away? Is one's access to new and different information being broadened or denied? Finally, does the individual assume personal responsibility and control or is it usurped by the group or by its leader?

The Peoples Temple attracted many of its members because it provided them an alternative way of viewing their lives; it gave many people who were downtrodden a sense of purpose, and even transcendence. But it did so at a cost, forcing them to disown their former friendships and beliefs and teaching them to fear anything outside of the Temple as "the enemy." Following Jones became the *only* alternative.

Indeed, most of the members grew increasingly unaware of the possibility of any other course. Within the Peoples Temple, and especially at Jonestown, Jim Jones controlled the information to which members would be exposed. He effectively stifled any dissent that might arise within the church and instilled a distrust in each member for contradictory messages from outside. After all, what credibility could be carried by information supplied by "the enemy" that was out to destroy the Peoples Temple with "lies"?

Seeing no alternatives and having no information, a member's capacity for dissent or resistance was minimized. Moreover, for most members, part of the Temple's attraction resulted from their willingness to relinquish much of the responsibility and control over their lives. These were primarily the poor, the minorities, the elderly, and the unsuccessful—they were happy to exchange personal autonomy (with its implicit assumption of personal responsibility for their plights) for security, brotherhood, the illusion of miracles, and the promise of salvation. Stanley Cath, a psychiatrist who has studied the conversion techniques used by cults, generalizes: "Converts have to believe only what they are told. They don't have to think, and this relieves tremendous tensions" (*Newsweek*, 1978a). Even Jeanne Mills, one of the better-educated Temple members, commented:

I was amazed at how little disagreement there was between the members of this church. Before we joined the church, Al and I couldn't even agree on whom to vote for in the presidential election. Now that we all belonged to a group, family arguments were becoming a thing of the past. There was never a question of who was right, because Jim was always right. When our large household met to discuss family problems, we didn't ask for opinions. Instead, we put the question to the children, "What would Jim do?" It took the difficulty out of life. There was a type of "manifest destiny" which said the Cause was right and would succeed. Jim was right and those who agreed with him were right. If you disagreed with Jim, you were wrong. It was as simple as that. [Mills, 1979.]

Though it is unlikely that he had any formal exposure to the social psychological literature, Jim Jones utilized several very powerful and effective techniques for controlling people's behavior and altering their attitudes. Some analyses have compared his tactics to those involved in "brainwashing," for both include the control of communication, the manipulation of guilt, and dispensing power over people's existence (Lifton, 1979), as well as isolation, an exacting regimen, physical pressure, and the use of confessions (Cahill, 1979). But using the term brainwashing makes the process sound too esoteric and unusual. There *were* some unique and scary elements in Jones's personality—paranoia, delusions of grandeur, sadism, and a preoccupation with suicide. Whatever his personal motivation, however, having formulated his plans and fantasies, he took advantage of well-established social psychological tactics to carry them out. The decision to have a community destroy itself was crazy, but those who performed the deed were "normal" people who were subjected to a tremendously impactful situation, the victims of powerful internal forces as well as external pressures.

POSTSCRIPT

Within a few weeks of the deaths at Jonestown, the bodies had been transported back to the United States, the remnants of the Peoples Temple membership were said to have disbanded, and the spate of stories and books about the suicide/murders had begun to lose the public's attention. Three months afterwards, Michael Prokes, who had escaped from Jonestown because he was assigned to carry away a box of Peoples Temple funds, called a press conference in a California motel room. After claiming that Jones had been misunderstood and demanding the release of a tape recording of the final minutes [quoted earlier], he stepped into the bathroom and shot himself in the head. He left behind a note, saying that if his death inspired another book about Jonestown, it was worthwhile (*Newsweek*, 1979).

POSTSCRIPT

Jeanne and Al Mills were among the most vocal of the Peoples Temple critics following their defection, and they topped an alleged "death list" of its enemies. Even after Jonestown, the Millses had repeatedly expressed fear for their lives. Well over a year after the Peoples Temple deaths, they and their daughter were murdered in their Berkeley home. Their teenage son, himself an ex–Peoples Temple member, has testified that he was in another part of the large house at the time. At this writing, no suspect has been charged. There are indications that the Millses knew their killer—there were no signs of forced entry, and they were shot at close range. Jeanne Mills had been quoted as saying, "It's going to happen. If not today, then tomorrow." On the final tape of Jonestown, Jim Jones had blamed Jeanne Mills by name, and had promised that his followers in San Francisco "will not take our death in vain" (*Newsweek*, 1980).

REFERENCES

ARONSON, E. *The social animal* (3rd ed.) San Francisco: W. H. Freeman and Company, 1980.

ARONSON, E. The theory of cognitive dissonance: A current perspective. In L. Berkowitz (ed.), *Advances in experimental social psychology*. Vol. 4. New York: Academic Press, 1969.

ARONSON, E., AND CARLSMITH, J. M. Effect of the severity of threat on the devaluation of forbidden behavior. *Journal of Abnormal and Social Psychology*, 1963, **66**, 584–588.

ARONSON, E., AND MILLS, J. The effects of severity of initiation on liking for a group. *Journal of Abnormal and Social Psychology*, 1959, **59**, 177–181.

ASCH, S. Opinions and social pressure. *Scientific American*, 1955, 193.

BLAKEY, D. Affidavit: Georgetown, Guyana. May 12, 1978.

BLAKEY, D. Affidavit: San Francisco. June 15, 1978.

BREHM, J. Increasing cognitive dissonance by a *fait-accompli*. *Journal of Abnormal and Social Psychology*, 1959, **58**, 379–382.

CAHILL, T. In the valley of the shadow of death. *Rolling Stone,* January 25, 1979.

Committee on Foreign Affairs, U.S. House of Representatives, Report of a staff investigative group. *The assassination of Representative Leo J. Ryan and the Jonestown, Guyana, tragedy.* Washington, D.C.: Government Printing Office, May 15, 1979.

CRAWFORD, Y. Affidavit: San Francisco. April 10, 1978.

DARLEY, J., AND BERSCHEID, E. Increased liking as a result of the anticipation of personal contact. *Human Relations,* 1967, **20,** 29–40.

DAVIS, K., AND JONES, E. Changes in interpersonal perception as a means of reducing cognitive dissonance. *Journal of Abnormal and Social Psychology,* 1960, **61,** 402–410.

"Don't be afraid to die" and another victim of Jonestown. *Newsweek,* March 10, 1980.

A fatal prophecy is fulfilled. *Newsweek,* March 10, 1980.

FREEDMAN, J. Long-term behavioral effects of cognitive dissonance. *Journal of Experimental Social Psychology,* 1965, **1,** 145–155.

FREEDMAN, J., AND FRASER, S. Compliance without pressure: The foot-in-the-door technique. *Journal of Personality and Social Psychology,* 1966, **4,** 195–202.

GALLAGHER, N. Jonestown: The survivors' story. *New York Times Magazine,* November 18, 1979.

KASINDORF, J. Jim Jones: The seduction of San Francisco. *New West,* December 18, 1978.

KILDUFF, M., AND JAVERS, R. *The suicide cult.* New York: Bantam, 1978, and *San Francisco Chronicle.*

KILDUFF, M., AND TRACY, P. Inside Peoples Temple. *New West,* August 1, 1977.

KRAUSE C. *Guyana massacre.* New York: Berkley, 1978, and *Washington Post.*

LIFTON, R. J. Appeal of the death trip. *New York Times Magazine,* January 7, 1979.

MILGRAM, S. Behavioral study of obedience. *Journal of Abnormal and Social Psychology,* 1963, **67,** 371–378. (Also reprinted in E. Aronson (ed.), *Readings about the social animal.*)

MILGRAM, S. Liberating effects of group pressure. *Journal of Personality and Social Psychology,* 1965, **1,** 127–134.

MILLS, J. *Six years with God.* New York: A & W Publishers, 1979.

REITERMAN, T. Scared too long. *San Francisco Examiner,* November 13, 1977.

The sounds of death. *Newsweek,* December 18, 1978b.

Special report: The cult of death. *Newsweek,* December 4, 1978a.

Tape hints early decision by Jones on mass suicide. *Baltimore Sun,* March 15, 1979.

TRACY, P. Jim Jones: The making of a madman. *New West,* December 18, 1978.

WINFREY, C. Why 900 died in Guyana. *New York Times Magazine,* February 25, 1979.

YOUNG, S. Report on Jonestown. *The CBS Evening News with Walter Cronkite,* November 16, 1979.

ZIMBARDO, P. *The cognitive control of motivation.* Glenview, Ill.: Scott Foresman, 1969.

ZIMBARDO, P., EBBESON, E., AND MASLACH, C. *Influencing attitudes and changing behavior* (2nd ed.). Reading, Mass.: Addison-Wesley, 1977.

INTELLECTUAL
FREEDOM

Leonard Everett Fisher

CENSORSHIP AND THE ARTS
(1993)

Let me at the outset thank the President's Advisory
Committee on Intellectual Freedom of the International Reading Association [the League of Women Voters, the Association of University Women, and the Y's Women] for inviting me to talk about censorship, the arts, and intellectual freedom. This is not going to be easy. Why would anyone want to listen to the intellectual exercising of a fellow Westporter—especially one born in New York during the Roaring Twenties—during the administration of Calvin Coolidge—while Civil War veterans still led Decoration Day parades?

I used to think that my late father, born during Benjamin Harrison's presidency, had nothing to say to *me*. His view—nineteenth-century manifest destiny and all that—was useless. My generation would do it all better. And now I have those muddleheaded ideas which newer humans see as having brought the twentieth century to ruin. The only thing my graying peers and I seem to be good for is sending our dues to the AARP and robbing our cynical young of their public inheritance. Ah, yes, youth will be served.

But I tell you this. I have heard two spirited, youthful U.S. presidents claim to have been passed the torch by a previous generation. What previous generation? I am not "previous," not as long as I can breathe and vote Democratic as I have done since casting my first vote for Harry Truman. I have never subscribed to divisiveness in these United States—ethnic, cultural, linguistic, biological, geographic, or generational. I am an ungrouped, unincorporated, unhyphenated American, however, much my mother was born elsewhere. As Christopher Gadsden of South Carolina was reported to have said, "I am not a New England man. I am not a New York man. I am not a South Carolinian. I am an American."

A child of the Great Depression, and war veteran, I am, nonetheless, an educated, skillful, hardworking male parent and grandparent. I make no apologies. I paid my dues only to find I am generationally separate, culturally obsolete, academically deceived, outwitted, and incorrect. The world moves on.

"Stay away from politics, religion, and money," my father advised, "and you'll be safe." My father, a marine designer who contributed to the construction of submarines and other naval vessels, was not interested in politics, religion, and money. His ships floated, however, from stem to stern.

Well, paternal advice being what it is, and youth being what it has always been, I did not listen to him and I shall not be safe—at least for the next few minutes. I shall be on dangerous ground weaving my way through the Bill of Rights, New Age Revisionism, twentieth-century flounderings, rage, hedonism, tribal priorities, and the moral-political cleansing that preoccupies so much of our time in these United States.

Censorship, the imposition of restraints by government decree or by unauthorized watchdogs upon what we hear, see, read, or even think and feel, has been with the human race since the beginning of recorded politics. Restraints on our intellectual freedom and other private rights have always been constructed either by those few who seize the mechanisms of government or academia for self serving interest, or by those few without fiat but with self anointed agendas for the rest of us who stagger through life's travail.

Throughout history, the human line of thought and intellect has been ragged. And it seems that it must forever be set in an orderly march from one end to the other by those who cannot abide a measure of human disarray and who think they know a better way. Books, reading, libraries, words, pictures, intellect, and progress have been, in their view, the unsettling of social order rather than the improvement of same. And that is just the beginning of a laundry list of provocations that keeps unsettling the social order.

Fear of different ideas, new experiences, and words to express these things are anathema to some private codes of behavior where narrow intellectual or spiritual discipline is the preferred route. That fear has caused governments to unravel, and cultures to be victimized. Nothing is ever learned from any of this. Michelangelo's nudes were covered and uncovered. They certainly were not an embarrassment to God who created us in His image—or is it Her image?

Common perceptions often have no vision. Someone is always trying to stop the clock. Take these observations, for example, collected by Father Stanley Bezuska of Boston College:

"Students today depend on expensive fountain pens. They can no longer write with a straight pen and nib. We parents must not allow them to wallow in such luxury to the detriment of learning" (*PTA Gazette,* 1941).

"Ballpoint pens will be the ruin of education in our country. American values of thrift and frugality are being discarded. Businesses and banks will never allow such luxuries" (*Federal Teachers*, 1950).

"Students today depend too much on handheld calculators" (unknown source, 1992).

In third century B.C. China, Emperor Ch'in Shi Huang Ti knew how to stop the clock.

"Off with their heads!"

He meant it. Confronted by words, ideas, and images—the expressions of minds other than his own, a perceived danger to his authority—he buried in the Great Wall, up to their necks, numerous scholars, writers, and artists who wrote poems, history books, and painted pictures, and sliced off their heads. Ch'in Shi Huang Ti, China's first emperor, from whence we get the name "China," wanted to end the memory of what came before him and assure his tenure as the only time and place in the history of the Middle Kingdom. Ch'in turned out to be a short-lived emperor—about ten years. He died of an overdose of the then current medicinal cure-all—the Uncle Jack's Wild West Snake Oil of that day—mercury! His body was carted out of town in a wagon load of dead fish to camouflage his demise and the odor of same. The clock resumed its ticking.

The mass decapitation on the Great Wall was the ultimate act of censorship. Together with rigid and traditional conservatism which shut out the world, that barbaric act deprived China of intellectual motion—of continuing education—and left her millions to wallow in unchanging ignorance and misery for centuries to come—until about 1912, as a matter of fact. That was the price of China's insular wisdom and paranoia.

In our century, Lenin and Stalin knew what to do about writers who strayed from the party line. The lucky ones froze in Siberia. The others were shot. The Soviet Union lasted less than seventy-five years.

Dr. Josef Goebbels knew what to do, too, about writers in Adolph Hitler's Third Reich. He burned books that did not fit his boss' view of the universe. Hitler didn't much care for books. He burned people. Nazi Germany's one thousand year vision lasted twelve years.

Torquemada, the Spanish Inquisitor, didn't bother with books much either. He just burned people alive whose preferences were different! The rest were sent packing. The Iberian light of learning and tolerance went out in 1492. Spain struggled in isolation for four hundred and fifty years.

What I have to say about present-day censorship I say against the background of global turmoil and intolerance that convulses our time, fed by religious fundamentalism, tribal messages, racial separatism, language independence, and gender divisionism. Herein is the breeding ground of a new Dark Age.

There is this great impulse to make our mad world better, to make people more responsive and obligated to one another. "For our children," we say, the noblest of all pursuits. But the routes being taken to mellow our hearts reek of the very intolerance that is being hunted down. Tyranny is at work in the land.

What we get is theocratic dogma of the right, a prescription for the end of religious tolerance in America; and word policing on the left, a prescription for the end of American free speech and dissent, all of which represent a formula for the disunion of America. The censorial bent of these fractious causes is the instrument of their designs. None of these groups are interested in America no matter their patriotic ardor and/or humanistic fervor. They are so fueled by tribal dominations—their own—that the focus becomes collective guilt and punishment. In that frame of action, the historical American idea begins to fade from view.

Books containing simple common expletives heard daily by every man, woman, and child—words like "damn" and "hell"—are removed from library shelves. A noun like "woman" is respelled "w-o-m-y-n" to delete the male implication. The pronoun "she," one concludes, will have to be reinvented to eliminate the male reference "h-e," used to construct that pronoun. In such a bias free world, suppression reigns supreme. A recent *New York Times* article, "The Word Police" (January 31, 1993, Michiko Kakatuni) asks: "Will tossing out Santa Claus, [accused] of reinforcing the cultural male-as-norm-system, truly help banish sexism? Can the avoidance of violent expressions and metaphors like 'sock it to 'em' or 'kick an idea around' actually promote a more harmonious world?"

There's more. The word police see Abraham Lincoln's Gettysburg Address as "phallocentric" in that it describes only what our "forefathers had brought forth." It follows that the Declaration of Independence is also "phallocentric" and will have to be rewritten as "humankind is created equal." But then again, the word "humankind," will have to go, too, since its second syllable, "man," is offensive to some. "Persons" won't do either. It contains "sons."

In paragraph three of its instructions to authors who wish to submit a book, monograph, or booklet manuscript for publication, the International Reading Association requires words that "do not carry a gender reference, such as 'postal worker' rather than 'mailman.'" The instructions continue by requiring the disuse of "so-called neutral pronouns he, his, and him"; the recasting of phrases to "avoid the use of pronouns, or use both masculine and feminine pronouns."

William Safire, a nationally syndicated columnist, claims there are those who wish to rename Yankee Stadium, the true icon of our national pastime, since "Yankee" is a slur upon the Southern ballplayers who appear there (*New York Times*, February 21, 1993). Given the state of baseball today, that idea regarding the "house that Ruth built"—Ruth?—may be purely academic. It may never see the light of day.

Another target of the word police is "zoo." The director of New York's Wildlife Conservation Parks—that is the replacement for "zoo"—urged the change because "zoo" had bad connotations when cities like New York or Chicago or San Francisco are sometimes referred to as "zoos." Pardon our sensitivity. With the banishment of "zoo," which is derived from "zoology" or "zoological," small readers of alphabet books will be left with "Zebra" and "Zanzibar." But "Zebra" will have to go, too, since its second syllable "bra," conjures up all kinds of mental images as does the "bar" in "Zanzibar." The whole effort is bizarre.

These revisions and prohibitions, seeded in the bastions of intellectual freedom, our university and college campuses, will be "purchased," as the *New York Times* article correctly reasons, "at the cost of freedom of expression and freedom of speech." The bottom line would be the silencing of America—the pulverization of American history, the dilution of our traditions, and the destruction of our institutions, which are, in my view, the only imperfect route to a better world.

In the year 1625, about the time the Massachusetts colonists had made up their minds that they were on the North American continent to stay, Baruch Spinoza, a Dutch lens-grinding philosopher, wrote in his work on ethics: "No man's mind," [and I add 'no woman's mind'—that was then—this is now]—"No man's mind," he wrote [and "no woman's mind"], "lies wholly at the disposition of another. And no one can abdicate their natural right of free reason even with their own consent or be compelled to do so."

In other words, no censor in the world, however much he or she restricts my work or speech because it is not to his or her liking, can change my train of thinking about anything I choose to think about, and the conclusions drawn therefrom. Spinoza didn't exactly have overt censorship on his mind—the banning of a specific children's book, for example, tainted with satanic undertones and the odor of hell's sulfur—like my *Warlock of Westfall*. I was not in vogue in 1625. Spinoza's concern was about mind management—rules to think by—political correctness, if you will, by today's definition.

There were many urgent reasons afoot that moved Spinoza to examine mind and matter, and the independence and interdependence of both. He was a pious man, living in his own godfearing and disruptive time. Yet he reserved for humankind the right of independent, interpretive roads to morality—to God—a Being he never denied. For this he was shunned by a Judeo-Christian Europe where the nature of divinity and the conduct of life had been prescribed by human beings.

Spinoza's concept of intellectual singularity and the natural right to choose foretold the manifest doctrine of our Founding Fathers. And upon this was eventually built the American ideal that magnetizes every lost soul in this world.

But we still had to jump over the likes of William Berkeley in the New World. A dozen years following

Spinoza's observation in the Netherlands, the printing press arrived in America. Fearing the printed word as a challenge to his authority, William Berkeley, governor of Virginia, proclaimed that "learning has brought disobedience, and heresy, and sects into the world, and printing has divulged them, and libels against the best government. God keep us from both."

The old poisons came across the ocean to what was supposed to have been the New World where there was space and opportunity—but not for everyone, I hasten to add. The Berkeleys are still with us and ever fearful.

It wasn't until we got to John F. Kennedy three hundred plus years later that who we really thought we ought to be was clearly articulated.

"A nation that is afraid to let its people judge the truth and falsehood in an open market," said President Kennedy on the Voice of America (February 25, 1962), "is a nation that is afraid of its own people." He went on to say, "We are not afraid to entrust the American people with unpleasant facts, foreign ideas, alien philosophies and competitive values."

This is what we were telling ourselves and the world. We and the world believed.

About a year ago, while on a visit to a far western state, I learned that a book I had written and illustrated in 1975, the aforementioned *Warlock of Westfall,* had been removed from some local school library shelves by literary vigilantes—thirty years following President Kennedy's idealistic view. This flying squad of watchdogs who presumed to protect public morality intimidated some school librarians and had the book removed. They decided that books about "warlocks"—witches of any kind—were "satanic" and not fit reading for children: theirs, yours, and mine. You and I had nothing to say about it. Never mind that this was a direct violation of the First Amendment—"that Congress shall make no laws abridging the freedom of speech or of the press." The government of the people, by the people, and for the people was silent, its vision limited by taxes, spending, and the deficit, the real occupation of America. "The business of America," said Calvin Coolidge, "is business." Well, I'd like to know who has been minding the store!

I tolerate those who refuse to permit their own children to read particular things that are offensive to their notion of an orderly universe. That is their privilege. But to deny my children—and now grandchildren—access to that literature is a violation of the Constitution and an affront to the American scheme of things.

The committee did not even allow that we nor'easterners know something about witches. We tried them, convicted them, and executed them. If the literary vigilantes will permit me, they can catch them every so often in the light of a full moon sitting and cackling away on my stone wall—my neighbors' stone walls too—or flying thru the crisp New England nightsky on a broomstick.

In my vivid historical imagination, I equated my banning with Robespierre and the French Reign of Terror—as I do the evangelical right, the word police, the political correctors. I have visions of the guillotine and Sydney Carton; of the revised calendar in which July became "Thermidor" (Heat), and August became "Fructidor" (Fruit), in the interest of a brave new politically correct French world. Napoleon took the "Ventose" (Wind) out of the calendar on January 1, 1806, and restored February, July, August, and the rest.

The French Revolutionary Calendar was imposed

between 1793 and 1805, reinforcing the country's chaos. No one knew the time of day, the day of the week, the week of the month, month, or year for twelve years. And at the end of which time Europe got Napoleon. *C'est la vie!*

But on second thought I liked the idea of being banned. Too bad the book went out of print thirteen years before. I could have sold a trillion copies and fixed my leaking roof. If people want to demolish a book, the best course would be to ignore it. Treat it with absolute indifference. But put the book on a list for punishment and it will surely be read—and then listen to the cash register ring.

I remember spending a hot summer on a hot beach under a hot blanket, during my teens in the late 1930s, reading James T. Farrell's hot book, *Studs Lonigan,* by the light of a flashlight. *Studs Lonigan,* a story of Chicago sex and other misdemeanors, was banned stuff—illegal. That's why we read it! Had it not been banned and illegal we would not have bothered. I do not remember how I came upon the contraband copy. But mine wasn't the only one. The beach was full of them. And all of us teens were reading it—under blankets with flashlights. We all turned out well, too. We went to war and served America's cause without complaint. Some of us died for our troubles. We Depression-War babies, untainted by Studs Lonigan, went on to value education, raise families, and happily tried to build a better America—so we thought—an America that has since become unstuck. Read *Studs Lonigan* today and one wonders about the fuss.

My book, *The Warlock of Westfall,* incidentally, had nothing to do with warlocks, save what some fictitious Colonial American villagers thought about an addled old man they didn't like because he was different. The book was about intolerance and retribution.

My adaptation of Genesis—*The Seven Days of Creation,* a picture book for young readers—has not been banned. I told a school audience that included three members of that same unsmiling watchful committee that that book took me six days to do. I rested on the seventh. They weren't going to take a chance and fool around with me!

That same year a publishing partnership decided not to use my thirty-two-page picture book, *Prince Henry the Navigator,* in a middle school anthology. Young students were thus deprived of reaching into one of the pivotal moments on history's time line—the subject of deep water navigation, Portuguese exploration, the beginnings of exportable West African slavery that would one day spill over onto the yet undiscovered North American continent, and the man who made it possible for Columbus to motivate the world in a compelling westerly direction, Prince Henry.

"It doesn't say what has to be said," they told me. "There were no women in the book and the events were Eurocentric."

True, there were no women on fifteenth-century Portuguese caravels, nor were there any at Prince Henry's School of Navigation on Cape Saint Vincent. Prince Henry was a bachelor, probably celibate. True, Prince Henry and his sailors were Europeans who were delving into oceanic sciences as no other people on earth had systematically done before. But the book had more to do with Africa, sailing east to India, than with Europe. This was a bum rap. My European origins notwithstanding, I could not reinvent history. Is this the meaning of inclusion?

Eventually, a children's magazine reprinted Prince Henry's tale of learning, oceanic and celestial navigation, discovery (or uncovery—whichever you prefer), and slavery—all of which contributed to civilization's westward momentum (or invasion—whichever you prefer) with its small pox, whooping cough, justice and injustice; the agonizing awakening of this hemisphere to new currents of learning; new social orders—good and bad; trade and commerce; the birth of this country, which most of the world's driven now aspire to reach; and the rough beginnings, here, of those possibilities of finally reaching a good and just world.

There was another time when I ran afoul of a censor. I wrote a letter to my parents describing an air raid I had experienced in North Africa. The writing was as vivid as I could make it. Maybe too vivid, given my creative inclination. But I was only twenty years old and everything looked larger than death to me in that place. Alas, the letter never got there whole. The U.S. Army censor had neatly cut out everything in it, including the date and place, with a razor blade. He saved "Dear Mom and Dad," a few conjunctions and prepositions, "Don't worry. See you soon. Love, Len."

Gone was the roar, the terror, the date, and the place of those ten minutes. I should have known better. After all, "Loose Lips [Sank] Ships." I understood the military censor. He was right! I was unthinking. It had nothing to do with free speech or ideologies, but everything to do with Allied lives, including my own. Besides, the censor did me a favor. He spared my parents an unnecessary sleepless night. Why did they have to know what a bomb over Algiers sounded like, especially one that was aimed at me.

Returning to today, the still rising tide of religious fundamentalism and historical revisionism is seen in some quarters as the antidote to a poisonous world, a world, we all acknowledge, gone mad with terror, crime, drugs, war, AIDS, abuse, and brutalities of every dimension. Great suffering and cruel indifference to it is nothing new in the long painful history of the human race. What makes ours so special is the inconceivable enormity of the excruciating pain of the twentieth century communicated and enlivened in an instant for all to see.

Enter stage front: those mortals who know how to fix it right by targeting the sins of the past and correcting those of the present by murdering our minds first, if not our bodies later—on occasion, both at the same time.

Remember Galileo?

Galileo was condemned and imprisoned for proving the Copernican theory that it isn't the earth that stands still at the center of the universe, but rather the sun that stands still while the earth and other planets revolve around it. He had shaken up a 2,000-year-old wrong idea. It took four hundred years to pardon Galileo, a cosmic event of the past year or two—the exoneration of a noncrime after having had a truth established four hundred years ago—unnoticed by a disinterested public.

Remember Veronese?

Paolo Caliari, a world famous painter known as Veronese, was brought before the Inquisition in July 1573. He was told that his painting, *The Last Supper,* created that April, was too fanciful and disrespectful. It contained a man with a bleeding nose, a dog, a parrot, a dwarf, and worst of all, some Germans— warts on the Italian heart. Moreover, everyone in the painting was dressed in sixteenth-century fashion. Unheard of! Jesus and the Disciples should have been dressed in belted desert robes and sandals. Veronese was told to get rid of these things or be stretched on the rack. They gave him ninety days. At the end of ninety days, the Tribunal of the Holy Office returned to Veronese's bottega. They looked at the painting with astonishment and dragged out the portable rack.

Veronese changed nothing except to clean up the man with the bloody nose.

"Stretch him," the black robed Inquisitors ordered.

"Wait," cried Veronese. "This is no longer *The Last Supper*."

"It looks the same to us! Stretch him!"

"Per favore," Veronese pleaded as he was dragged to the rack. "It's not the same picture! The painting is now *The Feast of the House of Levi*." The artist changed the title and saved his life and soul. The work now belongs to the ages.

Remember Salman Rushdie?

Imagine! Ordering the execution of someone for writing a book in our day and age, regardless of its contents! Two thousand years separate the Emperor Ch'in Shi Huang Ti and his decapitation of book writers and artists from the Iranian order to execute a book writer. That censorial connection is the ultimate obscenity. The human family has *not* come a long way, baby. Not on your life!

"That's not us," you say. "That is not America," you say. "It's the madness of Old World, Far East/Middle East Byzantine sociology. We are the New World."

Well, think again, my friends. How far from that are we in our grand illusion of life, liberty and the pursuit of happiness when we ban an edition of "Little Red Riding Hood" for carrying a bottle of wine in a picnic hamper to her grandmother while we allow drug traffickers and gunrunners to proliferate like wildflowers. One can eliminate a bottle of wine with a single complaint. But try tampering with the National Rifle Association's notion of the right to bear arms. And just for the record, let me quote the Constitution's Second Amendment on that score: "A well-regulated militia being necessary to the security of a free state, the right of the people to keep and bear arms shall not be infringed."

The Constitution never gave an unqualified right to private citizens to bear arms to suit any private purpose beyond self-preservation and national defense. When the first ten amendments, the Bill of Rights, became part of the Constitution on December 15, 1791, there was still need for a "well-regulated" citizen's militia to protect the young nation—and stated such in the Second Amendment. That militia became today's National Guard, authorized by Congress a year later, in 1792. The intent and interpretation of the Second Amendment notwithstanding, the Bill of Rights is so inviolable a package, that no one feels compelled to disarm the private citizen of murderous weapons which are not maintained today for either self preservation or the "security of a free state." Too many of these weapons have caught our children in the haphazard crossfire of ugly purposes. But it is no trouble at all to remove a book from the reach of a private citizen. Today, the net effect of the Second Amendment is to terrorize the First Amendment.

The banishment of "Little Red Riding Hood" and her bottle of wine, by the way, took place in the vineyard country of northern California.

In October 1990, the Associated Press reported that *My Friend Flicka*, a children's classic these past fifty-three years, was pulled from fifth and sixth grade optional reading lists in Green Cove Springs, Florida, when parents complained it contained vulgar words. The words? "Bitch" in reference to a female dog; and "damn" in reference to God knows what! Our focus on what is important not only leaves something to be desired, it saps our will and ability to control our national destiny.

Killing our bodies to save our souls in the name of

the universal moral good is not half as important as killing and mutilating our minds. It's easy to make and kill bodies. It is not so easy to make or even kill minds—especially young minds. And there are people out there who are desperately afraid of what the mind can do—more afraid of that than they are of drugs and guns. And they have honed in on children's literature lest the young grow up to know something different. Guns? No problem. Words? Big problem. Pictures? Bigger problem.

This is not to let off the hook those people who bear their crosses dipped in you-know-what; tear up papal photographs while belting out forgettable songs, or rapping about killing cops. In this world, I suppose you are what you say you are and do whatever your rage tells you to do so long as someone pays. We may be the world's wealthiest nation, but we are ethically and aesthetically poverty-stricken, among other impoverishments.

I have no high regard for these nihilists, their audiences, or their paymasters. They are social floggers void of obligation to the society that nurtures them. They take and give back nothing. They have a destructive bent in the name of improvement—their own; and by their very nature they will destroy improvement as well—including their own. Theirs is a tyrannical, self-perpetuating pseudo–avant garde whose excesses and silliness are some of the cause from the left that has produced the effect on the right (and vice versa). They are unacceptable self-imagemakers, but nevertheless, permissible. They have a right to express their outrageous selves, whatever my personal opinion.

To shut them up and close them down is to censor me, in the long run. And that I cannot abide. America and its children are still strong enough, I trust, to shake off the vacancies that assault our sensibilities without limiting our right of literary or artistic choice. To use censorship as an instrument of closure in our society, however well intended, will destroy us all in the end—including the censor. There is no place for censorship of any kind in our pluralistic society.

I do not expect to persuade those who presume the right to protect public morality by removing books from library shelves or those who must alter history to suit special interest preference or adjust history to amend past cultural injury to come over to my side, either. I can understand the conservative right along with the radical left and the divergent moral indignation with which they each sizzle at opposite ends of the spectrum. I understand and sympathize with the urgent and intense desire to right what is so wrong and unjust about the world in which we live. But to presume an authority to enforce a singular code of behavior and preference, right or left, on the rest of us, flies in the face of our founding spirit, of the First Amendment, the essential glue of this diverse society, and holds in contempt everything we hold dear. Such imposition is an unproductive exercise which can ultimately lead to the surrender of our unity and nationhood.

No one is free from guilt and accusation in this matter of blame and censorship. The banning of books is but one manifestation of enforcement. Everyone has had a hand in it. Writers and artists do not spare the public in often disconnected, unimportant self expression. And the public, its representatives, elected or not, often show great zeal for intolerance of the unimportant out of all proportion to merit. In that climate, what is literarily or visually important becomes a tragic casualty. Whatever happened to "I disagree with everything you say, but I shall defend to the death your right to say it"?

We Americans do allow a fearful, raging few to try and diminish the rest of us by determining what we say, read, see, and hear because they do not approve of some descriptive imagery or language—from Mark Twain to William Faulkner; or because they campaign against the terror of their own minds; or because their narrow vision supersedes the national ideal; or because the politics of academia dictates the rewriting of thought according to politics au courant.

There is a long list of books, both children's and adult, on the unwanted list. The list includes *Huckleberry Finn, The Wizard of Oz, Of Mice and Men, Where's Waldo?, Peter Pan, Romeo and Juliet* and works by of all people, Dr. Seuss, A. A. Milne, Rudyard Kipling, and Martin Luther King, Jr. These titles and authors, and more, have been targeted by those—right and left—who would shorten our intellectual reach by imposing on the human race collective guilts for past sins so that our punishment may be continued and our ignorance redefined ad nauseam.

These cravings do not represent the America I grew up in and whose positive ideals I fought for as imperfect as the nation was. Unhappily, I remember the hateful preachings of Father Coughlin, Gerald K. Nye, and Fritz Kuhn. I shudder with personal recollections of Jim Crow, and shiver at the pitiless betrayal of native Americans for the sake of the railroad's transcontinental destiny and profit. I am embarrassed by the long disenfranchisement of women. We have tried to move on. Move on to where? To the hate and distortions of Louis Farakhan. At times, I do not recognize the promise of America today. Where are we? Where are our good manners? Where is equality? Where is freedom?

"Is this what we won the Battle of Midway for?" asked *New York Times* columnist Russell Baker.

There needs to be a great awakening to the intellectual perils our democratic republic faces before it is too late. There needs to be a clear definition of education in our American democracy, a great deal less snarling, and a start on better behavior if our children are going to have role models from which to create a more civil world. In that regard, education, the lesson of *how* to think not *what* to think, must be confronted without constraining agendas if we are to see our humanity maintained with a sense of social obligation and historical perspective. The approach to information in that process ought not to be politically focused, culturally and/or ethnically selective, or privately eradicated. Learning should be left to the educator with respect to the level of educational appropriateness of literature and art in a school setting. Education should not be left to the courts, as in the Hazelwood School District vs. Kuhlmeier, 1988, where the Supreme Court allowed that a school principal had the right to remove material from a school newspaper he, the principal, found personally offensive. The issue is not the material, or the principal, his school, or the student newspaper. The issue is: can school principals summarily go beyond the paper, into the school library, reading lists, and curriculum and remove material on their own offended authority? The answer, according to the decision of the court, is seemingly yes.

People, of whatever stripe, bent on censoring to satisfy personal codes of behavior or changing our historical focus outside of a national consensus, or deleting material they find personally disturbing, certainly in our scholastic scheme of things, should be given little room in which to permit their private aims to diminish our global knowledge base by throwing a blanket of ignorance over our intellectual freedoms and history. Our humanity, our legitimacy, our survival as a truly free people, and everyone's better world is at stake, if indeed we are sincerely interested in these things. I hope we are.

"I have sworn," wrote Thomas Jefferson, ". . . eternal hostility against every form of tyranny over the mind of man"—to which I add "women" and "children." This is where I stand. And this is where every American should stand.

In the end, this forever passing world remains the sum of our failures. I do not know what each generation thinks it is contributing as it arrogantly bequeaths its selfrighteousness to the next. But in the soul-searing commotion that drives us toward the end of this century in a furious storm of destructive constructionism we ought to heed the advice of Samuel Johnson, who cautioned us about two hundred fifty years ago to "pause a while from learning to be wise."

Lance Morrow

IN PRAISE OF
HUCKLEBERRY FINN
(1995)

Reading these lists of the proscribed is a little like walking into a police station and seeing an unexpected lineup of suspects under glaring lights: The authors, who had seemed to be familiar, even admirable citizens, now look shifty and disheveled, their respectability torn aside to disclose their secret lives—corrupters of the young.

Isn't that John Steinbeck, guiltily clutching a copy of *Of Mice and Men*? J. D. Salinger—who would have thought it?—cringing there with *The Catcher in the Rye*? Roald Dahl, the filthy beast, holding *The Witches*? Shifty-eyed Maya Angelou trying to conceal *I Know Why the Caged Bird Sings*?

These authors and books are at the top of the list of those most frequently challenged or removed from course lists and shelves, or otherwise anathematized in public schools and libraries across America. When I see the lists I am amazed and half-amused. *Of Mice and Men*? Really!? (Ah: The notorious glove.)

When I find Mark Twain in the lineup (and he is

always there, around No. 5 in the rank of suspects), holding a copy of *The Adventures of Huckleberry Finn,* I am appalled and saddened. To sweep Salinger or Angelou from the shelves is bush-league intellectual folly, mere vigilante provincialism. But it is an act of real moral stupidity, and a desecration, to try to deprive the young of the voice of Huck Finn.

Most of the challenges to the books in the lineup come from religious conservatives. It is easy to sympathize with them, up to a point. The first rule of life is to protect the young—to do so even fanatically. In a culture saturated with sex, violence, drugs and other secular recreations, all pouring out of televisions or otherwise vividly displayed in technology that goes dazzling up toward virtual reality, it seems quaint for parents to get exercised about Holden Caulfield's bad example. I would be thrilled to learn that a kid was reading books at all, not stir-frying his neurons in MTV. Still, if schools and libraries stand *in loco parentis,* one understands beleaguered parents trying to draw some lines inside the small remaining sanctuaries.

The objections to *Huck Finn* arise mostly from African-American parents, who are also trying to draw some lines. With *Huck,* the argument focuses not upon sex or profanity but rather upon race, and the deepest, most painful American memory, slavery. The institution of slavery ended, of course, during the Civil War. The institution of racism still flourishes. And it is in the context of enduring racism that black parents naturally enough may wish to protect their children from *Huck Finn.*

I hope, however, that it is possible to honor the wishes of some black parents while at the same time keeping *Huck* on shelves and reading lists. To do so, it may be necessary to stipulate that children of twelve or so are a little too young to absorb the book's complexities. Better to wait until they are fourteen or fifteen.

If *Huck Finn* were merely a nineteenth-century minstrel show—the n-word slurring around in an atmosphere of casual hatred above a subtext of white supremacy—then no one could object to African-American parents removing the book as a precaution to keep gratuitous germs away from their children. Taking books out of the hands of children, after all, does not raise the same absolute censorship issues posed when an adult audience is involved.

But American life, hardly a sanitary environment, harbors millions of germs that may be dangerous to the young. Black children should be judged quite capable, I think, of making certain moral and artistic distinctions. To focus upon *Huck Finn* as some kind of racist tract, and to suppress the book with all its countervailing glories, seems to me, in the end, both unimaginative and wrong.

The Merchant of Venice, an old staple of sophomore high school English, presents an analogous moral dilemma. Should it not be taught because Shylock is such an evilly cartoonish Jew? Surely Native Americans are entitled to take all the works of James Fenimore Cooper to the dumpster? To carry dilemma mongering further, I can see a clear feminist argument against teaching any of the novels of Ernest Hemingway, on the perfectly accurate grounds that his women are offensively two-dimensional. Would a Spanish-speaking constituency be justified in removing *For Whom the Bell Tolls,* with all of its preposterous what-passes-with-you-Little-Rabbit diction?

In any case, permit me to argue that *Huck Finn*—intelligently taught, and understood—belongs on an infinitely higher artistic and moral plane. A teacher should be able to show the young of any race the book's grace and virtues.

In the story of Huck and Jim and the river, Twain confronts *the* American problems. *Huck Finn* is one of the earliest and deepest texts on race and slavery, on violence, on child abuse, alcoholism, class distinctions in America, hatred, hypocrisy, fraud, gaudily manifold stupidity, backwoods brainlessness, and lying in all its forms—creative, vicious and otherwise. *Huck Finn* is about American civilization and about what it means to be civilized in a vast, experimental, provisional and morally unsettled territory. Huck, who spells it "sivilized," is one of the most truly civilized characters in American letters. For a work often paired with *Tom Sawyer* as the *Iliad* and *Odyssey* of idealized American boyhood, *Huck Finn* carries an almost magic cargo of deeper grownup meanings. How racially condescending to assume that such meanings of American civilization—even as they are relayed by Huck through his white genius/ventriloquist, Mark Twain—cannot concern blacks. A number of black writers in the past, uncontaminated by the ideologies of correctness, have agreed.

Huck Finn is also, as Hemingway understood, the source from which modern American literature has flowed. Twain turned the American vernacular into literature, and an enormous number of later American writers, black and white, have been in his debt. Huck's voice echoes in Langston Hughes and Ralph Ellison and Alice Walker as well as in William Faulkner. In an interview with Shelley Fisher Fishkin, professor of American studies at the University of Texas, Ellison said that Twain's use of comedy and vernacular "allow us to deal with the unspeakable," meaning "the moral situation of the United States and the contrast between our ideals and our activities."

Is *Huck Finn* about kids' adventures on the Mississippi? In the same sense that *Moby-Dick* is about commercial fishing. Everyone should understand what is lost in shelving *Huck Finn*. On one level, it operates as a children's book, but if it were merely a children's book, then we would not miss it when we put it aside. No: Twain (to make the sort of grand claim that he would have had fun with) created in *Huck* an origin myth of the nation's moral struggles.

Huck Finn is also one of the funniest books to be written in America. Sometimes the humor is gentle enough, and spoofy at the *Tom Sawyer* level of prankery. Much of the wit is deliciously literate, as in the duke's magnificent compression of the Shakespeare soliloquy:

> *To be, or not to be; that is the bare bodkin*
> *That makes calamity of so long life;*
> *For who would fardels bear, till Birnam Wood do*
>   *come to Dunsinane,*
> *But that the fear of something after death*
> *Murders the innocent sleep,*
> *Great nature's second course,*
> *And makes us rather sling the arrows of outra-*
>   *geous fortune*
> *Than fly to others that we know not of.*

But more often the humor has a philosophical savagery about it—as in this exchange toward the end of the book, when Huck shows up at Aunt Sally's, impersonating Tom and lying about a mythical steamboat trip downriver:

HUCK: "We blowed out a cylinder head."
AUNT SALLY: "Good gracious! anybody hurt?"
HUCK: "No'm. Killed a nigger."

AUNT SALLY: "Well, it's lucky; because sometimes people do get hurt."

Twain comes down to the moral core of *Huck Finn* in a chapter called "You Can't Play a Lie," wherein Huck wrestles with his conscience about whether to turn Jim in as a runaway slave. Huck's most attractive quality—one worth calling to the attention of school-children—is that for an inveterate and accomplished liar, he has a powerful need to find the truth, and to act on it.

Huck's two-page struggle over whether to betray Jim is a masterpiece of metaphysically comic inversion, a sardonic, hilarious examination of conscience. Huck accuses himself of low-down, ornery wickedness "in stealing a poor old woman's nigger." The law—righteousness, the society's definition of good—says Huck is doing an awful thing in harboring Jim. Huck tries to pray, but "my heart warn't right." At last, Huck decides he cannot turn in his friend Jim. In one of the great moments of American literature, a cousin to Melville's "No! In thunder!", Huck says, "All right, then, I'll *go* to hell." He tears up the note to Miss Watson in which he meant to betray his friend. He has done the loneliest, bravest work there is—making a life-or-death decision against the law and custom of his own tribe.

For all its deep indignation, *Huck Finn* is the tenderest and most decent of stories. When the king and the duke are finally caught, tarred and feathered, and run out of town, Huck, who has every reason to cheer the spectacle, instead reacts this way: "Well, it made me sick to see it; and I was sorry for them poor pitiful rascals, it seemed like I couldn't ever feel any hardness against them any more in the world. It was a dreadful thing to see. Human beings *can* be awful cruel to one another."

The book is an inventory of essential values: kindness, courage, loyalty to friends, abhorrence of cruelty, independence of conscience, the need to think through moral choices, and, of course, the inexhaustible power of creative lying—which is to say (putting a more edifying light on it) the inexhaustible power of imagination.

Let me propose a way of teaching *Huck*.

The key to appreciating *Huck Finn*'s moral dimensions (and, for a black pupil, the key to tolerating the disturbing universe of white supremacy in which the story is told) is to understand that here, nothing is what it seems. At the beginning of *Huckleberry Finn*, Mark Twain placed his famous "Notice":

"Persons attempting to find a motive in this narrative will be prosecuted; persons attempting to find a moral in it will be banished; persons attempting to find a plot in it will be shot."

Meaning: Watch out for all three of those items, for they will surely turn up—motive and moral unfolding just as plot unfolds. The "Notice" was the trickster declaring himself. Twain was saying one thing and meaning the opposite, lying and yarning his way along, spinning the moral landscape into a sort of trompe l'oeil tapestry wherein lies and the real thing play hide-and-seek with one another.

Twain's pseudo-stern, eyebrow-wagging opener (*I'm just here to tell some colorful provincial stories, so don't you dare go deep and moralistic on me*) goes to the secret of his game: the narrative sleight of hand, with the reversal that sets up one expectation in the reader's mind and then (*poof!*) replaces it with another. A theater of dancing contraries.

The minstrelsy is the surface stuff, just as the boys' adventure story is the shallowest dimension of the book. The first lesson to teach is that here, in some immense metaphysics of democracy's beatitudes, virtually everything and everyone swaps places and meanings: The first shall be last; the civilized shall be uncivilized; the king and the duke shall be white trash (these two white con men are, in fact, the Amos 'n' Andy of the plot—another racial switcheroo); the slave shall be free, betimes, on the river, and the free whites shall be enchained in various ways (by hereditary blood feud, by their own casually institutionalized hate, by alcoholism, by sheer bucolic idiocy); the child shall be wise and the grownup irresponsible; the boy shall be a philosopher and the father, Pap, a monster of the American id; the sub-adolescents' lark shall be profound in its consequence (Jim's life is at stake), and the allegedly profound (the Shakespeare soliloquy, for example) shall be a travesty.

In other words, *Huckleberry Finn* is, among other things, a complex, serious book. And it should be taught as such—to children old enough to think and read with imagination. The supposedly racially insensitive tale, with its repeated use of the word "nigger," is the most devastating portrait of American white trash and white-trash racism that has ever been written. *Huck Finn* savages racism as thoroughly as any document in American history.

But all of this is a lot for students to take in. I would suggest that in order to stabilize *The Adventures of Huckleberry Finn* in students' minds, and to neutralize the surface hurts of apparent minstrelsy and race epithets, *Huck* should be taught with two accompanying texts that will serve, so to speak, as moral outriggers: (1) *Narrative of the Life of Frederick Douglass* and (2) *Was Huck Black?: Mark Twain and African-American Voices,* by Shelley Fisher Fishkin.

Twain and Douglass were friends. I would use Douglass's autobiography, a noble document by a noble man, as a kind of stringent reality enforcer. The narrative is, after all, a loftily pitiless record of what it was like to be a slave on Maryland's Eastern Shore in the first half of the nineteenth century. *Huck Finn* is slavery and the rest of the rural America of that time seen fictionally through the eyes of a kind of wild child. Frederick Douglass's narrative is an adult former slave's recollection of what it was like to be a slave child in that world.

At one point an eerie intersection occurs between Twain's novel and the ex-slave's story. Douglass records that on the plantation where he lived, property of a Colonel Lloyd, there was an overseer named Austin Gore. One day, Gore was whipping a slave named Demby, who "to get rid of the scourging, . . . ran and plunged himself into the creek, and stood there at the depth of his shoulders, refusing to come out. Mr. Gore told him that he would give him three calls, and that, if he did not come out at the third call, he would shoot him." Gore gave the three calls, then "raised his musket to his face, taking deadly aim at his standing victim, and in an instant, poor Demby was no more. His mangled body sank out of sight, and blood and brains marked the water where he had stood."

This incident is strangely similar to the Colonel Sherburn story in *Huck Finn:* In the street of a river town, a drunk named Boggs starts railing and hurling boozy abuse against a local merchant named Colonel Sherburn. Sherburn finally comes out of his store and warns Boggs that he has until one o'clock to shut up. One o'clock comes. Boggs rants on. Sherburn coolly shoots him dead in the street and walks away.

In both stories, there is a note of absolute authenticity, a kind of savage Americana that is perfectly recognizable today.

Frederick Douglass's eyesight is clear and merciless

on the subject of slavery. His story of painstakingly and surreptitiously learning how to read and write—activities that were forbidden to slaves—casts a complicated light on efforts in the late twentieth century to keep other children from reading a book, *Huck Finn,* on grounds that it might offend them. Any kind of censorship, of course, implies a condescension toward the audience being "protected," but the ironies here are especially poignant.

The second book, Fishkin's *Was Huck Black?*, explores a fascinating thesis. The author's tabloid-headline title does not mean that Fishkin thinks Huck had African blood but rather that Huck's speech, the splendid, never-before-heard American voice that was Twain's great contribution to the stream of American letters, was based, in very large part, upon the vernacular and speech rhythms of blacks. *Le style, c'est l'homme.* Dr. Fishkin argues that *l'homme* in this case, meaning Mark Twain/Huck Finn, owed a huge debt, in vocabulary, syntax, verbal strategy and style, to the blacks who were young Samuel Clemens's preferred playmates in Hannibal, Missouri, and to other blacks whom Mark Twain knew and listened to attentively in later life. The result, argues Fishkin, is that Huck, in his speech and his point of view, was black to a significant degree. And if that is true—Fishkin makes a scholarly and fascinatingly plausible case—then the most original voice in American literature, the source from which so much else has flowed, is black, or half-black, or anyway immensely tinted by precisely the African consciousness so long excluded from the official cultural life of the country.

All of that is worth teaching to schoolchildren, once they are old enough to absorb it. Fishkin's thesis is not another dreary exercise in political correctness. When you have read her book, you say, Of course.

The black component of *Huck*—and of the immense literature that derives from it—becomes as self-evident as the influence of African voices in American music.

After *Huckleberry Finn* was published in 1885, the Public Library in Concord, Massachusetts, banned the book. As the *Boston Transcript* reported: "One member of the committee says that, while he does not wish to call it immoral, he thinks it contains but little humor, and that of a very coarse type. He regards it as the veriest trash. The librarian and the other members of the committee entertain similar views, characterizing it as rough, coarse and inelegant."

The ambient light in Concord at the time was the Transcendental Emersonian moonbeam. The prevailing light in American education at the moment, unfortunately, is that pitiless, accusatory glare—flat and harsh as a zealot's mind—that pours down upon the lineup of suspect authors at the police station. That light is blinding. It is time to turn it off, at least where *Huck Finn* is concerned, in order to appreciate the novel's amazing play of intelligence and morality and shadow.

Judith F. Krug

INTELLECTUAL FREEDOM, LIBRARIES, AND CENSORSHIP
(2004)

Intellectual freedom is freedom of the mind. It is the freedom to think as you wish, and believe what you want to believe, without the government or any individual telling you what to think or believe. It is both a personal liberty and a prerequisite for all other freedoms.

Intellectual freedom can exist only when two essential conditions are met: first, that all individuals have the right to hold any belief on any subject and to convey those ideas in any form they deem appropriate; and second, that society makes an absolute commitment to the right of unrestricted access to information and ideas regardless of the medium of communication used, the content of the work, or the viewpoints of both the author and the receiver of the information.

Moreover, intellectual freedom forms the bulwark of any constitutional republic. It is an essential part of government by the people. The right to vote alone is not sufficient to give citizens effective control of the government's actions and policies. Citizens must be able to take part in the formation of public opinion by engaging in vigorous and wide-ranging debate on controversial matters. Censorship stifles this debate, thus weakening government by the people.

The founders of this country recognized these truths, securing each citizen's intellectual freedom by incorporating the First Amendment into the Constitution. Its guarantees of free speech, a free press, and free conscience assure each person the autonomy and the security to debate and to form one's own convictions about what it means to be a citizen and a member of society, without the government or any other group or individual intruding upon that process.

These freedoms—the freedom to express yourself, the freedom to form your own beliefs, and their necessary corollary, the freedom to read—are uniquely fulfilled by the library. The library assures that any person, regardless of status, income, education, or station in life, can have access to information, ideas, and opinions. Librarians fulfill this promise by bringing people and information together, making sure libraries have information and ideas across the spectrum of social and political thought, so people can choose what they want to read or view or listen to. Libraries and librarians give substance to intellectual freedom by acquiring and providing information without prejudice or restriction.

Yet, there are those who challenge the freedom to speak and read as one wishes. These individuals and groups believe that access to some ideas, opinions, or materials should be restricted because they find them to be untrue, offensive, harmful, or even dangerous. Today, conservatives and liberals alike are using old-fashioned political organizing and newer, nontraditional methods to silence critics, suppress dissent, and prevent audiences from accessing ideas they deem objectionable. Conservative Christian organizations seek to remove materials on witchcraft, mythology, and fantasy, including the *Harry Potter* series, on the grounds that these works promote occultism or Satanic religion. Individuals and groups across the political spectrum are engaging in campaigns to require labels warning consumers about books, films, television programs, video games, comic books and musical lyrics whose content offends them for a variety of reasons. Others campaign to purge schools and library collections of works deemed offensive because of racist, sexist, homophobic, ethnic, or religious stereotyping or themes, or because the works advocate ideas such as evolution or promote equal rights for all persons, regardless of their religion or sexuality.

Those advocating censorship might sincerely believe that certain materials are so offensive, or present ideas that are so hateful and destructive to society, that they simply must not see the light of day. Others are worried that younger or weaker people will be badly influenced by bad ideas, and will do bad things as a result. Still others believe that there is a very clear distinction between ideas that are right and morally uplifting, and ideas that are wrong and morally corrupting, and wish to ensure that society has the benefit of their perception. They believe that certain individuals, certain institutions, even society itself, will be endangered if particular ideas are disseminated without restriction.

Though such censors claim to be upholding American values by restricting access to information and ideas they find harmful or threatening, they actually undermine the values of tolerance, free inquiry, and self-determination that inform and sustain our democratic way of life. Moreover, what censors often don't consider is that if they succeed in suppressing the ideas they don't like today, others may use that precedent to suppress the ideas they do like tomorrow.

Libraries and librarians resist censorship. A library's role never has been, is not currently and will not be in the future to keep people from the information they need and want. Librarians know that a diverse and robust library collection reaffirms the importance and value of freedom to read and sends a message to all persons that they have the right to choose what they will read and think about, rather than allowing others to think for them.

Librarians also recognize that a wide range of ideas and information must be available in the library because libraries serve the information needs of all of the people in the community. That means every person who uses the library, not just the loudest, not just the most powerful, not even just the majority. If the material is legal, it can legitimately be in the library and often is.

For the uniqueness of the First Amendment lies not only in its guarantees, but also in its lack of proscriptions. The First Amendment assures freedom of speech, but it doesn't mandate that the speech be truthful, honest, equal, sensitive, tasteful, showing good judgment, respectful or any other adjective you can think of. If a speaker chooses to lie through his teeth, the First Amendment gives him (or any other speaker) the right to do so.

Censorship denies the individual's First Amendment right to read, watch, and listen, to freely access ideas, and to think about them. Now, more than ever, we must be vigilant in the fight against censorship. As individuals and as a nation, we must understand the importance of ideas and the importance of the right to express ideas and the right of others to be able to hear them. Each successful act of censorship strikes at the core of our democracy, for without information, without debate, our democracy will wither and die.

James Madison defined the situation almost two hundred years ago: "A popular government, without popular information or the means of acquiring it, is but a prologue to a farce or a tragedy; or perhaps both. Knowledge will forever govern ignorance; and a people who mean to be their own governors must arm themselves with the power knowledge gives."*

---

*James Madison to W. T. Barry, August 4, 1822, *Letters and Other Writings of James Madison,* ed. Philip R. Fendall, vol. 3 (Philadelphia: Lippincott, 1867).

WOMEN SPEAK OUT

Abigail Adams

LETTERS TO JOHN ADAMS
(1776)

Braintree, 31 March

I wish you would ever write me a letter half as long
as I write you, and tell me, if you may, where your
fleet are gone; what sort of defense Virginia can make
against our common enemy; whether it is so situated
as to make an able defense. Are not the gentry lords,
and the common people vassals? Are they not like the
uncivilized vassals Britain represents us to be? I hope
their riflemen, who have shown themselves very savage and even blood-thirsty, are not a specimen of the
generality of the people. I am willing to allow the
colony great merit for having produced a Washington;
but they have been shamefully duped by a Dunmore.

I have sometimes been ready to think that the passion for liberty cannot be equally strong in the breasts
of those who have been accustomed to deprive their
fellow-creatures of theirs. Of this I am certain, that it
is not founded upon that generous and Christian prin-

ciple of doing to others as we would that others should do unto us.

Do not you want to see Boston? I am fearful of the small-pox, or I should have been in before this time. I got Mr. Crane to go to our house and see what state it was in. I find it has been occupied by one of the doctors of a regiment; very dirty, but no other damage has been done to it. The few things which were left in it are all gone. Cranch has the key, which he never delivered up. I have wrote to him for it and am determined to get it cleaned as soon as possible and shut it up. I look upon it as a new acquisition of property— a property which one month ago I did not value at a single shilling, and would with pleasure have seen it in flames.

The town in general is left in a better state than we expected; more owing to a precipitate flight than any regard to the inhabitants; though some individuals discovered a sense of honor and justice, and have left the rent of the houses in which they were, for the owners, and the furniture unhurt, or, if damaged, sufficient to make it good. Others have committed abominable ravages. The mansion-house of your President is safe, and the furniture unhurt; while the house and furniture of the Solicitor General have fallen a prey to their own merciless party. Surely the very fiends feel a reverential awe for virtue and patriotism, whilst they detest the parricide and traitor.

I feel very differently at the approach of spring from what I did a month ago. We knew not then whether we could plant or sow with safety, whether where we had tilled we could reap the fruits of our own industry, whether we could rest in our own cottages or whether we should be driven from the seacoast to seek shelter in the wilderness; but now we feel as if we might sit under our own vine and eat the good of the land.

I feel a *gaieté de cœur* to which before I was a stranger. I think the sun looks brighter, the birds sing more melodiously, and Nature puts on a more cheerful countenance. We feel a temporary peace, and the poor fugitives are returning to their deserted habitation.

Though we felicitate ourselves, we sympathize with those who are trembling lest the lot of Boston should be theirs. But they cannot be in similar circumstances unless pusillanimity and cowardice should take possession of them. They have time and warning given them to see the evil and shun it.

I long to hear that you have declared an independency. And, by the way, in the new code of laws which I suppose it will be necessary for you to make, I desire you would remember the ladies and be more generous and favorable to them than your ancestors. Do not put such unlimited power into the hands of the husbands. Remember, all men would be tyrants if they could. If particular care and attention is not paid to the ladies, we are determined to foment a rebellion, and will not hold ourselves bound by any laws in which we have no voice or representation.

That your sex are naturally tyrannical is a truth so thoroughly established as to admit of no dispute; but such of you as wish to be happy willingly give up the harsh title of master for the more tender and endearing one of friend. Why, then, not put it out of the power of the vicious and the lawless to use us with cruelty and indignity with impunity? Men of sense in all ages abhor those customs which treat us only as the vassals of your sex; regard us then as beings placed by Providence under your protection, and in imitation of the Supreme Being make use of that power only for our happiness.

April 5

Not having an opportunity of sending this I shall add
a few lines more; though not with a heart so gay. I
have been attending the sick chamber of our neighbor
Trott whose affliction I most sensibly feel but cannot
describe, stripped of two lovely children in one week.
George the eldest died on Wednesday and Billy the
youngest on Friday, with the canker fever, a terrible
disorder so much like the throat distemper that it dif-
fers but little from it. Betsy Cranch has been very bad,
but upon the recovery. Becky Peck they do not expect
will live out the day. Many grown persons are now
sick with it, in this street. It rages much in other towns.
The mumps too are very frequent. Isaac is now confined with it. Our own little flock are yet well. My
heart trembles with anxiety for them. God preserve
them.

I want to hear much oftener from you than I do.
March 8th was the last date of any that I have yet had.
You inquire of me whether I am making saltpetre. I
have not yet attempted it, but after soap-making believe I shall make the experiment. I find as much as I
can do to manufacture clothing for my family, which
would else be naked. I know of but one person in this
part of the town who has made any. That is Mr. Ter-
tius Bass, as he is called, who has got very near a
hundred-weight which has been found to be very
good. I have heard of some others in the other par-
ishes. Mr. Reed, of Weymouth, has been applied to,
to go to Andover to the mills which are now at work,
and he has gone.

I have lately seen a small manuscript describing the
proportions of the various sorts of powder fit for can-
non, small arms, and pistols. If it would be of any
service your way I will get it transcribed and send it

to you. Every one of your friends sends regards, and all the little ones. Your brother's youngest child lies bad with convulsion fits. Adieu. I need not say how much I am your ever faithful friend.

Gloria Steinem

A NEW EGALITARIAN LIFE STYLE

(1971)

The first problem for all of us, men and women, is not to learn, but to unlearn. We are filled with the popular wisdom of several centuries just past, and we are terrified to give it up. Patriotism means obedience, age means wisdom, woman means submission, black means inferior: these are preconceptions imbedded so deeply in our thinking that we honestly may not know that they are there.

Whether it's woman's secondary role in society or the paternalistic role of the United States in the world, the old assumptions just don't work anymore.

Part of living this revolution is having the scales fall from our eyes. Every day, we see small obvious truths that we had missed before. Our histories, for instance, have generally been written for and about white men. Inhabited countries were "discovered" when the first white male set foot there, and most of us learned more about any one European country than we did about Africa and Asia combined.

We need Women's Studies courses just as much as we need Black Studies. We need courses on sexism and American law just as much as we need them on racism. The number of laws that discriminate against women is staggering. At least to women.

"Anonymous," as Virginia Woolf once said bitterly, "was a woman."

If we weren't studying white paternalistic documents, after all, we might start long before Charlemagne in history, or Blackstone in law. More than 5,000 years before, in fact, when women were treated as equals or superiors. When women were the gods, and worshipped because they had the children. Men didn't consider child-bearing a drawback, and in fact imitated that envied act in their ceremonies. It was thought that women bore fruit when they were ripe, like trees.

When paternity was discovered—a day I like to imagine as a gigantic light bulb over someone's head, as he says, "Oh, *that's* why"—the idea of ownership of children began. And the possibility of passing authority and goods down to them. And the origin of marriage—which was locking women up long enough to make sure who the father was. Women were subjugated, the original political subjugation and the pattern which others were to follow, as the means of production. They were given whatever tasks the men considered odious, and they became "feminine," a cultural habit which has continued till today.

When other tribes or groups were captured, they were given the least desirable role: that of women. When black people were brought to these shores as slaves, for instance, they were given the legal status of wives; that is, chattel. Since then, our revolutions have followed, each on the heels of the other.

I don't mean to equate women's problems with the sufferings of slavery. Women lose their identities: black men lose their lives. But, as Gunnar Myrdal pointed out more than thirty years ago, the parallel between women and blacks—the two largest second-class groups—is the deepest truth of American life.

We suffer from the same myths—childlike natures, smaller brains, naturally passive, lack of objectivity (Harvard Law School professors are still peddling that), inability to govern ourselves, identity as sex objects, supernatural powers—usually evil, and special job skills. We're great at detail work for instance, as long as it's poorly paid, but brain surgery is something else.

When we make a generalization about women, it helps if we substitute black, or Chicano or Puerto Rican. Then we see what we are saying.

The truth is that women are so much more durable than men at every stage of life, so much less subject to diseases of stress, for instance. Child-bearing shouldn't mean child-rearing. Motherhood is not all-consuming, nor is fatherhood a sometime thing. In fact, there are tribes in which the fathers rear the children, and the famous mother instinct turns out to be largely cultural.

The problem is achieving a compassionate balance, something this society has not done. It's clear that most American children suffer from too much mother and too little father.

Women employees in general lose no more time from work than men do, even including childbirth. They change jobs less, since they have less chance of trading upward, and tend to leave only after long periods of no promotion; thus benefiting male employees by financing their retirement plans.

Women don't want to imitate the male pattern of obsessive work ending up with a heart attack and an engraved wrist watch. We want to humanize the work pattern, to make new, egalitarian life styles.

We are not more moral, we are only less corrupted

by power. But we haven't been culturally trained to feel our identity depends on money, manipulative power, or a gun.

From now on, no man can call himself liberal, or radical, or even a conservative advocate of fair play, if his work depends in any way on the unpaid or underpaid labor of women at home, or in the office. Politics doesn't begin in Washington. Politics begins with those who are oppressed right here.

And maybe, if we live this revolution every day, we will put a suitable end to this second 5,000-year period: that of patriarchy and racism. Perhaps we have a chance for a third and new period—one of humanism.

Sandra Cisneros

ONLY DAUGHTER
(1990)

Once, several years ago, when I was just starting
out my writing career, I was asked to write my
own contributor's note for an anthology I was part of.
I wrote: "I am the only daughter in a family of six
sons. *That* explains everything."

Well, I've thought about that ever since, and yes, it
explains a lot to me, but for the reader's sake I should
have written: "I am the only daughter in a *Mexican*
family of six sons." Or even: "I am the only daughter
of a Mexican father and a Mexican-American mother."
Or: "I am the only daughter of a working-class family
of nine." All of these had everything to do with who
I am today.

I was/am the only daughter and *only* a daughter.
Being an only daughter in a family of six sons forced
me by circumstance to spend a lot of time by myself
because my brothers felt it beneath them to play with a
girl in public. But that aloneness, that loneliness, was
good for a would-be writer—it allowed me time to think
and think, to imagine, to read and prepare myself.

Being only a daughter for my father meant my des-

204

tiny would lead me to become someone's wife. That's what he believed. But when I was in fifth grade and shared my plans for college with him, I was sure he understood. I remember my father saying, "*Que bueno, mi'ja,* that's good." That meant a lot to me, especially since my brothers thought the idea hilarious. What I didn't realize was that my father thought college was good for girls—for finding a husband. After four years in college and two more in graduate school, and still no husband, my father shakes his head even now and says I wasted all that education.

In retrospect, I'm lucky my father believed daughters were meant for husbands. It meant it didn't matter if I majored in something silly like English. After all, I'd find a nice professional eventually, right? This allowed me the liberty to putter about embroidering my little poems and stories without my father interrupting with so much as a "What's that you're writing?"

But the truth is, I wanted him to interrupt. I wanted my father to understand what it was I was scribbling, to introduce me as "My only daughter, the writer." Not as "This is my only daughter. She teaches." *El maestra*—teacher. Not even *profesora.*

In a sense, everything I have ever written has been for him, to win his approval even though I know my father can't read English words, even though my father's only reading includes the brown-ink *Esto* sports magazines from Mexico City and the bloody *¡Alarma!* magazines that feature yet another sighting of *La Virgen de Guadalupe* on a tortilla or a wife's revenge on her philandering husband by bashing his skull in with a *molcajete* (a kitchen mortar made of volcanic rock). Or the *fotonovelas,* the little picture paperbacks with tragedy and trauma erupting from the characters' mouths in bubbles.

My father represents, then, the public majority. A public who is uninterested in reading, and yet one whom I am writing about and for, and privately trying to woo.

When we were growing up in Chicago, we moved a lot because of my father. He suffered periodic bouts of nostalgia. Then we'd have to let go our flat, store the furniture with mother's relatives, load the station wagon with baggage and bologna sandwiches, and head south. To Mexico City.

We came back, of course. To yet another Chicago flat, another Chicago neighborhood, another Catholic school. Each time, my father would seek out the parish priest in order to get a tuition break, and complain or boast: "I have seven sons."

He meant *siete hijos,* seven children, but he translated it as "sons." "I have seven sons." To anyone who would listen. The Sears Roebuck employee who sold us the washing machine. The short-order cook where my father ate his ham-and-eggs breakfasts. "I have seven sons." As if he deserved a medal from the state.

My papa. He didn't mean anything by that mistranslation, I'm sure. But somehow I could feel myself being erased. I'd tug my father's sleeve and whisper: "Not seven sons. Six! And *one daughter.*"

When my oldest brother graduated from medical school, he fulfilled my father's dream that we study hard and use this—our heads, instead of this—our hands. Even now my father's hands are thick and yellow, stubbed by a history of hammer and nails and twine and coils and springs. "Use this," my father said, tapping his head, "and not this," showing us those hands. He always looked tired when he said it.

Wasn't college an investment? And hadn't I spent all those years in college? And if I didn't marry, what was it all for? Why would anyone go to college and then choose to be poor? Especially someone who had always been poor.

Last year, after ten years of writing professionally, the financial rewards started to trickle in. My second National Endowment for the Arts Fellowship. A guest professorship at the University of California, Berkeley. My book, which sold to a major New York publishing house.

At Christmas, I flew home to Chicago. The house was throbbing, same as always; hot *tamales* and sweet *tamales* hissing in my mother's pressure cooker, and everybody—mother, six brothers, wives, babies, aunts, cousins—talking too loud and at the same time, like in a Fellini film, because that's just how we are.

I went upstairs to my father's room. One of my stories had just been translated into Spanish and published in an anthology of Chicano writing, and I wanted to show it to him. Ever since he recovered from a stroke two years ago, my father likes to spend his leisure hours horizontally. And that's how I found him, watching a Pedro Infante movie on Galavision and eating rice pudding.

There was a glass filmed with milk on the bedside table. There were several vials of pills and balled Kleenex. And on the floor, one black sock and a plastic urinal that I didn't want to look at but looked at anyway. Pedro Infante was about to burst into song, and my father was laughing.

I'm not sure if it was because my story was translated into Spanish, or because it was published in Mexico, or perhaps because the story dealt with Tepeyac, the *colonia* my father was raised in, but at any rate, my father punched the mute button on his remote control and read my story.

I sat on the bed next to my father and waited. He

read it very slowly. As if he were reading each line over and over. He laughed at all the right places and read lines he liked out loud. He pointed and asked questions: "Is this So-and-so?" "Yes," I said. He kept reading.

When he was finally finished, after what seemed like hours, my father looked up and asked: "Where can we get more copies of this for the relatives?"

Of all the wonderful things that happened to me last year, that was the most wonderful.

Hillary Rodham Clinton

————— ~~~ —————

REMARKS TO THE UNITED NATIONS FOURTH WORLD CONFERENCE ON WOMEN PLENARY SESSION
(1995)

Mrs. Mongella, Under Secretary Kittani, distinguished delegates and guests:

I would like to thank the Secretary General of the United Nations for inviting me to be a part of the United Nations Fourth World Conference on Women. This is truly a celebration—a celebration of the contributions women make in every aspect of life: in the home, on the job, in their communities, as mothers, wives, sisters, daughters, learners, workers, citizens and leaders.

It is also a coming together, much of the way women come together every day in every country.

We come together in fields and in factories. We come together in village markets and supermarkets. We come together in living rooms and board rooms.

Whether it is while playing with our children in the park, or washing clothes in a river, or taking a break at the office water cooler, we come together and talk about our aspirations and concern. And time and again, our talk turns to our children and our families. However different we may be, there is far more that unites us than divides us. We share a common future, and are here to find common ground so that we may help bring new dignity and respect to women and girls all over the world. By doing this, we bring new strength and stability to families as well.

By gathering in Beijing, we are focusing world attention on issues that matter most in the lives of women and their families: access to education, health care, jobs and credit, the chance to enjoy basic legal and human rights and participate fully in the political life of their countries.

There are some who question the reason for this conference.

Let them listen to the voices of women in their homes, neighborhoods, and workplaces.

There are some who wonder whether the lives of women and girls matter to economic and political progress around the globe.

Let them look at the women gathered here and at Huairou—the homemakers, nurses, teachers, lawyers, policymakers, and women who run their own businesses.

It is conferences like this that compel governments and people everywhere to listen, look and face the world's most pressing problems.

Wasn't it after the women's conference in Nairobi ten years ago that the world focused for the first time on the crisis of domestic violence?

Earlier today, I participated in a World Health Organization forum, where government officials, NGOs, and individual citizens are working on ways to address the health problems of women and girls.

Tomorrow, I will attend a gathering of the United

Nations Development Fund for Women. There, the discussion will focus on local—and highly successful—programs that give hardworking women access to credit so they can improve their own lives and the lives of their families.

What we are learning around the world is that if women are healthy and educated, their families will flourish. If women are free from violence, their families will flourish. If women have a chance to work and earn as full and equal partners in society, their families will flourish.

And when families flourish, communities and nations will florish.

That is why every woman, every man, every child, every family, and every nation on our planet has a stake in the discussion that takes place here.

Over the past twenty-five years, I have worked persistently on issues relating to women, children, and families. Over the past two and a half years, I have had the opportunity to learn more about the challenges facing women in my own country and around the world.

I have met new mothers in Jojakarta and Indonesia, who come together regularly in their village to discuss nutrition, family planning, and baby care.

I have met working parents in Denmark who talk about the comfort they feel in knowing that their children can be cared for in creative, safe, and nurturing after-school centers.

I have met women in South Africa who helped lead the struggle to end apartheid and are now helping build a new democracy.

I have met with the leading women of the Western Hemisphere who are working every day to promote literacy and better health care for the children of their countries.

I have met women in India and Bangladesh who are taking out small loans to buy milk cows, rickshaws, thread and other materials to create a livelihood for themselves and their families.

I have met doctors and nurses in Belarus and Ukraine who are trying to keep children alive in the aftermath of Chernobyl.

The great challenge of this Conference is to give voice to women everywhere whose experiences go unnoticed, whose words go unheard.

Women comprise more than half the world's population. Women are 70 percent of the world's poor, and two-thirds of those are not taught to read and write.

Women are the primary caretakers for most of the world's children and elderly. Yet much of the work we do is not valued—not by economists, not by historians, not by popular culture, not by government leaders.

At this very moment, as we sit here, women around the world are giving birth, raising children, cooking meals, washing clothes, cleaning houses, planting crops, working on assembly lines, running companies, and running countries.

Women also are dying from diseases that should have been prevented or treated. They are watching their children succumb to malnutrition caused by poverty and economic deprivation. They are being denied the right to go to school by their own fathers and brothers. They are being forced into prostitution, and they are being barred from the ballot box and the bank-lending office.

Those of us who have the opportunity to be here have the responsibility to speak for those who could not.

As an American, I want to speak up for those women in my own country—women who are raising children on the minimum wage, women who can't afford health care or child care, women whose lives are threatened by violence, including violence in their own homes.

I want to speak up for mothers who are fighting for good schools, safe neighborhoods, clean air, and clean airwaves; for older women, some of them widows, who have raised their families and now find their skills and life experiences are not valued in the workplace; for women who are working all night as nurses, hotel clerks, and fast food cooks so that they can be at home during the day with their kids; and for women everywhere who simply don't have time to do everything they are called upon to do each day.

Speaking to you today, I speak for them, just as each of us speaks for women around the world who are denied the chance to go to school, or see a doctor, or own property, or have a say about the direction of their lives, simply because they are women. The truth is that most women around the world work both inside and outside the home, usually by necessity.

We need to understand that there is no formula for how women should lead their lives.

That is why we must respect the choices that each woman makes for herself and her family. Every woman deserves the chance to realize her own God-given potential.

We also must recognize that women will never gain full dignity until their human rights are respected and protected.

Our goals for this Conference, to strengthen families and societies by empowering women to take greater control over their destinies, cannot be fully achieved unless all governments—here and around the world—accept their responsibility to protect and promote internationally recognized human rights.

The international community has long acknowledged—and recently affirmed at Vienna—that both women and men are entitled to a range of protections and personal freedoms, from the right of personal security to the right to determine freely the number and spacing of the children they bear.

No one should be forced to remain silent for fear of religious or political persecution, arrest, abuse or torture.

Tragically, women are most often the ones whose human rights are violated.

Even in the late-twentieth century, the rape of women continues to be used as an instrument of armed conflict. Women and children make up a large majority of the world's refugees. When women are excluded from the political process, they become even more vulnerable to abuse.

I believe that, on the eve of a new millennium, it is time to break our silence. It is time for us to say here in Beijing, and the world to hear, that it is no longer acceptable to discuss women's rights as separate from human rights.

These abuses have continued because, for too long, the history of women has been a history of silence. Even today, there are those who are trying to silence our words.

The voices of this conference and of the women at Huairou must be heard loud and clear:

It is a violation of *human* rights when babies are denied food, or drowned, or suffocated, or their spines broken, simply because they are born girls.

It is a violation of *human* rights when women are doused with gasoline, set on fire and burned to death because their marriage dowries are deemed too small.

It is a violation of *human* rights when individual women are raped in their own communities and when thousands of women are subjected to rape as a tactic or prize of war.

It is a violation of *human* rights when a leading cause of death worldwide among women ages fourteen to forty-four is the violence they are subjected to in their own homes.

It is a violation of *human* rights when women are denied the right to plan their own families, and that includes being forced to have abortions or being sterilized against their will.

If there is one message that echoes forth from this conference, it is that human rights are women's rights—and women's rights are human rights. Let us not forget that among those rights are the right to speak freely—and the right to be heard.

Women must enjoy the right to participate fully in the social and political lives of their countries if we want freedom and democracy to thrive and endure.

It is indefensible that many women in nongovernmental organizations who wished to participate in this conference have not been able to attend—or have been prohibited from fully taking part.

Let me be clear. Freedom means the right of people to assemble, organize and debate openly. It means respecting the views of those who may disagree with the views of their governments. It means not taking citizens away from their loved ones and jailing them, mistreating them, or denying them their freedom or dignity because of the peaceful expression of their ideas and opinions.

In my country, we recently celebrated the seventy-fifth anniversary of women's suffrage. It took 150 years after the signing of our Declaration of Independence for women to win the right to vote.

It took seventy-two years of organized struggle on

the part of many courageous women and men. It was one of America's most divisive philosophical wars. But it was also a bloodless war. Suffrage was achieved without a shot being fired.

We have also been reminded, in VJ Day observances last weekend, of the good that comes when men and women join together to combat the forces of tyranny and build a better world.

We have seen peace prevail in most places for a half century. We have avoided another world war.

But we have not solved older, deeply rooted problems that continue to diminish the potential of half the world's population.

Now it is time to act on behalf of women everywhere.

If we take bold steps to better the lives of women, we will be taking bold steps to better the lives of children and families too.

Families rely on mothers and wives for emotional support and care; families rely on women for labor in the home; and increasingly, families rely on women for income needed to raise healthy children and care for other relatives.

As long as discrimination and inequities remain so commonplace around the world—as long as girls and women are valued less, fed less, fed last, overworked, underpaid, not schooled and subjected to violence in and out of their homes—the potential of the human family to create a peaceful, prosperous world will not be realized.

Let this Conference be our—and the world's—call to action.

And let us heed the call so that we can create a world in which every woman is treated with respect and dignity, every boy and girl is loved and cared for equally, and every family has the hope of a strong and stable future.

Thank you very much.

May God bless you, your work and all who will benefit from it.

Anna Quindlen

THE WAR WE HAVEN'T WON
(2004)

In 1964 Lyndon B. Johnson made history during his first State of the Union speech with this sentence: "This administration today, here and now, declares unconditional war on poverty in America."

From that declaration a host of government initiatives sprang, including Head Start, an expanded food-stamp program, and sweeping reforms in health care for the needy. It worked. The poverty rates fell and living standards for many in poor communities rose. And all because the president had had the political will to say that having one in five Americans living in the kind of abject conditions their fellow citizens associated with Third World countries and the novels of Dickens was as dangerous as any battlefield enemy.

The problem with declaring war, of course, is that sooner or later people believe the conflict will end and peace will break out. But forty years after Johnson led the charge, the battle against poverty still rages. The biggest difference today is that there is no call to arms by those in power.

Recently released figures from the Census Bureau

show that for the third year in a row the number of Americans living below the poverty line has increased. It's no longer Johnson's one in five, but it's still more than one in eight. There were 1.3 million more people defined as poor in 2003 than there were in 2002; more than 700,000 of those were kids. And that's with the bar set extraordinarily low, at just over $18,000 a year for a family of four. When you adjust the level to reflect reality, you come closer to 35 percent of all Americans who are having a hard time providing the basics for their families, what the Community Service Society of New York calls "The Unheard Third."

Who cares? Well, some people who have been pushing the rock of need uphill for a long time. There are the food-pantry folks, handing out more meals, and the shelter folks, looking for more beds. Deborah Weinstein's been in the business for a quarter century and now runs Coalition on Human Needs, an umbrella group that advocates for its members in Washington. In other words, she lobbies for the disenfranchised. "It's been my privilege," she says. "I wish I had better success with it."

Her frustration, and that of others who do this work, is that it's pretty clear what brings results. Some of the solutions are similar to the ones LBJ talked about in his speech. Raising the minimum wage, which hasn't been adjusted in seven years. Expanding unemployment insurance. Really grappling with health care. Poor kids are much more likely to become sick than their richer counterparts, but much less likely to have health insurance. Talk about a double whammy.

But politicians are inclined to support those programs their most vocal constituents support, and part of the problem with a war on poverty today is that many Americans have decided that being poor is a character defect, not an economic condition. For those who think poor parents are hanging around the house watching the soaps and waiting for a government check, it's worth noting, says Weinstein, that 70 percent of our poorest kids live in households where someone works.

One teacher in a New York City school in which roughly half the kids qualify for free lunch says she can measure which of her first and second graders are poor by how many jobs their parents have. Two or three, and she knows they're probably really needy. She also says the poorest kids are terribly afraid of playing too hard and so messing up their clothes. "Maybe because they don't have very many," she said. "And probably it's pride."

Just before these dispiriting new poverty statistics were released, the Bush administration took a bow for a decrease in caseloads in the government program for needy families. A press release said that Americans were "improving their lives by leaving public assistance and entering the workforce." But the poverty figures that followed a few days later, and the marked decrease in the employment rate among single mothers, revealed the bait-and-switch: a growing population of the poor that had lost both their jobs and their benefits and gone, not from welfare to work, but to what now? Which means no breakfast for you, little boy.

An attitude check is no substitute for food on the table, but the first might lead to the second. Weinstein says she sits in focus groups in which middle-class citizens say, "Poor people get help and rich people get help and people in the middle don't get anything." Adds Weinstein, "They're right about the rich people." Statistics show that the wealthy have prospered most in our current economy, and the unheard third at the bottom least. (But who are you gonna believe, government rhetoric about fairness for all, or your lying eyes?) Given how much influence the wealthy exert over the political process, there's really only one reason to champion programs for the poor. But it's a reason well worth remembering at a time when elected officials are inclined to make much of the state of their souls: it's the moral thing to do. LBJ said of the war on poverty, "The richest nation on earth can afford to win it." That's still true. Now all we need are some generals.

INDIVIDUAL
RIGHTS

Henry David Thoreau

CIVIL DISOBEDIENCE
(1849)

I heartily accept the motto,—"That government is best which governs least;" and I should like to see it acted up to more rapidly and systematically. Carried out, it finally amounts to this, which also I believe,— "That government is best which governs not at all;" and when men are prepared for it, that will be the kind of government which they will have. Government is at best but an expedient; but most governments are usually, and all governments are sometimes, inexpedient. The objections which have been brought against a standing army, and they are many and weighty, and deserve to prevail, may also at last be brought against a standing government. The standing army is only an arm of the standing government. The government itself, which is only the mode which the people have chosen to execute their will, is equally liable to be abused and perverted before the people can act through it. Witness the present Mexican war, the work of comparatively a few individuals using the standing government as their tool; for, in the outset, the people would not have consented to this measure.

This American government,—what is it but a tradition, though a recent one, endeavoring to transmit itself unimpaired to posterity, but each instant losing some of its integrity? It has not the vitality and force of a single living man; for a single man can bend it to his will. It is a sort of wooden gun to the people themselves; and, if ever they should use it in earnest as a real one against each other, it will surely split. But it is not the less necessary for this; for the people must have some complicated machinery or other, and hear its din, to satisfy that idea of government which they have. Governments show thus how successfully men can be imposed on, even impose on themselves, for their own advantage. It is excellent, we must all allow; yet this government never of itself furthered any enterprise, but by the alacrity with which it got out of its way. *It* does not keep the country free. *It* does not settle the West. *It* does not educate. The character inherent in the American people has done all that has been accomplished; and it would have done somewhat more, if the government had not sometimes got in its way. For government is an expedient by which men would fain succeed in letting one another alone; and, as has been said, when it is most expedient, the governed are most let alone by it. Trade and commerce, if they were not made of India rubber, would never manage to bounce over the obstacles which legislators are continually putting in their way; and, if one were to judge these men wholly by the effects of their actions, and not partly by their intentions, they would deserve to be classed and punished with those mischievous persons who put obstructions on the railroads.

But, to speak practically and as a citizen, unlike those who call themselves no-government men, I ask for, not at once no government, but *at once* a better government. Let every man make known what kind of government would command his respect, and that will be one step toward obtaining it.

After all, the practical reason why, when the power is once in the hands of the people, a majority are permitted, and for a long period continue, to rule, is not because they are most likely to be in the right, nor because this seems fairest to the minority, but because they are physically the strongest. But a government in which the majority rule in all cases cannot be based on justice, even as far as men understand it. Can there not be a government in which majorities do not virtually decide right and wrong, but conscience?— in which majorities decide only those questions to which the rule of expediency is applicable? Must the citizen ever for a moment, or in the least degree, resign his conscience to the legislator? Why has every man a conscience, then? I think that we should be men first, and subjects afterward. It is not desirable to cultivate a respect for the law, so much as for the right. The only obligation which I have a right to assume, is to do at any time what I think right. It is truly enough said, that a corporation has no conscience; but a corporation of conscientious men is a corporation *with* a conscience. Law never made men a whit more just; and, by means of their respect for it, even the well-disposed are daily made the agents of injustice. A common and natural result of an undue respect for law is, that you may see a file of soldiers, colonel, captain, corporal, privates, powder-monkeys and all, marching in admirable order over hill and dale to the wars, against their wills, aye, against their common sense and consciences, which makes it very steep marching indeed, and produces a palpitation of the heart. They have no doubt that it is a damnable business in which they are concerned; they are all peaceably inclined. Now, what are they? Men at all? or small moveable forts and magazines, at the service of some unscrupulous man in power? Visit the Navy Yard, and behold a marine, such a man as an American government can make, or such as it can make a man with its black arts, a mere shadow and reminiscence of humanity, a man laid out alive and standing, and already, as one may say, buried under arms with funeral accompaniments, though it may be

> "Not a drum was heard, nor a funeral note,
>   As his corse to the ramparts we hurried;
> Not a soldier discharged his farewell shot
>   O'er the grave where our hero we buried."

The mass of men serve the State thus, not as men mainly, but as machines, with their bodies. They are the standing army, and the militia, jailers, constables, *posse comitatus,* &c. In most cases there is no free exercise whatever of the judgment or of the moral sense; but they put themselves on a level with wood and earth and stones; and wooden men can perhaps be manufactured that will serve the purpose as well. Such command no more respect than men of straw, or a lump of dirt. They have the same sort of worth only as horses and dogs. Yet such as these even are commonly esteemed good citizens. Others, as most legislators, politicians, lawyers, ministers, and office-holders, serve the State chiefly with their heads; and, as they rarely make any moral distinctions, they are as likely to serve the devil, without intending it, as God. A very few, as heroes, patriots, martyrs, reformers in the great sense, and *men,* serve the State with their consciences also, and so necessarily resist it for the most part; and they are commonly treated by it as enemies. A wise man will only be useful as a man, and will not submit to be "clay," and "stop a hole to keep the wind away," but leave that office to his dust at least:—

> "I am too high-born to be propertied,
> To be a secondary at control,
> Or useful serving-man and instrument
> To any sovereign state throughout the world."

He who gives himself entirely to his fellow-men appears to them useless and selfish; but he who gives himself partially to them is pronounced a benefactor and philanthropist.

How does it become a man to behave toward this American government to-day? I answer that he cannot without disgrace be associated with it. I cannot for an instant recognize that political organization as *my* government which is the *slave's* government also.

All men recognize the right of revolution; that is, the right to refuse allegiance to and to resist the government, when its tyranny or its inefficiency are great and unendurable. But almost all say that such is not the case now. But such was the case, they think, in the Revolution of '75. If one were to tell me that this was a bad government because it taxed certain foreign commodities brought to its ports, it is most probable that I should not make an ado about it, for I can do without them: all machines have their friction; and possibly this does enough good to counterbalance the evil. At any rate, it is a great evil to make a stir about it. But when the friction comes to have its machine, and oppression and robbery are organized, I say, let us not have such a machine any longer. In other words, when a sixth of the population of a nation which has undertaken to be the refuge of liberty are slaves, and a whole country is unjustly overrun and conquered by a foreign army, and subjected to military law, I think that it is not too soon for honest men to rebel and revolutionize. What makes this duty the more urgent is the fact, that the country so overrun is not our own, but ours is the invading army.

Paley, a common authority with many on moral questions, in his chapter on the "Duty of Submission to Civil Government," resolves all civil obligation into expediency; and he proceeds to say, "that so long as the interest of the whole society requires it, that is, so long as the established government cannot be resisted or changed without public inconveniency, it is the will of God that the established government be obeyed, and no longer."— "This principle being admitted, the justice of every particular case of resistance is reduced to a computation of the quantity of the danger and grievance on the one side, and of the probability and expense of redressing it on the other." Of this, he says, every man shall judge for himself. But Paley appears never to have contemplated those cases to which the rule of expediency does not apply, in which a people, as well as an individual, must do justice, cost what it may. If I have unjustly wrested a plank from a drowning man, I must restore it to him though I drown myself. This, according to Paley, would be inconvenient. But he that would save his life, in such a case, shall lose it. This people must cease to hold slaves, and to make war on Mexico, though it cost them their existence as a people.

In their practice, nations agree with Paley; but does any one think that Massachusetts does exactly what is right at the present crisis?

"A drab of state, a cloth-o'-silver slut,
   To have her train borne up, and her soul trail in
   the dirt."

Practically speaking, the opponents to a reform in Massachusetts are not a hundred thousand politicians at the South, but a hundred thousand merchants and farmers here, who are more interested in commerce and agriculture than they are in humanity, and are not prepared to do justice to the slave and to Mexico, *cost what it may*. I quarrel not with far-off foes, but with those who, near at home, co-operate with, and do the bidding of those far away, and without whom the latter would be harmless. We are accustomed to say, that the mass of men are unprepared; but improvement is slow, because the few are not materially wiser or better than the many. It is not so important that many should be as good as you, as that there be some absolute goodness somewhere; for that will leaven the whole lump. There are thousands who are *in opinion* opposed to slavery and to the war, who yet in effect do nothing to put an end to them; who, esteeming themselves children of Washington and Franklin, sit down with their hands in their pockets, and say that they know not what to do, and do nothing; who even postpone the question of freedom to the question of free-trade, and quietly read the prices-current along with the latest advices from Mexico, after dinner, and, it may be, fall asleep over them both. What is the price-current of an honest man and patriot to-day? They hesitate, and they regret, and sometimes they petition; but they do nothing in earnest and with effect. They will wait, well disposed, for others to remedy the evil, that they may no longer have it to regret. At most, they give only a cheap vote, and a feeble countenance and God-speed, to the right, as it goes by them. There are nine hundred and ninety-nine patrons of virtue to one virtuous man; but it is easier to deal with the real possessor of a thing than with the temporary guardian of it.

All voting is a sort of gaming, like chequers or back-gammon, with a slight moral tinge to it, a playing with right and wrong, with moral questions; and betting naturally accompanies it. The character of the voters is not staked. I cast my vote, perchance, as I think right; but I am not vitally concerned that that right should prevail. I am willing to leave it to the majority. Its obligation, therefore, never exceeds that of expediency. Even voting *for the right* is *doing* nothing for it. It is only expressing to men feebly your desire that it should prevail. A wise man will not leave the right to the mercy of chance, nor wish it to prevail through the power of the majority. There is but little virtue in the action of masses of men. When the majority shall at length vote for the abolition of slavery, it will be because they are indifferent to slavery, or because there is but little slavery left to be abolished by their vote. *They* will then be the only slaves. Only *his* vote can hasten the abolition of slavery who asserts his own freedom by his vote.

I hear of a convention to be held at Baltimore, or elsewhere, for the selection of a candidate for the Presidency, made up chiefly of editors, and men who are politicians by profession; but I think, what is it to any independent, intelligent, and respectable man what decision they may come to, shall we not have the advantage of his wisdom and honesty, nevertheless? Can we not count upon some independent votes? Are there not many individuals in the country who do not attend conventions? But no: I find that the respectable man, so called, has immediately drifted from his position, and despairs of his country, when his country has more reason to despair of him. He forthwith adopts one of the candidates thus selected as the only *available* one, thus proving that he is himself *available* for any purposes of the demagogue. His vote is of no more worth than that of any unprincipled foreigner or hireling native, who may have been bought. Oh for a man who is a *man,* and, as my neighbor says, has a bone in his back which you cannot pass your hand through! Our statistics are at fault: the population has been returned too large. How many *men* are there to a square thousand miles in this country? Hardly one. Does not America offer any inducement for men to settle here? The American has dwindled into an Odd Fellow,—one who may be known by the development of his organ of gregariousness, and a manifest lack of intellect and cheerful self-reliance; whose first and chief concern, on coming into the world, is to see that the alms-houses are in good repair; and, before yet he has lawfully donned the virile garb, to collect a fund for the support of the widows and orphans that may be; who, in short, ventures to live only by the aid of the mutual insurance company, which has promised to bury him decently.

It is not a man's duty, as a matter of course, to devote himself to the eradication of any, even the most enormous wrong; he may still properly have other concerns to engage him; but it is his duty, at least, to wash his hands of it, and, if he gives it no thought longer, not to give it practically his support. If I devote myself to other pursuits and contemplations, I must first see, at least, that I do not pursue them sitting upon another man's shoulders. I must get off him first, that he may pursue his contemplations too. See what gross inconsistency is tolerated. I have heard some of my townsmen say, "I should like to have them order me out to help put down an insurrection of the slaves, or to march to Mexico,—see if I would go;" and yet these very men have each, directly by their allegiance, and so indirectly, at least, by their money, furnished a substitute. The soldier is applauded who refuses to serve in an unjust war by those who do not refuse to sustain the unjust government which makes the war; is applauded by those whose own act and authority he disregards and sets at nought; as if the State were penitent to that degree that it hired one to scourge it while it sinned, but not to that degree that it left off sinning for a moment. Thus, under the name of order and civil government, we are all made at last to pay homage to and support our own meanness. After the first blush of sin, comes its indifference; and from immoral it becomes, as it were, *un*moral, and not quite unnecessary to that life which we have made.

The broadest and most prevalent error requires the most disinterested virtue to sustain it. The slight reproach to which the virtue of patriotism is commonly liable, the noble are most likely to incur. Those who, while they disapprove of the character and measures of a government, yield to it their allegiance and support, are undoubtedly its most conscientious supporters, and so frequently the most serious obstacles to reform. Some are petitioning the State to dissolve the Union, to disregard the requisitions of the President. Why do they not dissolve it themselves,—the union between themselves and the State,—and refuse to pay their quota into its treasury? Do not they stand in the same relation to the State, that the State does to the Union? And have not the same reasons prevented the State from resisting the Union, which have prevented them from resisting the State?

How can a man be satisfied to entertain an opinion merely, and enjoy *it*? Is there any enjoyment in it, if his opinion is that he is aggrieved? If you are cheated out of a single dollar by your neighbor, you do not rest satisfied with knowing that you are cheated, or with saying that you are cheated, or even with petitioning him to pay you your due; but you take effectual steps at once to obtain the full amount, and see that you are never cheated again. Action from principle,—the perception and the performance of right,—changes things and relations; it is essentially revolutionary, and does not consist wholly with any thing which was. It not only divides states and churches, it divides families; aye, it divides the *individual*, separating the diabolical in him from the divine.

Unjust laws exist: shall we be content to obey them, or shall we endeavor to amend them, and obey them until we have succeeded, or shall we transgress them at once? Men generally, under such a government as this, think that they ought to wait until they have persuaded the majority to alter them. They think that, if they should resist, the remedy would be worse than the evil. But it is the fault of the government itself that the remedy *is* worse than the evil. *It* makes it worse. Why is it not more apt to anticipate and provide for reform? Why does it not cherish its wise minority? Why does it cry and resist before it is hurt? Why does it not encourage its citizens to be on the alert to point out its faults, and *do* better than it would have them? Why does it always crucify Christ, and excommunicate Copernicus and Luther, and pronounce Washington and Franklin rebels?

One would think, that a deliberate and practical denial of its authority was the only offence never contemplated by government; else, why has it not assigned its definite, its suitable and proportionate penalty? If a man who has no property refuses but once to earn nine shillings for the State, he is put in prison for a period unlimited by any law that I know, and determined only by the discretion of those who placed him there; but if he should steal ninety times nine shillings from the State, he is soon permitted to go at large again.

If the injustice is part of the necessary friction of the machine of government, let it go, let it go: perchance it will wear smooth,—certainly the machine will wear out. If the injustice has a spring, or a pulley, or a rope, or a crank, exclusively for itself, then perhaps you may consider whether the remedy will not be worse than the evil; but if it is of such a nature that it requires you to be the agent of injustice to another, then, I say, break the law. Let your life be a counter friction to stop the machine. What I have to do is to see, at any rate, that I do not lend myself to the wrong which I condemn.

As for adopting the ways which the State has provided for remedying the evil, I know not of such ways. They take too much time, and a man's life will be gone. I have other affairs to attend to. I came into this world, not chiefly to make this a good place to live in, but to live in it, be it good or bad. A man has not every thing to do, but something; and because he cannot do *every thing,* it is not necessary that he should do *something* wrong. It is not my business to be petitioning the governor or the legislature any more than it is theirs to petition me; and, if they should not hear my petition, what should I do then? But in this case the State has provided no way: its very Constitution is the evil. This may seem to be harsh and stubborn and unconciliatory; but it is to treat with the utmost kindness and consideration the only spirit that can appreciate or deserves it. So is all change for the better, like birth and death which convulse the body.

I do not hesitate to say, that those who call themselves abolitionists should at once effectually withdraw their support, both in person and property, from the government of Massachusetts, and not wait till they constitute a majority of one, before they suffer the right to prevail through them. I think that it is enough if they have God on their side, without waiting for that other one. Moreover, any man more right than his neighbors, constitutes a majority of one already.

I meet this American government, or its representative the State government, directly, and face to face, once a year, no more, in the person of its tax-gatherer; this is the only mode in which a man situated as I am necessarily meets it; and it then says distinctly, Recognize me; and the simplest, the most effectual, and, in the present posture of affairs, the indispensablest mode of treating with it on this head, of expressing your little satisfaction with and love for it, is to deny it then. My civil neighbor, the tax-gatherer, is the very man I have to deal with,—for it is, after all, with men and not with parchment that I quarrel,— and he has voluntarily chosen to be an agent of the government. How shall he ever know well what he is and does as an officer of the government, or as a man, until he is obliged to consider whether he shall treat me, his neighbor, for whom he has respect, as a neighbor and well-disposed man, or as a maniac and disturber of the peace, and see if he can get over this obstruction to his neighborliness without a ruder and more impetuous thought or speech corresponding with his action? I know this well, that if one thousand, if one hundred, if ten men whom I could name,—if ten *honest* men only,—aye, if *one* HONEST man, in this State of Massachusetts, *ceasing to hold slaves,* were actually to withdraw from this copartnership, and be locked up in the county jail therefor, it would be the abolition of slavery in America. For it matters not how small the beginning may seem to be: what is once well done is done for ever. But we love better to talk

about it: that we say is our mission. Reform keeps
many scores of newspapers in its service, but not one
man. If my esteemed neighbor, the State's ambassador, who will devote his days to the settlement of
the question of human rights in the Council Chamber,
instead of being threatened with the prisons of Carolina, were to sit down the prisoner of Massachusetts,
that State which is so anxious to foist the sin of slavery
upon her sister,—though at present she can discover
only an act of inhospitality to be the ground of a quarrel with her,—the Legislature would not wholly waive
the subject the following winter.

Under a government which imprisons any unjustly,
the true place for a just man is also a prison. The
proper place to-day, the only place which Massachusetts has provided for her freer and less desponding
spirits, is in her prisons, to be put out and locked out
of the State by her own act, as they have already put
themselves out by their principles. It is there that the
fugitive slave, and the Mexican prisoner on parole,
and the Indian come to plead the wrongs of his race,
should find them; on that separate, but more free and
honorable ground, where the State places those who
are not *with* her but *against* her,—the only house in a
slave-state in which a free man can abide with honor.
If any think that their influence would be lost there,
and their voices no longer afflict the ear of the State,
that they would not be as an enemy within its walls,
they do not know by how much truth is stronger than
error, nor how much more eloquently and effectively
he can combat injustice who has experienced a little
in his own person. Cast your whole vote, not a strip
of paper merely, but your whole influence. A minority
is powerless while it conforms to the majority; it is
not even a minority then; but it is irresistible when it
clogs by its whole weight. If the alternative is to keep

all just men in prison, or give up war and slavery, the State will not hesitate which to choose. If a thousand men were not to pay their tax-bills this year, that would not be a violent and bloody measure, as it would be to pay them, and enable the State to commit violence and shed innocent blood. This is, in fact, the definition of a peaceable revolution, if any such is possible. If the tax-gatherer, or any other public officer, asks me, as one has done, "But what shall I do?" my answer is, "If you really wish to do any thing, resign your office." When the subject has refused allegiance, and the officer has resigned his office, then the revolution is accomplished. But even suppose blood should flow. Is there not a sort of blood shed when the conscience is wounded? Through this wound a man's real manhood and immortality flow out, and he bleeds to an everlasting death. I see this blood flowing now.

I have contemplated the imprisonment of the offender, rather than the seizure of his goods,—though both will serve the same purpose,—because they who assert the purest right, and consequently are most dangerous to a corrupt State, commonly have not spent much time in accumulating property. To such the State renders comparatively small service, and a slight tax is wont to appear exorbitant, particularly if they are obliged to earn it by special labor with their hands. If there were one who lived wholly without the use of money, the State itself would hesitate to demand it of him. But the rich man—not to make any invidious comparison—is always sold to the institution which makes him rich. Absolutely speaking, the more money, the less virtue; for money comes between a man and his objects, and obtains them for him; and it was certainly no great virtue to obtain it. It puts to rest many questions which he would otherwise be taxed to answer; while the only new question which it puts is the hard but superfluous one, how to spend it. Thus his moral ground is taken from under his feet. The opportunities of living are diminished in proportion as what are called the "means" are increased. The best thing a man can do for his culture when he is rich is to endeavour to carry out those schemes which he entertained when he was poor. Christ answered the Herodians according to their condition. "Show me the tribute-money," said he;—and one took a penny out of his pocket;—If you use money which has the image of Cæsar on it, and which he has made current and valuable, that is, *if you are men of the State,* and gladly enjoy the advantages of Cæsar's government, then pay him back some of his own when he demands it; "Render therefore to Cæsar that which is Cæsar's, and to God those things which are God's,"—leaving them no wiser than before as to which was which; for they did not wish to know.

When I converse with the freest of my neighbors, I perceive that, whatever they may say about the magnitude and seriousness of the question, and their regard for the public tranquillity, the long and the short of the matter is, that they cannot spare the protection of the existing government, and they dread the consequences of disobedience to it to their property and families. For my own part, I should not like to think that I ever rely on the protection of the State. But, if I deny the authority of the State when it presents its tax-bill, it will soon take and waste all my property, and so harass me and my children without end. This is hard. This makes it impossible for a man to live honestly and at the same time comfortably in outward respects. It will not be worth the while to accumulate property; that would be sure to go again. You must hire or squat somewhere, and raise but a small crop, and eat that soon. You must live within yourself, and depend upon yourself, always tucked up and ready for a start, and not have many affairs. A man may grow rich in Turkey even, if he will be in all respects a good subject of the Turkish government. Confucius said,— "If a State is governed by the principles of reason, poverty and misery are subjects of shame; if a State is not governed by the principles of reason, riches and honors are the subjects of shame." No: until I want the protection of Massachusetts to be extended to me in some distant southern port, where my liberty is endangered, or until I am bent solely on building up an estate at home by peaceful enterprise, I can afford to refuse allegiance to Massachusetts, and her right to my property and life. It costs me less in every sense to incur the penalty of disobedience to the State, than it would to obey. I should feel as if I were worth less in that case.

Some years ago, the State met me in behalf of the church, and commanded me to pay a certain sum toward the support of a clergyman whose preaching my father attended, but never I myself. "Pay it," it said, "or be locked up in the jail." I declined to pay. But, unfortunately, another man saw fit to pay it. I did not see why the schoolmaster should be taxed to support the priest, and not the priest the schoolmaster; for I was not the State's schoolmaster, but I supported myself by voluntary subscription. I did not see why the lyceum should not present its tax-bill, and have the State to back its demand, as well as the church. However, at the request of the selectmen, I condescended to make some such statement as this in writing:—"Know all men by these presents, that I, Henry Thoreau, do not wish to be regarded as a member of any incorporated society which I have not joined." This I gave to the town-clerk; and he has it. The State, having thus learned that I did not wish to be regarded as a member of that church, has never made a like demand on me since; though it said that it must adhere to its original presumption that time. If I had known how to name them, I should then have signed off in detail from all the societies which I never signed on to; but I did not know where to find a complete list.

I have paid no poll-tax for six years. I was put into a jail once on this account, for one night; and, as I stood considering the walls of solid stone, two or three feet thick, the door of wood and iron, a foot thick, and the iron grating which strained the light, I could not help being struck with the foolishness of that institution which treated me as if I were mere flesh and blood and bones, to be locked up. I wondered that it should have concluded at length that this was the best use it could put me to, and had never thought to avail itself of my services in some way. I saw that, if there was a wall of stone between me and my townsmen, there was a still more difficult one to climb or break through, before they could get to be as free as I was. I did not for a moment feel confined, and the walls seemed a great waste of stone and mortar. I felt as if I alone of all my townsmen had paid my tax. They plainly did not know how to treat me, but behaved like persons who are underbred. In every threat and in every compliment there was a blunder; for they thought that my chief desire was to stand the other side of that stone wall. I could not but smile to see how industriously they locked the door on my meditations, which followed them out again without let or hinderance, and *they* were really all that was dangerous. As they could not reach me, they had resolved to punish my body; just as boys, if they cannot come at some person against whom they have a spite, will abuse his dog. I saw that the State was half-witted, that it was timid as a lone woman with her silver spoons, and that it did not know its friends from its foes, and I lost all my remaining respect for it, and pitied it.

Thus the State never intentionally confronts a man's sense, intellectual or moral, but only his body, his senses. It is not armed with superior wit or honesty, but with superior physical strength. I was not born to be forced. I will breathe after my own fashion. Let us see who is the strongest. What force has a multitude? They only can force me who obey a higher law than I. They force me to become like themselves. I do not hear of *men* being *forced* to live this way or that by masses of men. What sort of life were that to live? When I meet a government which says to me, "Your money or your life," why should I be in haste to give it my money? It may be in a great strait, and not know what to do: I cannot help that. It must help itself; do as I do. It is not worth the while to snivel about it. I am not responsible for the successful working of the machinery of society. I am not the son of the engineer. I perceive that, when an acorn and a chestnut fall side by side, the one does not remain inert to make way for the other, but both obey their own laws, and spring and grow and flourish as best they can, till one, perchance, overshadows and destroys the other. If a plant cannot live according to its nature, it dies; and so a man.

The night in prison was novel and interesting enough. The prisoners in their shirt-sleeves were enjoying a chat and the evening air in the door-way, when I entered. But the jailer said, "Come, boys, it is time to lock up;" and so they dispersed, and I heard the sound of their steps returning into the hollow apartments. My roommate was introduced to me by the jailer, as "a first-rate fellow and a clever man." When the door was locked, he showed me where to hang my hat, and how he managed matters there. The rooms were whitewashed once a month; and this one, at least, was the whitest, most simply furnished, and probably the neatest apartment in the town. He naturally wanted to know where I came from, and what brought me there; and, when I had told him, I asked him in my turn how he came there, presuming him to be an honest man, of course; and, as the world goes, I believe he was. "Why," said he, "they accuse me of burning a barn; but I never did it." As near as I could discover, he had probably gone to bed in a barn when drunk, and smoked his pipe there; and so a barn was burnt. He had the reputation of being a clever man, had been there some three months waiting for his trial to come on, and would have to wait as much longer; but he was quite domesticated and contented, since he got his board for nothing, and thought that he was well treated.

He occupied one window, and I the other; and I saw, that, if one stayed there long, his principal business would be to look out the window. I had soon read all the tracts that were left there, and examined where former prisoners had broken out, and where a grate had been sawed off, and heard the history of the various occupants of that room; for I found that even here there was a history and a gossip which never circulated beyond the walls of the jail. Probably this is the only house in the town where verses are composed, which are afterward printed in a circular form, but not published. I was shown quite a long list of verses which were composed by some young men who had been detected in an attempt to escape, who avenged themselves by singing them.

I pumped my fellow-prisoner as dry as I could, for fear I should never see him again; but at length he showed me which was my bed, and left me to blow out the lamp.

It was like travelling into a far country, such as I had never expected to behold, to lie there for one night. It seemed to me that I never had heard the town-clock strike before, nor the evening sounds of the village; for we slept with the windows open, which were inside the grating. It was to see my native village in the light of the middle ages, and our Concord was turned into a Rhine stream, and visions of knights and castles passed before me. They were the voices of old burghers that I heard in the streets. I was an involuntary spectator and auditor of whatever was done and said in the kitchen of the adjacent village-inn,—a wholly new and rare experience to me. It was a closer view of my native town. I was fairly inside of it. I never had seen its institutions before. This is one of its peculiar institutions; for it is a shire town. I began to comprehend what its inhabitants were about.

In the morning, our breakfasts were put through the hole in the door, in small oblong-square tin pans, made to fit, and holding a pint of chocolate, with brown bread, and an iron spoon. When they called for the vessels again, I was green enough to return what bread I had left; but my comrade seized it, and said that I should lay that up for lunch or dinner. Soon after, he was let out to work at haying in a neighboring field, whither he went every day, and would not be back till noon; so he bade me good-day, saying that he doubted if he should see me again.

When I came out of prison,—for some one interfered, and paid the tax,—I did not perceive that great changes had taken place on the common, such as he observed who went in a youth, and emerged a tottering and gray-headed man; and yet a change had to my eyes come over the scene,—the town, and State, and country,—greater than any that mere time could effect. I saw yet more distinctly the State in which I lived. I saw to what extent the people among whom I lived could be trusted as good neighbors and friends; that their friendship was for summer weather only; that they did not greatly purpose to do right; that they were a distinct race from me by their prejudices and superstitions, as the Chinamen and Malays are; that, in their sacrifices to humanity, they ran no risks, not even to their property; that, after all, they were not so noble but they treated the thief as he had treated them, and hoped, by a certain outward observance and a few prayers, and by walking in a particular straight though useless path from time to time, to save their souls. This may be to judge my neighbors harshly; for I believe that most of them are not aware that they have such an institution as the jail in their village.

It was formerly the custom in our village, when a poor debtor came out of jail, for his acquaintances to salute him, looking through their fingers, which were crossed to represent the grating of a jail window, "How do ye do?" My neighbors did not thus salute me, but first looked at me, and then at one another, as if I had returned from a long journey. I was put into jail as I was going to the shoemaker's to get a shoe which was mended. When I was let out the next morning, I proceeded to finish my errand, and, having put on my mended shoe, joined a huckleberry party, who were impatient to put themselves under my conduct; and in half an hour,—for the horse was soon tackled,—was in the midst of a huckleberry field, on one of our highest hills, two miles off; and then the State was nowhere to be seen.

This is the whole history of "My Prisons."

I have never declined paying the highway tax, because I am as desirous of being a good neighbor as I am of being a bad subject; and, as for supporting schools, I am doing my part to educate my fellow-countrymen now. It is for no particular item in the tax-bill that I refuse to pay it. I simply wish to refuse allegiance to the State, to withdraw and stand aloof from it effectually. I do not care to trace the course of my dollar, if I could, till it buys a man, or a musket to shoot one with,—the dollar is innocent,—but I am concerned to trace the effects of my allegiance. In fact, I quietly declare war with the State, after my fashion, though I will still make what use and get what advantage of her I can, as is usual in such cases.

If others pay the tax which is demanded of me, from a sympathy with the State, they do but what they have already done in their own case, or rather they abet injustice to a greater extent than the State requires. If they pay the tax from a mistaken interest in the individual taxed, to save his property or prevent his going to jail, it is because they have not considered wisely how far they let their private feelings interfere with the public good.

This, then, is my position at present. But one cannot be too much on his guard in such a case, lest his action be biased by obstinacy, or an undue regard for the opinions of men. Let him see that he does only what belongs to himself and to the hour.

I think sometimes, Why, this people mean well; they are only ignorant; they would do better if they knew how: why give your neighbors this pain to treat you as they are not inclined to? But I think, again, this is no reason why I should do as they do, or permit others to suffer much greater pain of a different kind. Again, I sometimes say to myself, When many millions of men, without heat, without ill-will, without personal feeling of any kind, demand of you a few shillings only, without the possibility, such is their constitution, of retracting or altering their present demand, and without the possibility, on your side, of appeal to any other millions, why expose yourself to this overwhelming brute force? You do not resist cold and hunger, the winds and the waves, thus obstinately; you quietly submit to a thousand similar necessities. You do not put your head into the fire. But just in proportion as I regard this as not wholly a brute force, but partly a human force, and consider that I have relations to those millions as to so many millions of men, and not of mere brute or inanimate things, I see that appeal is possible, first and instantaneously, from them to the Maker of them, and, secondly, from them to themselves. But, if I put my head deliberately into the fire, there is no appeal to fire or to the Maker of fire, and I have only myself to blame. If I could convince myself that I have any right to be satisfied with men as they are, and to treat them accordingly, and not according, in some respects, to my requisitions and expectations of what they and I ought to be, then, like a good Mussulman and fatalist, I should endeavor to be satisfied with things as they are, and say it is the will of God. And, above all, there is this difference between resisting this and a purely brute or natural force, that I can resist this with some effect; but I cannot expect, like Orpheus, to change the nature of the rocks and trees and beasts.

I do not wish to quarrel with any man or nation. I do not wish to split hairs, to make fine distinctions, or set myself up as better than my neighbors. I seek rather, I may say, even an excuse for conforming to the laws of the land. I am but too ready to conform to them. Indeed I have reason to suspect myself on this head; and each year, as the tax-gatherer comes round, I find myself disposed to review the acts and position of the general and state governments, and the spirit of the people, to discover a pretext for conformity. I believe that the State will soon be able to take all my work of this sort out of my hands, and then I shall be no better a patriot than my fellow-countrymen. Seen from a lower point of view, the Constitution, with all its faults, is very good; the law and the courts are very respectable; even this State and this American government are, in many respects, very admirable and rare things, to be thankful for, such as a great many have described them; but seen from a point of view a little higher, they are what I have described them; seen from a higher still, and the highest, who shall say what they are, or that they are worth looking at or thinking of at all?

However, the government does not concern me much, and I shall bestow the fewest possible thoughts on it. It is not many moments that I live under a government, even in this world. If a man is thought-free, fancy-free, imagination-free, that which *is not* never for a long time appearing *to be* to him, unwise rulers or reformers cannot fatally interrupt him.

I know that most men think differently from myself; but those whose lives are by profession devoted to the study of these or kindred subjects, content me as little as any. Statesmen and legislators, standing so completely within the institution, never distinctly and nakedly behold it. They speak of moving society, but have no resting-place without it. They may be men of a certain experience and discrimination, and have no doubt invented ingenious and even useful systems, for which we sincerely thank them; but all their wit and usefulness lie within certain not very wide limits. They are wont to forget that the world is not governed by policy and expediency. Webster never goes behind government, and so cannot speak with authority about it. His words are wisdom to those legislators who contemplate no essential reform in the existing government; but for thinkers, and those who legislate for all time, he never once glances at the subject. I know of those whose serene and wise speculations on this theme would soon reveal the limits of his mind's range and hospitality. Yet, compared with the cheap professions of most reformers, and the still cheaper wisdom and eloquence of politicians in general, his are almost the only sensible and valuable words, and we thank Heaven for him. Comparatively, he is always strong, original, and, above all, practical. Still his quality is not wisdom, but prudence. The lawyer's truth is not Truth, but consistency, or a consistent expediency. Truth is always in harmony with herself, and is not concerned chiefly to reveal the justice that may consist with wrong-doing. He well deserves to be called, as he has been called, the Defender of the Constitution. There are really no blows to be given by him but defensive ones. He is not a leader, but a follower. His leaders are the men of '87. "I have never made an effort," he says, "and never propose to make an effort; I have never countenanced an effort, and never mean to countenance an effort, to disturb the arrangement as originally made, by which the various States came into the Union." Still thinking of the sanction which the Constitution gives to slavery, he says, "Because it was a part of the original compact,—let it stand." Notwithstanding his special acuteness and ability, he is unable to take a fact out of its merely political relations, and behold it as it lies absolutely to be disposed of by the intellect,—what, for instance, it behoves a man to do here in America to-day with regard to slavery, but ventures, or is driven, to make some such desperate answer as the following, while professing to speak absolutely, and as a private man,—from which what new and singular code of social duties might be inferred?—"The manner," says he, "in which the government of those States where slavery exists are to regulate it, is for their own consideration, under their responsibility to their constituents, to the general laws of priority, humanity, and justice, and to God. Associations formed elsewhere, springing from a feeling of humanity, or any other cause, have nothing whatever to do with it. They have never received any encouragement from me, and they never will."*

They who know of no purer sources of truth, who have traced up its stream no higher, stand, and wisely stand, by the Bible and the Constitution, and drink at it there with reverence and humility; but they who behold where it comes trickling into this lake or that pool, gird up their loins once more, and continue their pilgrimage toward its fountain-head.

*These extracts have been inserted since the Lecture was read. [Thoreau's note.]

No man with a genius for legislation has appeared in America. They are rare in the history of the world. There are orators, politicians, and eloquent men, by the thousand; but the speaker has not yet opened his mouth to speak, who is capable of settling the much-vexed questions of the day. We love eloquence for its own sake, and not for any truth which it may utter, or any heroism it may inspire. Our legislators have not yet learned the comparative value of free-trade and of freedom, of union, and of rectitude, to a nation. They have no genius or talent for comparatively humble questions of taxation and finance, commerce and manufactures and agriculture. If we were left solely to the wordy wit of legislators in Congress for our guidance, uncorrected by the seasonable experience and the effectual complaints of the people, America would not long retain her rank among the nations. For eighteen hundred years, though perchance I have no right to say it, the New Testament has been written; yet where is the legislator who has wisdom and practical talent enough to avail himself of the light which it sheds on the science of legislation?

The authority of government, even such as I am willing to submit to,—for I will cheerfully obey those who know and can do better than I, and in many things even those who neither know nor can do so well,—is still an impure one: to be strictly just, it must have the sanction and consent of the governed. It can have no pure right over my person and property but what I concede to it. The progress from an absolute to a limited monarchy, from a limited monarchy to a democracy, is a progress toward a true respect for the individual. Is a democracy, such as we know it, the last improvement possible in government? Is it not possible to take a step further towards recognizing and organizing the rights of man? There will never be a really free and enlightened State, until the State comes to recognize the individual as a higher and independent power, from which all its own power and authority are derived, and treats him accordingly. I please myself with imagining a State at last which can afford to be just to all men, and to treat the individual with respect as a neighbor; which even would not think it inconsistent with its own repose, if a few were to live aloof from it, not meddling with it, nor embraced by it, who fulfilled all the duties of neighbors and fellowmen. A State which bore this kind of fruit, and suffered it to drop off as fast as it ripened, would prepare the way for a still more perfect and glorious State, which also I have imagined, but not yet anywhere seen.

Martin Luther King, Jr.

LETTER FROM BIRMINGHAM JAIL

(1963)

Bishop C.C.J. Carpenter, *Bishop* Joseph A. Durick,
Rabbi Milton L. Grafman, *Bishop* Paul Hardin,
Bishop Nolan B. Harmon, *The Rev.* George M.
  Murray,
The Rev. Edward V. Ramage, *The Rev.* Earl Stallings

My dear Fellow Clergymen,

While confined here in the Birmingham City Jail, I came across your recent statement calling our present activities "unwise and untimely." Seldom, if ever, do I pause to answer criticism of my work and ideas. If I sought to answer all of the criticisms that cross my desk, my secretaries would be engaged in little else in the course of the day and I would have no time for constructive work. But since I feel that you are men of genuine good will and your criticisms are sincerely set forth, I would like to answer your statement in what I hope will be patient and reasonable terms.

I think I should give the reason for my being in

Birmingham, since you have been influenced by the argument of "outsiders coming in." I have the honor of serving as president of the Southern Christian Leadership Conference, an organization operating in every Southern state with headquarters in Atlanta, Georgia. We have some eighty-five affiliate organizations all across the South—one being the Alabama Christian Movement for Human Rights. Whenever necessary and possible we share staff, educational, and financial resources with our affiliates. Several months ago our local affiliate here in Birmingham invited us to be on call to engage in a nonviolent direct action program if such were deemed necessary. We readily consented and when the hour came we lived up to our promises. So I am here, along with several members of my staff, because we were invited here. I am here because I have basic organizational ties here. Beyond this, I am in Birmingham because injustice is here. Just as the eighth century prophets left their little villages and carried their "thus saith the Lord" far beyond the boundaries of their home town, and just as the Apostle Paul left his little village of Tarsus and carried the gospel of Jesus Christ to practically every hamlet and city of the Graeco-Roman world, I too am compelled to carry the gospel of freedom beyond my particular home town. Like Paul, I must constantly respond to the Macedonian call for aid.

Moreover, I am cognizant of the interrelatedness of all communities and states. I cannot sit idly by in Atlanta and not be concerned about what happens in Birmingham. Injustice anywhere is a threat to justice everywhere. We are caught in an inescapable network of mutuality tied in a single garment of destiny. Whatever affects one directly affects all indirectly. Never again can we afford to live with the narrow, provincial "outside agitator" idea. Anyone who lives inside the United States can never be considered an outsider anywhere in this country.

You deplore the demonstrations that are presently taking place in Birmingham. But I am sorry that your statement did not express a similar concern for the conditions that brought the demonstrations into being. I am sure that each of you would want to go beyond the superficial social analyst who looks merely at effects, and does not grapple with underlying causes. I would not hesitate to say that it is unfortunate that so-called demonstrations are taking place in Birmingham at this time, but I would say in more emphatic terms that it is even more unfortunate that the white power structure of this city left the Negro community with no other alternative.

In any nonviolent campaign there are four basic steps: (1) collection of the facts to determine whether injustices are alive; (2) negotiation; (3) self-purification; and (4) direct action. We have gone through all of these steps in Birmingham. There can be no gainsaying of the fact that racial injustice engulfs this community. Birmingham is probably the most thoroughly segregated city in the United States. Its ugly record of police brutality is known in every section of this country. Its unjust treatment of Negroes in the courts is a notorious reality. There have been more unsolved bombings of Negro homes and churches in Birmingham than any city in this nation. These are the hard, brutal, and unbelievable facts. On the basis of these conditions Negro leaders sought to negotiate with the city fathers. But the political leaders consistently refused to engage in good faith negotiation.

Then came the opportunity last September to talk with some of the leaders of the economic community. In these negotiating sessions certain promises were made by the merchants—such as the promise to remove the humiliating racial signs from the stores. On the basis of these promises Rev. Shuttlesworth and the leaders of the Alabama Christian Movement for Human Rights agreed to call a moratorium on any type of demonstrations. As the weeks and months unfolded we realized that we were the victims of a broken promise. The signs remained. As in so many experiences of the past we were confronted with blasted hopes, and the dark shadow of a deep disappointment settled upon us. So we had no alternative except that of preparing for direct action, whereby we would present our very bodies as a means of laying our case before the conscience of the local and national community. We were not unmindful of the difficulties involved. So we decided to go through a process of self-purification. We started having workshops on nonviolence and repeatedly asked ourselves the questions, "Are you able to accept blows without retaliating?" "Are you able to endure the ordeals of jail?"

We decided to set our direct action program around the Easter season, realizing that with the exception of Christmas, this was the largest shopping period of the year. Knowing that a strong economic withdrawal program would be the by-product of direct action, we felt that this was the best time to bring pressure on the merchants for the needed changes. Then it occurred to us that the March election was ahead, and so we speedily decided to postpone action until after election day. When we discovered that Mr. Connor was in the run-off, we decided again to postpone so that the demonstrations could not be used to cloud the issues. At this time we agreed to begin our nonviolent witness the day after the run-off.

This reveals that we did not move irresponsibly into

direct action. We too wanted to see Mr. Connor defeated; so we went through postponement after postponement to aid in this community need. After this
we felt that direct action could be delayed no longer.

You may well ask, "Why direct action? Why sit-ins,
marches, etc.? Isn't negotiation a better path?" You
are exactly right in your call for negotiation. Indeed,
this is the purpose of direct action. Nonviolent direct
action seeks to create such a crisis and establish such
creative tension that a community that has constantly
refused to negotiate is forced to confront the issue. It
seeks so to dramatize the issue that it can no longer
be ignored. I just referred to the creation of tension
as a part of the work of the nonviolent resister. This
may sound rather shocking. But I must confess that I
am not afraid of the word tension. I have earnestly
worked and preached against violent tension, but
there is a type of constructive nonviolent tension that
is necessary for growth. Just as Socrates felt that it
was necessary to create a tension in the mind so that
individuals could rise from the bondage of myths and
half-truths to the unfettered realm of creative analysis
and objective appraisal, we must see the need of having nonviolent gadflies to create the kind of tension
in society that will help men rise from the dark depths
of prejudice and racism to the majestic heights of understanding and brotherhood. So the purpose of the
direct action is to create a situation so crisis-packed
that it will inevitably open the door to negotiation.
We, therefore, concur with you in your call for negotiation. Too long has our beloved Southland been
bogged down in the tragic attempt to live in monologue rather than dialogue.

One of the basic points in your statement is that
our acts are untimely. Some have asked, "Why didn't
you give the new administration time to act?" The

only answer that I can give to this inquiry is that the new administration must be prodded about as much as the outgoing one before it acts. We will be sadly mistaken if we feel that the election of Mr. Boutwell will bring the millennium to Birmingham. While Mr. Boutwell is much more articulate and gentle than Mr. Connor, they are both segregationists dedicated to the task of maintaining the status quo. The hope I see in Mr. Boutwell is that he will be reasonable enough to see the futility of massive resistance to desegregation. But he will not see this without pressure from the devotees of civil rights. My friends, I must say to you that we have not made a single gain in civil rights without determined legal and nonviolent pressure. History is the long and tragic story of the fact that privileged groups seldom give up their privileges voluntarily. Individuals may see the moral light and voluntarily give up their unjust posture; but as Reinhold Niebuhr has reminded us, groups are more immoral than individuals.

We know through painful experience that freedom is never voluntarily given by the oppressor; it must be demanded by the oppressed. Frankly I have never yet engaged in a direct action movement that was "well timed," according to the timetable of those who have not suffered unduly from the disease of segregation. For years now I have heard the word "Wait!" It rings in the ear of every Negro with a piercing familiarity. This "wait" has almost always meant "never." It has been a tranquilizing thalidomide, relieving the emotional stress for a moment, only to give birth to an ill-formed infant of frustration. We must come to see with the distinguished jurist of yesterday that "justice too long delayed is justice denied." We have waited for more than three hundred and forty years for our constitutional and God-given rights. The nations of

Asia and Africa are moving with jetlike speed toward the goal of political independence, and we still creep at horse and buggy pace toward the gaining of a cup of coffee at a lunch counter.

I guess it is easy for those who have never felt the stinging darts of segregation to say wait. But when you have seen vicious mobs lynch your mothers and fathers at will and drown your sisters and brothers at whim; when you have seen hate filled policemen curse, kick, brutalize, and even kill your black brothers and sisters with impunity; when you see the vast majority of your twenty million Negro brothers smothering in an air-tight cage of poverty in the midst of an affluent society; when you suddenly find your tongue twisted and your speech stammering as you seek to explain to your six-year-old daughter why she can't go to the public amusement park that has just been advertised on television, and see tears welling up in her little eyes when she is told that Funtown is closed to colored children, and see the depressing clouds of inferiority begin to form in her little mental sky, and see her begin to distort her little personality by unconsciously developing a bitterness toward white people; when you have to concoct an answer for a five-year-old son asking in agonizing pathos: "Daddy, why do white people treat colored people so mean?"; when you take a cross country drive and find it necessary to sleep night after night in the uncomfortable corners of your automobile because no motel will accept you; when you are humiliated day in and day out by nagging signs reading "white" men and "colored"; when your first name becomes "nigger" and your middle name becomes "boy" (however old you are) and your last name becomes "John," and when your wife and mother are never given the respected title "Mrs."; when you are harried by day and haunted by night by the fact that you are a Negro, living constantly at tip-toe stance never quite knowing what to expect next, and plagued with inner fears and outer resentments; when you are forever fighting a degenerating sense of "nobodiness";—then you will understand why we find it difficult to wait. There comes a time when the cup of endurance runs over, and men are no longer willing to be plunged into an abyss of injustice where they experience the bleakness of corroding despair. I hope, sirs, you can understand our legitimate and unavoidable impatience.

You express a great deal of anxiety over our willingness to break laws. This is certainly a legitimate concern. Since we so diligently urge people to obey the Supreme Court's decision of 1954 outlawing segregation in the public schools, it is rather strange and paradoxical to find us consciously breaking laws. One may well ask, "How can you advocate breaking some laws and obeying others?" The answer is found in the fact that there are two types of laws. There are *just* laws and there are *unjust* laws. I would be the first to advocate obeying just laws. One has not only a legal but moral responsibility to obey just laws. Conversely, one has a moral responsibility to disobey unjust laws. I would agree with Saint Augustine that "An unjust law is no law at all."

Now what is the difference between the two? How does one determine when a law is just or unjust? A just law is a man-made code that squares with the moral law or the law of God. An unjust law is a code that is out of harmony with the moral law. To put it in the terms of Saint Thomas Aquinas, an unjust law is a human law that is not rooted in eternal and natural law. Any law that uplifts human personality is just. Any law that degrades human personality is unjust. All segregation statutes are unjust because segregation distorts the soul and damages the personality. It gives the segregator a false sense of superiority and the segregated a false sense of inferiority. To use the words of Martin Buber, the great Jewish philosopher, segregation substitutes an "I-it" relationship for the "I-thou" relationship, and ends up relegating persons to the status of things. So segregation is not only politically, economically, and sociologically unsound, but it is morally wrong and sinful. Paul Tillich has said that sin is separation. Isn't segregation an existential expression of man's tragic separation, an expression of his awful estrangement, his terrible sinfulness? So I can urge men to obey the 1954 decision of the Supreme Court because it is morally right, and I can urge them to disobey segregation ordinances because they are morally wrong.

Let us turn to a more concrete example of just and unjust laws. An unjust law is a code that a majority inflicts on a minority that is not binding on itself. This is *difference* made legal. On the other hand a just law is a code that a majority compels a minority to follow that it is willing to follow itself. This is *sameness* made legal.

Let me give another explanation. An unjust law is a code inflicted upon a minority which that minority had no part in enacting or creating because they did not have the unhampered right to vote. Who can say the legislature of Alabama which set up the segregation laws was democratically elected? Throughout the state of Alabama all types of conniving methods are used to prevent Negroes from becoming registered voters and there are some counties without a single Negro registered to vote despite the fact that the Negro constitutes a majority of the population. Can any law set up in such a state be considered democratically structured?

These are just a few examples of unjust and just laws. There are some instances when a law is just on its face but unjust in its application. For instance, I was arrested Friday on a charge of parading without a permit. Now there is nothing wrong with an ordinance which requires a permit for a parade, but when the ordinance is used to preserve segregation and to deny citizens the First Amendment privilege of peaceful assembly and peaceful protest, then it becomes unjust.

I hope you can see the distinction I am trying to point out. In no sense do I advocate evading or defying the law as the rabid segregationist would do. This would lead to anarchy. One who breaks an unjust law must do it *openly, lovingly* (not hatefully as the white mothers did in New Orleans when they were seen on television screaming "nigger, nigger, nigger") and with a willingness to accept the penalty. I submit that an individual who breaks a law that conscience tells him is unjust, and willingly accepts the penalty by staying in jail to arouse the conscience of the community over its injustice, is in reality expressing the very highest respect for law.

Of course there is nothing new about this kind of civil disobedience. It was seen sublimely in the refusal of Shadrach, Meshach, and Abednego to obey the laws of Nebuchadnezzar because a higher moral law was involved. It was practiced superbly by the early Christians who were willing to face hungry lions and the excruciating pain of chopping blocks, before submitting to certain unjust laws of the Roman Empire. To a degree academic freedom is a reality today because Socrates practiced civil disobedience.

We can never forget that everything Hitler did in Germany was "legal" and everything the Hungarian freedom fighters did in Hungary was "illegal." It was "illegal" to aid and comfort a Jew in Hitler's Germany. But I am sure that, if I had lived in Germany during that time, I would have aided and comforted my Jewish brothers even though it was illegal. If I lived in a communist country today where certain principles dear to the Christian faith are suppressed, I believe I would openly advocate disobeying those antireligious laws.

I must make two honest confessions to you, my Christian and Jewish brothers. First I must confess that over the last few years I have been gravely disappointed with the white moderate. I have almost reached the regrettable conclusion that the Negroes' great stumbling block in the stride toward freedom is not the White Citizens' "Counciler" or the Ku Klux Klanner, but the white moderate who is more devoted to "order" than to justice; who prefers a negative peace which is the absence of tension to a positive peace which is the presence of justice; who constantly says "I agree with you in the goal you seek, but I can't agree with your methods of direct action"; who paternalistically feels that he can set the timetable for another man's freedom; who lives by the myth of time and who constantly advises the Negro to wait until a "more convenient season." Shallow understanding from people of good will is more frustrating than absolute misunderstanding from people of ill will. Lukewarm acceptance is much more bewildering than outright rejection.

I had hoped that the white moderate would understand that law and order exist for the purpose of establishing justice, and that when they fail to do this they become the dangerously structured dams that block the flow of social progress. I had hoped that the white moderate would understand that the present tension in the South is merely a necessary phase of the transition from an obnoxious negative peace, where the Negro passively accepted his unjust plight, to a substance-filled positive peace, where all men will respect the dignity and worth of human personality. Actually, we who engage in nonviolent direct action are not the creators of tension. We merely bring to the surface the hidden tension that is already alive. We bring it out in the open where it can be seen and dealt with. Like a boil that can never be cured as long as it is covered up but must be opened with all its pus-flowing ugliness to the natural medicines of air and light, injustice must likewise be exposed, with all of the tension its exposing creates, to the light of human conscience and the air of national opinion before it can be cured.

In your statement you asserted that our actions, even though peaceful, must be condemned because they precipitate violence. But can this assertion be logically made? Isn't this like condemning the robbed man because his possession of money precipitated the evil act of robbery? Isn't this like condemning Socrates because his unswerving commitment to truth and his philosophical delvings precipitated the misguided popular mind to make him drink the hemlock? Isn't this like condemning Jesus because His unique God consciousness and never-ceasing devotion to His will precipitated the evil act of crucifixion? We must come to see, as federal courts have consistently affirmed, that it is immoral to urge an individual to withdraw his efforts to gain his basic constitutional rights because the quest precipitates violence. Society must protect the robbed and punish the robber.

I had also hoped that the white moderate would reject the myth of time. I received a letter this morning from a white brother in Texas which said: "All Christians know that the colored people will receive equal rights eventually, but is it possible that you are in too great of a religious hurry? It has taken Christianity almost 2000 years to accomplish what it has. The teachings of Christ take time to come to earth." All that is said here grows out of a tragic misconception of time. It is the strangely irrational notion that there is something in the very flow of time that will inevitably cure all ills. Actually time is neutral. It can be used either destructively or constructively. I am coming to feel that the people of ill will have used time much more effectively than the people of good will. We will have to repent in this generation not merely for the vitriolic words and actions of the bad people, but for the appalling silence of the good people. We must come to see that human progress never rolls in on wheels of inevitability. It comes through the tireless efforts and persistent work of men willing to be coworkers with God, and without this hard work time itself becomes an ally of the forces of social stagnation.

We must use time creatively, and forever realize that the time is always ripe to do right. Now is the time to make real the promise of democracy, and transform our pending national elegy into a creative psalm of brotherhood. Now is the time to lift our national policy from the quicksand of racial injustice to the solid rock of human dignity.

You spoke of our activity in Birmingham as extreme. At first I was rather disappointed that fellow clergymen would see my nonviolent efforts as those of the extremist. I started thinking about the fact that I stand in the middle of two opposing forces in the Negro community. One is a force of complacency made up of Negroes who, as a result of long years of oppression, have been so completely drained of self-respect and a sense of "somebodiness" that they have adjusted to segregation, and of a few Negroes in the middle class who, because of a degree of academic and economic security, and because at points they profit by segregation, have unconsciously become insensitive to the problems of the masses. The other force is one of bitterness and hatred and comes perilously close to advocating violence. It is expressed in the various black nationalist groups that are springing up over the nation, the largest and best known being Elijah Muhammad's Muslim movement. This movement is nourished by the contemporary frustration over the continued existence of racial discrimination. It is made up of people who have lost faith in America, who have absolutely repudiated Christianity, and who have concluded that the white man is an incurable "devil." I have tried to stand between these two forces saying that we need not follow the "do-nothingism" of the complacent or the hatred and despair of the black nationalist. There is the more excellent way of love and nonviolent protest. I'm grateful to God that, through the Negro church, the dimension of nonviolence entered our struggle. If this philosophy had not emerged I am convinced that by now many streets of the South would be flowing with floods of blood. And I am further convinced that if our white brothers dismiss us as "rabble rousers" and "outside agitators"— those of us who are working through the channels of nonviolent direct action—and refuse to support our nonviolent efforts, millions of Negroes, out of frustration and despair, will seek solace and security in black nationalist ideologies, a development that will lead inevitably to a frightening racial nightmare.

Oppressed people cannot remain oppressed forever. The urge for freedom will eventually come. This is what has happened to the American Negro. Something within has reminded him of his birthright of freedom; something without has reminded him that he can gain it. Consciously and unconsciously, he has been swept in by what the Germans call the *Zeitgeist,* and with his black brothers of Africa, and his brown and yellow brothers of Asia, South America, and the Caribbean, he is moving with a sense of cosmic urgency toward the promised land of racial justice. Recognizing this vital urge that has engulfed the Negro community, one should readily understand public demonstrations. The Negro has many pent-up resentments and latent frustrations. He has to get them out. So let him march sometime; let him have his prayer pilgrimages to the city hall; understand why he must have sit-ins and freedom rides. If his repressed emotions do not come out in these nonviolent ways, they will come out in ominous expressions of violence. This is not a threat; it is a fact of history. So I have not said to my people, "Get rid of your discontent." But I have tried to say that this normal and healthy discontent can be channeled through the creative outlet of nonviolent direct action. Now this approach is being dismissed as extremist. I must admit that I was initially disappointed in being so categorized.

But as I continued to think about the matter I gradually gained a bit of satisfaction from being considered an extremist. Was not Jesus an extremist in love? "Love your enemies, bless them that curse you, pray for them that despitefully use you." Was not Amos an extremist for justice—"Let justice roll down like waters and righteousness like a mighty stream." Was not Paul an extremist for the gospel of Jesus Christ— "I bear in my body the marks of the Lord Jesus." Was not Martin Luther an extremist—"Here I stand; I can do none other so help me God." Was not John Bunyan an extremist—"I will stay in jail to the end of my days before I make a butchery of my conscience." Was not Abraham Lincoln an extremist—

"This nation cannot survive half slave and half free."
Was not Thomas Jefferson an extremist—"We hold
these truths to be self evident that all men are created
equal." So the question is not whether we will be extremist but what kind of extremist will we be. Will we
be extremists for hate or will we be extremists for
love? Will we be extremists for the preservation of
injustice—or will we be extremists for the cause of
justice? In that dramatic scene on Calvary's hill three
men were crucified. We must never forget that all
three were crucified for the same crime—the crime of
extremism. Two were extremists for immorality, and
thus fell below their environment. The other, Jesus
Christ, was an extremist for love, truth, and goodness,
and thereby rose above His environment. So, after all,
maybe the South, the nation, and the world are in dire
need of creative extremists.

I had hoped that the white moderate would see this.
Maybe I was too optimistic. Maybe I expected too
much. I guess I should have realized that few members
of a race that has oppressed another race can understand or appreciate the deep groans and passionate
yearnings of those that have been oppressed, and still
fewer have the vision to see that injustice must be
rooted out by strong, persistent, and determined action. I am thankful, however, that some of our white
brothers have grasped the meaning of this social revolution and committed themselves to it. They are still
all too small in quantity, but they are big in quality.
Some like Ralph McGill, Lillian Smith, Harry Golden,
and James Dabbs have written about our struggle in
eloquent, prophetic, and understanding terms. Others
have marched with us down nameless streets of the
South. They have languished in filthy, roach-infested
jails, suffering the abuse and brutality of angry policemen who see them as "dirty nigger lovers." They, un-

like so many of their moderate brothers and sisters, have recognized the urgency of the moment and sensed the need for powerful "action" antidotes to combat the disease of segregation.

Let me rush on to mention my other disappointment. I have been so greatly disappointed with the white Church and its leadership. Of course there are some notable exceptions. I am not unmindful of the fact that each of you has taken some significant stands on this issue. I commend you, Rev. Stallings, for your Christian stand on this past Sunday, in welcoming Negroes to your worship service on a nonsegregated basis. I commend the Catholic leaders of this state for integrating Springhill College several years ago.

But despite these notable exceptions I must honestly reiterate that I have been disappointed with the Church. I do not say that as one of those negative critics who can always find something wrong with the Church. I say it as a minister of the gospel, who loves the Church; who was nurtured in its bosom; who has been sustained by its spiritual blessings and who will remain true to it as long as the cord of life shall lengthen.

I had the strange feeling when I was suddenly catapulted into the leadership of the bus protest in Montgomery several years ago that we would have the support of the white Church. I felt that the white ministers, priests, and rabbis of the South would be some of our strongest allies. Instead, some have been outright opponents, refusing to understand the freedom movement and misrepresenting its leaders; all too many others have been more cautious than courageous and have remained silent behind the anesthetizing security of stained glass windows.

In spite of my shattered dreams of the past, I came to Birmingham with the hope that the white religious

leadership of the community would see the justice of
our cause and, with deep moral concern, serve as the
channel through which our just grievances could get
to the power structure. I had hoped that each of you
would understand. But again I have been disappointed.

I have heard numerous religious leaders of the
South call upon their worshippers to comply with a
desegregation decision because it is the law, but I have
longed to hear white ministers say follow this decree
because integration is morally right and the Negro is
your brother. In the midst of blatant injustices inflicted
upon the Negro, I have watched white churches stand
on the sideline and merely mouth pious irrelevancies
and sanctimonious trivialities. In the midst of a mighty
struggle to rid our nation of racial and economic injustice, I have heard so many ministers say, "Those are
social issues with which the Gospel has no real concern," and I have watched so many churches commit
themselves to a completely otherworldly religion
which made a strange distinction between body and
soul, the sacred and the secular.

So here we are moving toward the exit of the twentieth century with a religious community largely adjusted to the status quo, standing as a tail light behind
other community agencies rather than a headlight
leading men to higher levels of justice.

I have travelled the length and breadth of Alabama,
Mississippi, and all the other Southern states. On swel-
tering summer days and crisp autumn mornings I have
looked at her beautiful churches with their spires
pointing heavenward. I have beheld the impressive
outlay of her massive religious education buildings.
Over and over again I have found myself asking:
"Who worships here? Who is their God? Where were
their voices when the lips of Governor Barnett

dripped with words of interposition and nullification? Where were they when Governor Wallace gave the clarion call for defiance and hatred? Where were their voices of support when tired, bruised, and weary Negro men and women decided to rise from the dark dungeons of complacency to the bright hills of creative protest?"

Yes, these questions are still in my mind. In deep disappointment, I have wept over the laxity of the Church. But be assured that my tears have been tears of love. There can be no deep disappointment where there is not deep love. Yes, I love the Church; I love her sacred walls. How could I do otherwise? I am in the rather unique position of being the son, the grandson, and the great grandson of preachers. Yes, I see the Church as the body of Christ. But, oh! How we have blemished and scarred that body through social neglect and fear of being nonconformists.

There was a time when the Church was very powerful. It was during that period when the early Christians rejoiced when they were deemed worthy to suffer for what they believed. In those days the Church was not merely a thermometer that recorded the ideas and principles of popular opinion; it was a thermostat that transformed the mores of society. Wherever the early Christians entered a town the power structure got disturbed and immediately sought to convict them for being "disturbers of the peace" and "outside agitators." But they went on with the conviction that they were a "colony of heaven" and had to obey God rather than man. They were small in number but big in commitment. They were too God-intoxicated to be "astronomically intimidated." They brought an end to such ancient evils as infanticide and gladiatorial contest.

Things are different now. The contemporary Church

is so often a weak, ineffectual voice with an uncertain sound. It is so often the archsupporter of the status quo. Far from being disturbed by the presence of the Church, the power structure of the average community is consoled by the Church's silent and often vocal sanction of things as they are.

But the judgment of God is upon the Church as never before. If the Church of today does not recapture the sacrificial spirit of the early Church, it will lose its authentic ring, forfeit the loyalty of millions, and be dismissed as an irrelevant social club with no meaning for the twentieth century. I am meeting young people every day whose disappointment with the Church has risen to outright disgust.

Maybe again I have been too optimistic. Is organized religion too inextricably bound to the status quo to save our nation and the world? Maybe I must turn my faith to the inner spiritual Church, the church within the Church, as the true *ecclesia* and the hope of the world. But again I am thankful to God that some noble souls from the ranks of organized religion have broken loose from the paralyzing chains of conformity and joined us as active partners in the struggle for freedom. They have left their secure congregations and walked the streets of Albany, Georgia, with us. They have gone through the highways of the South on torturous rides for freedom. Yes, they have gone to jail with us. Some have been kicked out of their churches and lost the support of their bishops and fellow ministers. But they have gone with the faith that right defeated is stronger than evil triumphant. These men have been the leaven in the lump of the race. Their witness has been the spiritual salt that has preserved the true meaning of the Gospel in these troubled times. They have carved a tunnel of hope through the dark mountain of disappointment.

I hope the Church as a whole will meet the challenge of this decisive hour. But even if the Church does not come to the aid of justice, I have no despair about the future. I have no fear about the outcome of our struggle in Birmingham, even if our motives are presently misunderstood. We will reach the goal of freedom in Birmingham and all over the nation, because the goal of America is freedom. Abused and scorned though we may be, our destiny is tied up with the destiny of America. Before the pilgrims landed at Plymouth, we were here. Before the pen of Jefferson etched across the pages of history the majestic words of the Declaration of Independence, we were here. For more than two centuries our foreparents labored in this country without wages; they made cotton "king"; and they built the homes of their masters in the midst of brutal injustice and shameful humiliation—and yet out of a bottomless vitality they continued to thrive and develop. If the inexpressible cruelties of slavery could not stop us, the opposition we now face will surely fail. We will win our freedom because the sacred heritage of our nation and the eternal will of God are embodied in our echoing demands.

I must close now. But before closing I am impelled to mention one other point in your statement that troubled me profoundly. You warmly commended the Birmingham police force for keeping "order" and "preventing violence." I don't believe you would have so warmly commended the police force if you had seen its angry violent dogs literally biting six unarmed, nonviolent Negroes. I don't believe you would so quickly commend the policemen if you would observe their ugly and inhuman treatment of Negroes here in the city jail; if you would watch them push and curse old Negro women and young Negro girls; if you would see them slap and kick old Negro men and young

Negro boys; if you will observe them, as they did on two occasions, refuse to give us food because we wanted to sing our grace together. I'm sorry that I can't join you in your praise for the police department.

It is true that they have been rather disciplined in their public handling of the demonstrators. In this sense they have been rather publicly "nonviolent." But for what purpose? To preserve the evil system of segregation. Over the last few years I have consistently preached that nonviolence demands that the means we use must be as pure as the ends we seek. So I have tried to make it clear that it is wrong to use immoral means to attain moral ends. But now I must affirm that it is just as wrong, or even more so, to use moral means to preserve immoral ends. Maybe Mr. Connor and his policemen have been rather publicly nonviolent, as Chief Pritchett was in Albany, Georgia, but they have used the moral means of nonviolence to maintain the immoral end of flagrant racial injustice. T. S. Eliot has said that there is no greater treason than to do the right deed for the wrong reason.

I wish you had commended the Negro sit-inners and demonstrators of Birmingham for their sublime courage, their willingness to suffer, and their amazing discipline in the midst of the most inhuman provocation. One day the South will recognize its real heroes. They will be the James Merediths, courageously and with a majestic sense of purpose, facing jeering and hostile mobs and the agonizing loneliness that characterizes the life of the pioneer. They will be old, oppressed, battered Negro women, symbolized in a seventy-two-year-old woman of Montgomery, Alabama, who rose up with a sense of dignity and with her people decided not to ride the segregated buses, and responded to one who inquired about her tiredness with ungrammatical

profundity: "My feets is tired, but my soul is rested."
They will be young high school and college students,
young ministers of the gospel and a host of the elders,
courageously and nonviolently sitting in at lunch
counters and willingly going to jail for conscience sake.
One day the South will know that when these disin-
herited children of God sat down at lunch counters
they were in reality standing up for the best in the
American dream and the most sacred values in our
Judeo-Christian heritage, and thus carrying our whole
nation back to great wells of democracy which were
dug deep by the founding fathers in the formulation of
the Constitution and the Declaration of Independence.

Never before have I written a letter this long (or
should I say a book?). I'm afraid that it is much too
long to take your precious time. I can assure you that
it would have been much shorter if I had been writing
from a comfortable desk, but what else is there to do
when you are alone for days in the dull monotony of
a narrow jail cell other than write long letters, think
strange thoughts, and pray long prayers?

If I have said anything in this letter that is an over-
statement of the truth and is indicative of an unreasonable impatience, I beg you to forgive me. If I have
said anything in this letter that is an understatement
of the truth and is indicative of my having a patience
that makes me patient with anything less than brotherhood, I beg God to forgive me.

I hope this letter finds you strong in the faith. I also
hope that circumstances will soon make it possible for
me to meet each of you, not as an integrationist or a
civil rights leader, but as a fellow clergyman and a
Christian brother. Let us all hope that the dark clouds
of racial prejudice will soon pass away and the deep
fog of misunderstanding will be lifted from our fear-
drenched communities and in some not too distant

tomorrow the radiant stars of love and brotherhood will shine over our great nation with all of their scintillating beauty.

Yours for the cause of Peace and Brotherhood,
Martin Luther King, Jr.

ON THE
LIGHTER SIDE

George Plimpton

DESPERATELY SEEKING HUMOR

(1996)

Some years ago I was persuaded—perhaps against my better judgment—to appear onstage at Caesar's Palace in Las Vegas as a stand-up comedian for one night. At the time, I was doing a series of participatory journalistic stints (football, auto racing, performing in the circus, movie acting, among them) for hour-long TV specials, which appeared on ABC. The world of comedy seemed like an appropriate subject. The special was called *Plimpton! Did You Hear the One About?*

I had the privilege of being coached for the Big Night by a remarkable cast of comedians—Buddy Hackett, Bob Hope, Woody Allen (who remarked he didn't think I'd have a very good time out there), Phyllis Diller, Steve Allen, Jonathan Winters, among others. My routine was put together by the star writers of one of the most successful comedy shows ever— the rube-dominated show called *Laugh-In*. I went to them and complained that I didn't think their John Wayne jokes had captured my style. They said to me as follows: "Plimpton, if we could capture your style we'd put it in a cage and club it to death!"—which I have always thought was a funnier remark than any of those they gave me to say from the stage.

The show was hardly a "wow." I finished it with a sigh of relief, and with a profound appreciation of how difficult it is to be a successful comedian.

It would seem a far jump from the stage of Las Vegas to the editor's desk of a literary quarterly. Certainly the comic mode is barely discernible in magazines like *The Paris Review,* which tend to be grim (short stories), difficult (poetry), academic (essays) and savage (criticism). Indeed, the same could be said of all magazines with a serious bent—*The Atlantic Monthly, Harper's.* But in fact humor is an ingredient eagerly sought by editors. Desperately so. They would gladly pull an article on global warming, say, and schedule it for a subsequent issue if they could replace it with something truly funny.

I think the notion of devoting an entire issue of *The Paris Review* to a study of humor originated with a story John Mortimer once told me—that a novelist friend of his had boarded the London subway (or tube, if you will) at Green Park, intending to get off at Piccadilly Circus, the next stop. As he sat down, he noticed that a young woman opposite was reading one of his novels. By surreptitiously looking, he was able to calculate that after a number of pages a big laugh was coming up. She went all the way to Cockfosters, at the end of the line, while he waited for a laugh that never came.

I don't suppose one should be all that surprised. Surely, of all the arts—excluding music, perhaps—the written word is the most ill-equipped to engender laughter. In my edition of the *Encyclopaedia Britannica,* the essay on humor is bisected by a color plate showing various hummingbirds—which seems appropriate enough considering the erratic flight of that bird. A commanding definition has never taken hold—starting with Aristotle's curious observation that comedy was "an imitation of men who are inferior but not altogether vicious." I have always liked what William Temple had to say on the subject. In his essay "Of Poetry" (1690), he suggested that the eminence of English humor had something to do (along with other things) with the uncertainty of the climate.

So it was with this curious disparity in mind that the editors of *The Paris Review* decided to address humor—examples of it in their selection of fiction and poetry, along with studies of its various aspects.

Actually, from the start, we had always hoped to leaven *The Paris Review* with humor—perhaps because two of the original editors, John Train and I, along with the magazine's first publisher, Sadruddin Aga Khan, spent undergraduate years at the *Harvard Lampoon,* the university's humor magazine. Back then, undergraduates who enjoyed the breezy camaraderie of that institution and wished to go on to a career in letters went to magazines like *The New Yorker* (John Updike, Michael Arlen) or *National Lampoon* (Chris Cerf, Henry Beard). Today, the *Lampoon* graduates who want to continue in communication move almost invariably to television sitcoms and talk shows; indeed one of them, Conan O'Brien, is a late-night talk-show host.

With the propagation of literate humor in mind, in 1960 we persuaded Gertrude Vanderbilt, who despaired at the solemn content of an average issue, to establish a humor prize. Its first winner was the late novelist Terry Southern, who won it with sketches about an eccentric billionaire, Grand Guy Grand, who spent his fortune startling the electorate with elaborate practical jokes . . . sketches that eventually became the novel *The Magic Christian*. The prize was discontinued after seven years, and then reinstituted by John Train. Unfortunately, there were disagreements between the donor of the prize and the editors as to what was funny. Train preferred the urbane, ironic wit typical of London's *Spectator*. His fellow editors had a more robust view of what they thought was amusing. Eventually, after another seven years, the prize was once again discontinued.

Many of the authors interviewed in the magazine's Writers at Work series have talked about humor. Bernard Malamud told his interviewer, "With me humor comes unexpectedly. . . . When something starts funny, I can feel my imagination eating and running. I love the distancing—the guise of invention—that humor gives fiction. Comedy, I imagine, is harder to do consistently than tragedy, but I like it spiced in the wine of sadness." Henry Green stated his intentions more succinctly: "If you can make the reader laugh he is apt to get careless and go on reading."

When the notion of devoting an entire issue of *The Paris Review* to humor was raised, Drue Heinz, the publisher, was delighted. She suggested a sobriquet derived from Hamlet's lament, "I have of late, but wherefore know not, lost all my mirth." Thus, "Whither mirth?" seemed an appropriate heading for the cover. Interviews were arranged with three writers known for their comic slant on things—Calvin Trillin, Garrison Keillor and Woody Allen. There were surprises in the results. I would not have guessed that Woody Allen (interviewed by Michiko Kakutani of *The New York Times*) does not have a particularly high opinion of humor in the arts and would not list any comedies among his favorite 10 films. Below the salt! Nor would I have thought that anybody (Calvin Trillin in this case) would have trouble being *serious*.

"It's a genetic thing—being funny—like being able to wiggle your ears," he confessed. "I don't have any trouble being funny, that's my turn of mind." Garrison Keillor talked about leaving *The New Yorker* when Tina Brown took over—I suspect a wrenching experience, since *The New Yorker* had made such an impression on him during his adolescence in the Midwest that he referred to the magazine as an "immense literary ocean liner off the coast of Minnesota." Now, he says, *The New Yorker*'s editors do not realize the Midwest exists, and the "ocean liner" has "moved off the coast of Minnesota, and now it is firmly anchored off the coast of Staten Island." And what does Keillor have to say about failed humorists? He suggests the ministry.

One of the earliest staff suggestions was to ask Harold Bloom, author of *The Western Canon*, to write an abbreviated canon of Western humor for the issue. Professor Bloom did not agree to write a canon, but he said he would be delighted to be interviewed at his home in New Haven. How simple it turned out to be! After the first question (What would he include in a syllabus if he were to teach a course on Western humor?), I hardly had to ask another. What was memorable about the afternoon was how much Bloom enjoyed recounting certain comic scenes from literature that he especially enjoyed—so consumed with laughter that he could barely continue. One of the scenes that particularly convulsed him appeared in Mark Twain's "Journalism in Tennessee"—the humorist crouched down in the offices of the *Morning Glory and Johnson County War-Whoop* to avoid the crossfire between rival editors shooting at each other. Just the name of the paper rendered Professor Bloom almost helpless.

One less risible but noteworthy part of his discourse was how few women writers—that is to say from the past—made a name as humorists. Indeed, he said, only Jane Austen would be secure in his canon. He felt that the reason for this curious lack might be that being in contention with the whole world of male writers, women have traditionally felt that they must elevate themselves to high seriousness. I pressed him a bit on this, knowing that I'd be questioned by female members of the staff. He said as follows: "If one thinks in general of the great tradition of British women novelists, George Eliot or the two Brontës, or Edith Wharton or Willa Cather in America, all remarkable writers, they are absolutely lacking in humor . . . there isn't a touch of it."

Along with Austen, he mentioned one British author (A. S. Byatt) and five American poets he felt could be characterized as great comic writers in their field: Emily Dickinson, Marianne Moore, Elizabeth Bishop, May Swenson and Amy Clampitt. I was tempted to ask him about Jane Smiley, among other fiction writers, but he had soared on to another topic.

Back in New York, the humor project continued. We sent out a questionnaire to writers to ask their opinions of humor, their answers to be published under the heading, "The Man in the Back Row Has a Question." John Updike (surely because of his status as a *Harvard Lampoon* alumnus) sent in a lengthy reply to the query "What is the state of humor today?" He mentioned his own absorption with the genre, his reasons for its demise—that a less literate culture can no longer appreciate the genteel tradition epitomized by Thurber, Benchley & Co.—and that as for himself he has discovered that "simply describing, as reverently and calmly as possible, my fellow Americans in action was fun enough, and funny enough, for me." The shortest response to the questionnaire was sent in by Dave Barry. To the same question, "What is the state of humor today?" he replied, "Without a doubt, Arkansas. (Rim shot.)"

Richard Howard, the poetry editor, provided a substantial number of poems with a humorous turn of mind. One of them (by Lloyd Schwartz) I especially enjoyed. Titled "Proverbs from Purgatory," it was a series of mixed proverbs: A bird in the hand makes waste; a rolling stone deserves another; a friend in need opens a can of worms; he smokes like a fish, etc.

We selected four fiction pieces whose plots suggest their appropriateness for a humor issue—T. Coraghessan Boyle's account of a mutiny aboard Jacques Cousteau's *Calypso* by a crew fed up with a constant diet of fish; Marcia Guthridge's story about a housewife who runs into Henry V in a supermarket and has an affair with him; Melvin Jules Bukiet's description of a man shadowing Vladimir Nabokov around New York City; and John Barth's desperate monologue of a master of ceremonies trapped at the lecture podium awaiting the arrival of the featured speaker.

For an art portfolio for the issue, we thought it would be interesting to get famous cartoonists to talk about their art—inspiration, how their ideas developed. A number of them contributed. I was astonished to hear from Lee Lorenz of *The New Yorker* (not surprisingly, almost all the artists who agreed to the exercise were from that magazine "firmly anchored off the coast of Staten Island") that George Price, surely one of *The New Yorker's* most distinguished cartoonists, had his ideas over a 50-year period supplied him by others. Only one of his own ever appeared in an issue—a cover, actually—of a large crowd of bemused and startled department-store Santa Clauses who find themselves by chance the only passengers in a subway car.

As for the cover of our humor issue, we decided to

use a portrait of a cat that Saul Steinberg gave us a number of years ago for a signed limited run of posters. In the poster, three bubbles rise from the cat's head to indicate he is wondering, *"The Paris Review?"* It seemed the appropriate image, particularly if the cat could be asking himself the humor issue's motto, "Whither mirth?" I telephoned Steinberg. Just a question of exchanging one thought for the other. Steinberg resisted: None of *his* cats would ever ask themselves something like "Whither mirth?" Alas! His cat *does* appear on the cover, deep in thought, but there is no suggestion as to what might be running through his mind.

Two pages of the humor issue were set aside for a list of those members of the House of Representatives who voted for even more drastic cuts in the National Endowment for the Arts budget. We couldn't resist it. The members were listed under the heading "Yahoos." It may well be that those pages are the funniest in the issue—depending upon one's view of government assistance to the arts.

The most ambitious attempt to look into the state of contemporary humor was arranged in Drue Heinz's villa on Lake Como—a conference chaired by Grey Gowrie and Malcolm Bradbury to which she was able to entice a number of wits from England, including John Wells, John Mortimer, John Gross, Tibor Fischer, Auberon Waugh and Mordecai Richler, actually a Canadian, but living in London at the time. A small American contingent consisted of Roy Blount Jr., Calvin Trillin and myself. We spent three days talking about various aspects of humor—the edited result taking up almost 50 pages in the magazine. Roy Blount Jr. suggested that tragedy was a lot harder to sustain than comedy, that being funny was a fallback, a consolation. To illustrate the slim margin of difference, he recounted that John Gielgud, on being asked how to stage *King Lear,* had said that his only advice was to be sure to have a "light Cordelia." If Lear weighed 150 pounds, Cordelia 149 pounds 15 ounces—tragedy. Lear 150 pounds and Cordelia 150 pounds 1 ounce—comedy.

John Mortimer totally disagreed; he said that anyone, as he put it, could "toss up a tragedy on a wet afternoon."

During the sessions I sat next to Auberon Waugh. On occasion he jotted notes with a fountain pen for his own publication, *The Literary Review*. He is well known for his querulous feelings about any number of things—especially but not exclusively feminism, modern art and the U.S.A.: In a recent column he wrote, "I begin to have the feeling that the time has come for another war. We have done the Germans and the Japanese, but Swedes are particularly annoying people. They have no body hair and never stop grumbling about all the acid rain and atmospheric pollution we send them."

At one point he announced: "I'm sorry to say that the feminist movement is the great area of opposition to humor in any form. They put on these absolutely frozen faces. That is the only point I wish to make at this plenary session."

Toward the end of the conference, the panelists were asked to make summary remarks. When my turn came, I recalled my stint in Las Vegas. I said that the analogy that came to mind being out there on the stage was that it was like fishing at night. I said: "You throw this joke far out into this black lake and you hope for a strike. It's exhilarating, of course, when there is one, and it's magical that somehow you've performed a kind of service in making people laugh. Sometimes you hurl the John Wayne joke, or whatever, far out into the darkness, and nothing happens. You keep on reeling in and nothing touches it. Despair. A numbness . . . what they call out there 'flop sweat.' "

I finished by remarking what an intrepid bunch had turned up for the conference—writers who in large part were attempting to engender laughter through their work. What a complicated topic! I reminded them that Grey Gowrie had mentioned that "a simple joke obviously makes one laugh more than many great works of literature which one could fairly call comedy." In that case, would anyone like to hear a musty John Wayne joke? I had one on tap. . . .

Mark Twain

ADVICE TO YOUTH

(1882)

Being told I would be expected to talk here, I inquired what sort of talk I ought to make. They
said it should be something suitable to youth—
something didactic, instructive, or something in the nature of good advice. Very well; I have a few things in
my mind which I have often longed to say for the
instruction of the young; for it is in one's tender early
years that such things will best take root and be most
enduring and most valuable. First, then, I will say to
you, my young friends—and say it beseechingly,
urgingly—.

Always obey your parents, when they are present.
This is the best policy in the long run; because if you
don't, they will make you. Most parents think they
know better than you do; and you can generally make
more by humoring that superstition than you can by
acting on your own better judgment.

Be respectful to your superiors, if you have any;
also to strangers, and sometimes to others. If a person
offend you, and you are in doubt as to whether it was
intentional or not, do not resort to extreme measures;

simply watch your chance and hit him with a brick. That will be sufficient. If you shall find that he had not intended any offense, come out frankly and confess yourself in the wrong when you struck him; acknowledge it like a man, and say you didn't mean to. Yes, always avoid violence; in this age of charity and kindliness, the time has gone by for such things. Leave dynamite to the low and unrefined.

Go to bed early, get up early—this is wise. Some authorities say get up with one thing, some with another. But a lark is really the best thing to get up with. It gives you a splendid reputation with everybody to know that you get up with the lark; and if you get the right kind of lark, and work at him right, you can easily train him to get up at half-past nine, every time—it is no trick at all.

Now as to the matter of lying. You want to be very careful about lying; otherwise you are nearly sure to get caught. Once caught, you can never again be, in the eyes of the good and the pure, what you were before. Many a young person has injured himself permanently through a single clumsy and ill-finished lie, the result of carelessness born of incomplete training. Some authorities hold that the young ought not to lie at all. That, of course, is putting it rather stronger than necessary; still, while I cannot go quite so far as that, I do maintain, and I believe I am right, that the young ought to be temperate in the use of this great art until practice and experience shall give them that confidence, elegance and precision which alone can make the accomplishment graceful and profitable. Patience, diligence, painstaking attention to detail—these are the requirements; these, in time, will make the student perfect; upon these, and upon these only, may he rely as the sure foundation for future eminence. Think what tedious years of study, thought, practice, experience, went to the equipment of that peerless old master who was able to impose upon the whole world the lofty and sounding maxim that "Truth is mighty and will prevail"—the most majestic compound fracture of fact which any of woman born has yet achieved. For the history of our race, and each individual's experience, are sown thick with evidences that a truth is not hard to kill, and that a lie well told is immortal. There in Boston is a monument to the man who discovered anesthesia; many people are aware, in these latter days, that that man didn't discover it at all, but stole the discovery from another man. Is this truth mighty, and will it prevail? Ah, no, my hearers, the monument is made of hardy material, but the lie it tells will outlast it a million years. An awkward, feeble, leaky lie is a thing which you ought to make it your unceasing study to avoid; such a lie as that has no more real permanence than an average truth. Why, you might as well tell the truth at once and be done with it. A feeble, stupid, preposterous lie will not live two years—except it be a slander upon somebody. It is indestructible, then, of course, but that is no merit of yours. A final word: begin your practice of this gracious and beautiful art early—begin now. If I had begun earlier, I could have learned how.

Never handle firearms carelessly. The sorrow and suffering that have been caused through the innocent but heedless handling of firearms by the young! Only four days ago, right in the next farmhouse to the one where I am spending the summer, a mother, old and gray and sweet, one of the loveliest spirits in the land, was sitting at her work, when her young son crept in and got down an old battered, rusty gun which had not been touched for many years, and was supposed not to be loaded, and pointed it at her, laughing and threatening to shoot. In her fright she ran screaming and pleading toward the door on the other side of the room; but as she passed him he placed the gun almost against her very breast and pulled the trigger! He had supposed it was not loaded. And he was right: it wasn't. So there wasn't any harm done. It is the only case of the kind I ever heard of. Therefore, just the same, don't you meddle with old unloaded firearms; they are the most deadly and unerring things that have ever been created by man. You don't have to take any pains at all, with them; you don't have to have a rest, you don't have to have any sights on the gun, you don't have to take aim, even. No, you just pick out a relative and bang away, and you are sure to get him. A youth who can't hit a cathedral at thirty yards with a Gatling gun in three-quarters of an hour, can take up an old empty musket and bag his mother every time, at a hundred. Think what Waterloo would have been if one of the armies had been boys armed with old rusty muskets supposed not to be loaded, and the other army had been composed of their female relations. The very thought of it makes me shudder.

There are many sorts of books; but good ones are the sort for the young to read. Remember that. They are a great, an inestimable, an unspeakable means of improvement. Therefore be careful in your selection, my young friends; be very careful; confine yourself exclusively to Robertson's *Sermons*, Baxter's *Saint's Rest*, *The Innocents Abroad*, and works of that kind.

Erma Bombeck

WARNING: FAMILIES MAY BE DANGEROUS TO YOUR HEALTH
(1971)

There's a lot of theories on why the American family is losing ground as an institution.

Some say it's economics . . . others say ecology . . . others blame lack of fulfillment . . . a few opt for priorities, or as one neighbor observed, "Would you want to bring a child into a world that wouldn't elect Ronald Reagan?"

I personally like the American family. It has a lot of potential. Besides, the world is not geared for two people. Twinkies come twelve to a box, kitchen chairs, four to a set, gum, five sticks to the package.

To my way of thinking, the American family started to decline when parents began to communicate with their children. When we began to "rap," "feed into one another," "let things hang out" that mother didn't know about and would rather not.

Foremost of the villains that ripped the American family to shreds was Education. It was a case of Hide-and-Seek meeting Show and Tell . . . the McGuffey reader crowd locking horns with the Henry Miller group.

295

The ignorance gap that the new math created between parent and child has not even begun to mend.

Before the new math, I had a mysterious aura about me. I never said anything, but my children were convinced I had invented fire.

When we began to have "input" with one another, my daughter said to me one day, "Mama, what's a variable?"

"It's a weirdo who hangs around the playground. Where did you read that word? On a restroom wall?"

"It's in my new math book," she said. "I was hoping you could help me. They want me to locate the mantissa in the body of the table and determine the associated antilog ten, and write the characteristics as an exponent on the base of ten."

I thought a minute. "How long has the mantissa been missing?"

She went to her room, locked her door and I never saw her again until after she graduated.

The metric system was no better. Once a child knows that a square millimeter is .00155 square inches, will he ever have respect for a mother who once measured the bathroom for carpeting and found out she had enough left over to slipcover New Jersey?

And what modern-day mother has never been intimidated when she has to communicate with a child's teacher?

I don't think there's anything that makes my morning like a kid looking up from his cereal and saying casually, "I gotta have a note saying I was sick or my teacher won't let me back into school."

"I suppose it has to be written on paper," I ask, slumping miserably over the bologna.

"The one you wrote on wax paper she couldn't read. But if you can't find paper, I could stay home for another day," he said.

I tore a piece of wallpaper off the wall and said, "Get me a pencil."

The pencil took a bit of doing. After a fifteen-minute search we finally found a stub in the lint trap of the dryer.

"You sure are whipped up about this note," I sighed.

"You don't understand," he said. "If we don't have one we don't go back to school."

I started to write. "Is your teacher a Miss, a Ms. or a Mrs.?"

"I don't know," he pondered. "She owns her own car and carries her own books."

"Dear Ms. Weems," I wrote.

"On the other hand, she stayed up to watch the Miss America Pageant."

"Dear Miss Weems," I wrote.

"It doesn't matter," he shrugged. "When she has her baby we'll have a new teacher."

"Dear MRS. Weems," I wrote. "Please excuse Brucie from school yesterday. When he awoke in the morning he complained of stomach cramps and . . ."

"Cross out stomach cramps," he ordered, "tell her I was too sick to watch TV."

"Dear Mrs. Weems, Brucie had the urgencies and . . ."

"What does urgencies mean?"

"Stomach cramps."

"Don't tell her that! The last time you wrote that she put me next to the door and didn't take her eyes off me all day long."

"It was your imagination," I said. "Do you need a note or not?"

"I told you I can't go to school without it."

"Okay then, get me the dictionary and turn to the D's."

He looked over my shoulder. "What does D-I-A-R-R-H-E-A mean?"

"It means you sit by the door again," I said, licking the envelope.

Composing the note took twenty-five minutes, which was eight minutes longer than the signing of the Declaration of Independence. I wouldn't bring it up, but only yesterday I was cleaning out a jacket pocket and there was the note: unread and unnecessary.

To me, modern education is a contradiction. It's like a three-year-old kid with a computer in his hand who can multiply 10.6 percent interest of $11,653, but doesn't know if a dime is larger or smaller than a nickel.

It is like your daughter going to college and taking all your small appliances, linens, beddings, furniture, luggage, TV set and car and then saying, "I've got to get away from your shallow materialism."

My kids always talk a great game of ecology. Yet, they harbor the No. 1 cause of pollution in this country: gym clothes.

A pair of shorts, a shirt and a pair of gym shoes walked into the utility room under their own steam last Wednesday and leaned helplessly against the wall. I stood there while I watched a pot of ivy shrivel and die before my eyes.

Blinking back the tears, I yelled to my son, "How long has it been since these clothes have been washed?"

"Since the beginning of the school year," he shouted back.

"What school year?"

"1972–1973."

"I thought so. You know, I don't know how your P.E. teacher stands it."

"He said we weren't too bad until yesterday."

"What happened yesterday?"

"It rained and we came inside."

"Don't you have rules about laundering these things?"

"Yeah. We have to have them washed every four months whether they need it or not."

Carefully, I unfolded the muddy shorts, the brittle T-shirt and the socks that were already in the final stages of rigor mortis.

As I tried to scrape off a French fry entangled in a gym shoestring, I couldn't help but reflect that this was a child who had been reared in an antiseptic world. When he was a baby, I used to boil his toys and sterilize his navel bands. I made the dog wear a mask when he was in the same room. I washed my hands BEFORE I changed his diapers.

Where had I failed?

Under his bed were dirty clothes that were harboring wildlife. In his drawers were pairs of soiled underwear so old that some had plastic liners in them. His closet had overalls and jeans that hung suspended without the need of hangers.

Opening the lid of the washer, I felt around trying to find the gym clothes that I had just washed. I retrieved a shoestring, two labels and a clean French fry.

"What happened to my gym clothes?" asked my son.

"After the sweat and dirt went, this was all that was left."

Probably the most blatant contradiction between what a child is at home and what he is at school manifests itself at the annual Athletic Banquet.

Next time you attend an athletic awards banquet, catch the look on the faces of mothers as the accomplishments of their sons and daughters are revealed.

It is as if they are talking about a different person with the same name as your youngster.

By intense concentration, you can sometimes read the parents' thoughts, as the coaches pay them homage.

"Mark is probably one of the best sprinters I've had in my entire career here at So. High. Hang onto your hats, people. Mark ran the hundred-yard dash in nine point nine!"

(Had to be nine days and nine hours. I once asked him to run out the garbage and it sat by the sink until it turned into a bookend.)

"I don't know what the baseball team would do without Charlie. We've had chatterers on the team before who get the guys whipped up, but Charlie is the all-time chatterer. There isn't a moment when he isn't saying something to spark the team."

(Charlie speaks six words to me in a week. "When you going to the store?")

"For those of you who don't really understand field events, I want to explain about the shotput. It's a ball weighing eight pounds that was thrown a hundred feet by an outstanding athlete here at So. . . . Wesley Whip."

(That's funny. Wesley looks like the same boy who delivers my paper and can't heave a six-ounce Saturday edition all the way from his bike to my porch.)

"Wolf Man Gus will go down in football annals as one of the all-time greats here at So. High. In the game with Central, Gus scored the winning touchdown despite a chipped bone in his ankle, a dislocated shoulder and a fever of a hundred and two."

(So how come Wolf Man Gus stays home from school every time he has his teeth cleaned?)

"I don't suppose anyone has better reflexes in this entire state than our outstanding basketball rebounder, Tim Rim. When the Good Lord passed out coordination, Tim was first in line."

(Tim is seventeen years old and I can still only pour him a half-glass of milk because that's all I want to clean up.)

"Tennis is a gentleman's game. This year's recipient of the Court Courtesy award is none other than So. High's Goodwill Ambassador, Stevie Cool."

(He's certainly come a long way since he tried to break his brother's face last week when he took a record album without asking.)

"The swimming team would never have made it this year without our plucky little manager, Paul Franswarth. Paul picks up those wet towels off the floor, hangs up the suits to dry, and is responsible for putting all the gear back where it belongs."

(Let's go home, Ed. I feel sick.)

AMERICA AT THE CROSSROADS

Abraham Lincoln

—〜〜—

SECOND INAUGURAL ADDRESS

(1865)

FELLOW-COUNTRYMEN:

At this second appearing to take the oath of the presidential office, there is less occasion for an extended address than there was at the first. Then a statement, somewhat in detail, of a course to be pursued, seemed fitting and proper. Now, at the expiration of four years, during which public declarations have been constantly called forth on every point and phase of the great contest which still absorbs the attention and engrosses the energies of the nation, little that is new could be presented. The progress of our arms, upon which all else chiefly depends, is as well known to the public as to myself; and it is, I trust, reasonably satisfactory and encouraging to all. With high hope for the future, no prediction in regard to it is ventured.

On the occasion corresponding to this four years ago, all thoughts were anxiously directed to an impending civil war. All dreaded it—all sought to avert it. While the inaugural address was being delivered from this place, devoted altogether to saving the Union without war, insurgent agents were in the city seeking to destroy it without war—seeking to dissolve the Union, and divide effects, by negotiation. Both parties deprecated war; but one of them would make war rather than let the nation survive; and the other would accept war rather than let it perish. And the war came.

One-eighth of the whole population were colored slaves, not distributed generally over the Union, but localized in the Southern part of it. These slaves constituted a peculiar and powerful interest. All knew that this interest was, somehow, the cause of the war. To strengthen, perpetuate, and extend this interest was the object for which the insurgents would rend the Union, even by war; while the government claimed no right to do more than to restrict the territorial enlargement of it.

Neither party expected for the war the magnitude or the duration which it has already attained. Neither anticipated that the cause of the conflict might cease with, or even before, the conflict itself should cease. Each looked for an easier triumph, and a result less fundamental and astounding. Both read the same Bible, and pray to the same God; and each invokes his aid against the other. It may seem strange that any men should dare to ask a just God's assistance in wringing their bread from the sweat of other men's faces; but let us judge not, that we be not judged. The prayers of both could not be answered—that of neither has been answered fully.

The Almighty has his own purposes. "Woe unto the world because of offences! for it must needs be that offences come; but woe to that man by whom the offence cometh." If we shall suppose that American slavery is one of those offences which, in the providence of God, must needs come, but which, having continued through His appointed time, He now wills to remove, and that He gives to both North and South this terrible war, as the woe due to those by whom the offence came, shall we discern therein any departure from those divine attributes which the believers in a Living God always ascribe to Him? Fondly do we hope—fervently do we pray—that this mighty scourge of war may speedily pass away. Yet, if God wills that it continue until all the wealth piled by the bondman's two hundred and fifty years of unrequited toil shall be sunk, and until every drop of blood drawn with the lash shall be paid by another drawn with the sword, as was said three thousand years ago, so still it must be said, "The judgments of the Lord are true and righteous altogether."

With malice toward none; with charity for all; with firmness in the right, as God gives us to see the right, let us strive on to finish the work we are in; to bind up the nation's wounds; to care for him who shall have borne the battle, and for his widow, and his orphan— to do all which may achieve and cherish a just and lasting peace, among ourselves, and with all nations.

Franklin Delano Roosevelt

JOINT ADDRESS TO CONGRESS LEADING TO A DECLARATION OF WAR AGAINST JAPAN

(1941)

Mr. Vice President, and Mr. Speaker, and Members of the Senate and House of Representatives:

Yesterday, December 7, 1941—a date which will live in infamy—the United States of America was suddenly and deliberately attacked by naval and air forces of the Empire of Japan.

The United States was at peace with that Nation and, at the solicitation of Japan, was still in conversation with its Government and its Emperor looking toward the maintenance of peace in the Pacific. Indeed, one hour after Japanese air squadrons had commenced bombing in the American Island of Oahu, the Japanese Ambassador to the United States and his colleague delivered to our Secretary of State a formal reply to a recent American message. And while this reply stated that it seemed useless to continue the existing diplomatic negotiations, it contained no threat or hint of war or of armed attack.

It will be recorded that the distance of Hawaii from Japan makes it obvious that the attack was deliberately planned many days or even weeks ago. During the intervening time the Japanese Government has deliberately sought to deceive the United States by false statements and expressions of hope for continued peace.

The attack yesterday on the Hawaiian Islands has caused severe damage to American naval and military forces. I regret to tell you that very many American lives have been lost. In addition American ships have been reported torpedoed on the high seas between San Francisco and Honolulu.

Yesterday the Japanese Government also launched an attack against Malaya.

Last night Japanese forces attacked Hong Kong.

Last night Japanese forces attacked Guam.

Last night Japanese forces attacked the Philippine Islands.

Last night the Japanese attacked Wake Island. And this morning the Japanese attacked Midway Island.

Japan has, therefore, undertaken a surprise offensive extending throughout the Pacific area. The facts of yesterday and today speak for themselves. The people of the United States have already formed their opinions and well understand the implications to the very life and safety of our Nation.

As Commander in Chief of the Army and Navy I have directed that all measures be taken for our defense.

But always will our whole Nation remember the character of the onslaught against us.

No matter how long it may take us to overcome this premeditated invasion, the American people in their righteous might will win through to absolute victory. I believe that I interpret the will of the Congress and of the people when I assert that we will not only defend ourselves to the uttermost but will make it very certain that this form of treachery shall never again endanger us.

Hostilities exist. There is no blinking at the fact that our people, our territory, and our interests are in grave danger.

With confidence in our armed forces—with the unbounding determination of our people—we will gain the inevitable triumph—so help us God.

I ask that the Congress declare that since the unprovoked and dastardly attack by Japan on Sunday, December 7, 1941, a state of war has existed between the United States and the Japanese Empire.

Dwight D. Eisenhower

FAREWELL ADDRESS

(1961)

My fellow Americans:

Three days from now, after half a century in the service of our country, I shall lay down the responsibilities of office as, in traditional and solemn ceremony, the authority of the presidency is vested in my successor.

This evening I come to you with a message of leave-taking and farewell, and to share a few final thoughts with you, my countrymen.

Like every other citizen, I wish the new president, and all who will labor with him, Godspeed. I pray that the coming years will be blessed with peace and prosperity for all.

Our people expect their president and the Congress to find essential agreement on issues of great moment, the wise resolution of which will better shape the future of the Nation.

My own relations with the Congress, which began on a remote and tenuous basis when, long ago, a member of the Senate appointed me to West Point, have since ranged to the intimate during the war and immediate postwar period, and, finally, to the mutually interdependent during these past eight years.

In this final relationship, the Congress and the Administration have, on most vital issues, cooperated well, to serve the national good rather than mere partisanship, and so have assured that the business of the Nation should go forward. So, my official relationship with the Congress ends in a feeling, on my part, of gratitude that we have been able to do so much together.

II

We now stand ten years past the midpoint of a century that has witnessed four major wars among great nations. Three of these involved our own country. Despite these holocausts America is today the strongest, the most influential and most productive nation in the world. Understandably proud of this preeminence, we yet realize that America's leadership and prestige depend, not merely upon our unmatched material progress, riches and military strength, but on how we use our power in the interests of world peace and human betterment.

III

Throughout America's adventure in free government, our basic purposes have been to keep the peace; to foster progress in human achievement, and to enhance liberty, dignity and integrity among people and among nations. To strive for less would be unworthy of a free and religious people. Any failure traceable to arrogance, or our lack of comprehension or readiness to sacrifice would inflict upon us grievous hurt both at home and abroad.

Progress toward these noble goals is persistently threatened by the conflict now engulfing the world. It commands our whole attention, absorbs our very beings. We face a hostile ideology—global in scope, atheistic in character, ruthless in purpose, and insidious in method. Unhappily the danger it poses promises to be of indefinite duration. To meet it successfully, there is called for, not so much the emotional and transitory sacrifices of crisis, but rather those which enable us to carry forward steadily, surely, and without complaint the burdens of a prolonged and complex struggle—with liberty at stake. Only thus shall we remain, despite every provocation, on our charted course toward permanent peace and human betterment.

Crises there will continue to be. In meeting them, whether foreign or domestic, great or small, there is a recurring temptation to feel that some spectacular and costly action could become the miraculous solution to all current difficulties. A huge increase in newer elements of our defense; development of unrealistic programs to cure every ill in agriculture; a dramatic expansion in basic and applied research—these and many other possibilities, each possibly promising in itself, may be suggested as the only way to the road we wish to travel.

But each proposal must be weighed in the light of a broader consideration: the need to maintain balance in and among national programs—balance between the private and the public economy, balance between cost and hoped-for advantage—balance between the clearly necessary and the comfortably desirable; balance between our essential requirements as a nation and the duties imposed by the nation upon the individual; balance between action of the moment and the national welfare of the future. Good judgment seeks balance and progress; lack of it eventually finds imbalance and frustration.

The record of many decades stands as proof that our people and their government have, in the main, understood these truths and have responded to them well, in the face of stress and threat. But threats, new in kind or degree, constantly arise. I mention two only.

IV

A vital element in keeping the peace is our military establishment. Our arms must be mighty, ready for instant action, so that no potential aggressor may be tempted to risk his own destruction.

Our military organization today bears little relation to that known by any of my predecessors in peace time, or indeed by the fighting men of World War II or Korea.

Until the latest of our world conflicts, the United States had no armaments industry. American makers of plowshares could, with time and as required, make swords as well. But now we can no longer risk emergency improvisation of national defense; we have been compelled to create a permanent armaments industry of vast proportions. Added to this, three and a half million men and women are directly engaged in the defense establishment. We annually spend on military security more than the net income of all United States corporations.

This conjunction of an immense military establishment and a large arms industry is new in the American experience. The total influence—economic, political, even spiritual—is felt in every city, every state house, every office of the Federal government. We recognize the imperative need for this development. Yet we must not fail to comprehend its grave implications. Our toil, resources and livelihood are all involved; so is the very structure of our society.

In the councils of government, we must guard against the acquisition of unwarranted influence, whether sought or unsought, by the military-industrial complex. The potential for the disastrous rise of misplaced power exists and will persist.

We must never let the weight of this combination endanger our liberties or democratic processes. We should take nothing for granted. Only an alert and knowledgeable citizenry can compel the proper meshing of huge industrial and military machinery of defense with our peaceful methods and goals, so that security and liberty may prosper together.

Akin to, and largely responsible for, the sweeping changes in our industrial-military posture, has been the technological revolution during recent decades.

In this revolution, research has become central; it also becomes more formalized, complex, and costly. A steadily increasing share is conducted for, by, or at the direction of, the Federal government.

Today, the solitary inventor, tinkering in his shop, has been overshadowed by task forces of scientists in laboratories and testing fields. In the same fashion, the free university, historically the fountainhead of free ideas and scientific discovery, has experienced a revolution in the conduct of research. Partly because of the huge costs involved, a government contract becomes virtually a substitute for intellectual curiosity. For every old blackboard there are now hundreds of new electronic computers.

The prospect of domination of the nation's scholars by Federal employment, project allocations, and the power of money is ever present and is gravely to be regarded.

Yet, in holding scientific research and discovery in respect, as we should, we must also be alert to the equal and opposite danger that public policy could itself become the captive of a scientific-technological elite.

It is the task of statesmanship to mold, to balance, and to integrate these and other forces, new and old, within the principles of our democratic system—ever aiming toward the supreme goals of our free society.

V

Another factor in maintaining balance involves the element of time. As we peer into society's future, we—you and I, and our government—must avoid the impulse to live only for today, plundering, for our own ease and convenience, the precious resources of tomorrow. We cannot mortgage the material assets of our grandchildren without risking the loss also of their political and spiritual heritage. We want democracy to survive for all generations to come, not to become the insolvent phantom of tomorrow.

VI

Down the long lane of the history yet to be written America knows that this world of ours, ever growing smaller, must avoid becoming a community of dreadful fear and hate, and be, instead, a proud confederation of mutual trust and respect.

Such a confederation must be one of equals. The weakest must come to the conference table with the same confidence as do we, protected as we are by our moral, economic, and military strength. That table, though scarred by many past frustrations, cannot be abandoned for the certain agony of the battlefield.

Disarmament, with mutual honor and confidence, is a continuing imperative. Together we must learn how to compose difference, not with arms, but with intellect and decent purpose. Because this need is so sharp and apparent I confess that I lay down my official responsibilities in this field with a definite sense of disappointment. As one who has witnessed the horror and the lingering sadness of war—as one who knows that another war could utterly destroy this civilization which has been so slowly and painfully built over thousands of years—I wish I could say tonight that a lasting peace is in sight.

Happily, I can say that war has been avoided. Steady progress toward our ultimate goal has been made. But, so much remains to be done. As a private citizen, I shall never cease to do what little I can to help the world advance along that road.

VII

So—in this my last good night to you as your president—I thank you for the many opportunities you have given me for public service in war and peace. I trust that in that service you find some things worthy; as for the rest of it, I know you will find ways to improve performance in the future.

You and I—my fellow citizens—need to be strong in our faith that all nations, under God, will reach the goal of peace with justice. May we be ever unswerving in devotion to principle, confident but humble with power, diligent in pursuit of the Nation's great goals.

To all the peoples of the world, I once more give expression to America's prayerful and continuing inspiration:

We pray that peoples of all faiths, all races, all nations, may have their great human needs satisfied; that those now denied opportunity shall come to enjoy it to the full; that all who yearn for freedom may experience its spiritual blessings; that those who have freedom will understand, also, its heavy responsibilities; that all who are insensitive to the needs of others will learn charity; that the scourges of poverty, disease and ignorance will be made to disappear from the earth, and that, in the goodness of time, all peoples will come to live together in a peace guaranteed by the binding force of mutual respect and love.

John F. Kennedy

~

SPECIAL MESSAGE TO THE CONGRESS ON THE DEFENSE BUDGET
(1961)

To the Congress of the United States:

In my role as Commander-in-Chief of the American Armed Forces, and with my concern over the security of this nation now and in the future, no single question of policy has concerned me more since entering upon these responsibilities than the adequacy of our present and planned military forces to accomplish our major national security objectives.

In January, while ordering certain immediately needed changes, I instructed the Secretary of Defense to reappraise our entire defense strategy, capacity, commitments and needs in the light of present and future dangers. The Secretary of State and others have been consulted in this reappraisal, and I have myself carefully reviewed their reports and advice.

Such a review is obviously a tremendous task and it still continues. But circumstances do not permit a postponement of all further action during the many additional months that a full reappraisal will require. Consequently we are now able to present the most urgent and obvious recommendations for inclusion in the fiscal 1962 Budget.

Meaningful defense budget decisions, however, are not possible without preliminary decisions on defense policy, reflecting both current strategic assumptions and certain fundamental principles. These basic policies or principles, as stated below, will constitute the essential guidelines and standards to be followed by all civilian and military personnel who work on behalf of our nation's security. The Budget which follows, if enacted by the Congress under its own solemn duty "to provide for the common defense," is designed to implement these assumptions as we now see them, and to chart a fresh, clear course for our security in a time of rising dangers and persistent hope.

I. BASIC DEFENSE POLICIES

1. The primary purpose of our arms is peace, not war—to make certain that they will never have to be used—to deter all wars, general or limited, nuclear or conventional, large or small—to convince all potential aggressors that any attack would be futile—to provide backing for diplomatic settlement of disputes—to insure the adequacy of our bargaining power for an end to the arms race. The basic problems facing the world today are not susceptible to a military solution. Neither our strategy nor our psychology as a nation—and certainly not our economy—must become dependent upon the permanent maintenance of a large military establishment. Our military posture must be sufficiently flexible and under control to be consistent with our efforts to explore all possibilities and to take every step to lessen tensions, to obtain peaceful solutions

and to secure arms limitations. Diplomacy and defense are no longer distinct alternatives, one to be used where the other fails—both must complement each other.

Disarmament, so difficult and so urgent, has been much discussed since 1945, but progress has not been made. Recrimination in such matters is seldom useful, and we for our part are determined to try again. In so doing, we note that, in the public position of both sides in recent years, the determination to be strong has been coupled with announced willingness to negotiate. For our part, we know there can be dialectical truth in such a position, and we shall do all we can to prove it in action. This budget is wholly consistent with our earnest desire for serious conversation with the other side on disarmament. If genuine progress is made, then as tension is reduced, so will be our arms.

2. Our arms will never be used to strike the first blow in any attack. This is not a confession of weakness but a statement of strength. It is our national tradition. We must offset whatever advantage this may appear to hand an aggressor by so increasing the capability of our forces to respond swiftly and effectively to any aggressive move as to convince any would-be aggressor that such a movement would be too futile and costly to undertake. In the area of general war, this doctrine means that such capability must rest with that portion of our forces which would survive the initial attack. We are not creating forces for a first strike against any other nation. We shall never threaten, provoke or initiate aggression—but if aggression should come, our response will be swift and effective.

3. Our arms must be adequate to meet our commitments and ensure our security, without being bound by arbitrary budget ceilings. This nation can afford to

be strong—it cannot afford to be weak. We shall do what is needed to make and to keep us strong. We must, of course, take advantage of every opportunity to reduce military outlays as a result of scientific or managerial progress, new strategic concepts, a more efficient, manageable and thus more effective defense establishment, or international agreements for the control and limitation of arms. But we must not shrink from additional costs where they are necessary. The additional $650 million in expenditures for fiscal 1962 which I am recommending today, while relatively small, are too urgent to be governed by a budget largely decided before our defense review had been completed. Indeed, in the long run the net effect of all the changes I am recommending will be to provide a more economical budget. But I cannot promise that in later years we need not be prepared to spend still more for what is indispensable. Much depends on the course followed by other nations. As a proportion of gross national product, as a share of our total Budget, and in comparison with our national effort in earlier times of war, this increase in Defense expenditures is still substantially below what our citizens have been willing and are now able to support as insurance on their security—insurance we hope is never needed— but insurance we must nevertheless purchase.

4. Our arms must be subject to ultimate civilian control and command at all times, in war as well as peace. The basic decisions on our participation in any conflict and our response to any threat—including all decisions relating to the use of nuclear weapons, or the escalation of a small war into a large one—will be made by the regularly constituted civilian authorities. This requires effective and protected organization, procedures, facilities and communication in the event of attack directed toward this objective, as well as de-

fensive measures designed to insure thoughtful and selective decisions by the civilian authorities. This message and budget also reflect that basic principle. The Secretary of Defense and I have had the earnest counsel of our senior military advisers and many others—and in fact they support the great majority of the decisions reflected in this Budget. But I have not delegated to anyone else the responsibilities for decision which are imposed upon me by the Constitution.

5. Our strategic arms and defenses must be adequate to deter any deliberate nuclear attack on the United States or our allies—by making clear to any potential aggressor that sufficient retaliatory forces will be able to survive a first strike and penetrate his defenses in order to inflict unacceptable losses upon him. As I indicated in an address to the Senate some 31 months ago, this deterrence does not depend upon a simple comparison of missiles on hand before an attack. It has been publicly acknowledged for several years that this nation has not led the world in missile strength. Moreover, we will not strike first in any conflict. But what we have and must continue to have is the ability to survive a first blow and respond with devastating power. This deterrent power depends not only on the number of our missiles and bombers, but on their state of readiness, their ability to survive attack, and the flexibility and sureness with which we can control them to achieve our national purpose and strategic objectives.

6. The strength and deployment of our forces in combination with those of our allies should be sufficiently powerful and mobile to prevent the steady erosion of the Free World through limited wars; and it is this role that should constitute the primary mission of our overseas forces. Non-nuclear wars, and sub-limited or guerrilla warfare, have since 1945 constituted the

most active and constant threat to Free World security. Those units of our forces which are stationed overseas, or designed to fight overseas, can be most usefully oriented toward deterring or confining those conflicts which do not justify and must not lead to a general nuclear attack. In the event of a major aggression that could not be repulsed by conventional forces, we must be prepared to take whatever action with whatever weapons are appropriate. But our objective now is to increase our ability to confine our response to non-nuclear weapons, and to lessen the incentive for any limited aggression by making clear what our response will accomplish. In most areas of the world, the main burden of local defense against overt attack, subversion and guerrilla warfare must rest on local populations and forces. But given the great likelihood and seriousness of this threat, we must be prepared to make a substantial contribution in the form of strong, highly mobile forces trained in this type of warfare, some of which must be deployed in forward areas, with a substantial airlift and sealift capacity and prestocked overseas bases.

7. Our defense posture must be both flexible and determined. Any potential aggressor contemplating an attack on any part of the Free World with any kind of weapons, conventional or nuclear, must know that our response will be suitable, selective, swift and effective. While he may be uncertain of its exact nature and location, there must be no uncertainty about our determination and capacity to take whatever steps are necessary to meet our obligations. We must be able to make deliberate choices in weapons and strategy, shift the tempo of our production and alter the direction of our forces to meet rapidly changing conditions or objectives at very short notice and under any cir-

cumstances. Our weapon systems must be usable in a manner permitting deliberation and discrimination as to timing, scope and targets in response to civilian authority; and our defenses must be secure against prolonged re-attack as well as a surprise first-strike. To purchase productive capacity and to initiate development programs that may never need to be used—as this Budget proposes—adopts an insurance policy of buying alternative future options.

8. Our defense posture must be designed to reduce the danger of irrational or unpremeditated general war—the danger of an unnecessary escalation of a small war into a large one, or of miscalculation or misinterpretation of an incident or enemy intention. Our diplomatic efforts to reach agreements on the prevention of surprise attack, an end to the spread of nuclear weapons—indeed all our efforts to end the arms race—are aimed at this objective. We shall strive for improved communication among all nations, to make clear our own intentions and resolution, and to prevent any nation from underestimating the response of any other, as has too often happened in the past. In addition our own military activities must be safeguarded against the possibility of inadvertent triggering incidents. But even more importantly, we must make certain that our retaliatory power does not rest on decisions made in ambiguous circumstances, or permit a catastrophic mistake.

It would not be appropriate at this time or in this message to either boast of our strength or dwell upon our needs and dangers. It is sufficient to say that the budgetary recommendations which follow, together with other policy, organizational and related changes and studies now underway administratively, are designed to provide for an increased strength, flexibility and control in our defense establishment in accordance with the above policies.

II. STRENGTHENING AND PROTECTING OUR STRATEGIC DETERRENT AND DEFENSES

A. *Improving our missile deterrent.* As a power which will never strike first, our hopes for anything close to an absolute deterrent must rest on weapons which come from hidden, moving, or invulnerable bases which will not be wiped out by a surprise attack. A retaliatory capacity based on adequate numbers of these weapons would deter any aggressor from launching or even threatening an attack—an attack he knew could not find or destroy enough of our force to prevent his own destruction.

1. *Polaris*—the ability of the nuclear-powered Polaris submarine to operate deep below the surface of the seas for long periods and to launch its ballistic, solid-fuel nuclear-armed missiles while submerged gives this weapons system a very high degree of mobility and concealment, making it virtually immune to ballistic missile attack.

In the light of the high degree of success attained to date in its development, production and operation, I strongly recommend that the Polaris program be greatly expanded and accelerated. I have earlier directed the Department of Defense, as stated in my State of the Union Message, to increase the fiscal year 1961 program from 5 submarine starts to 10, and to accelerate the delivery of these and other Polaris submarines still under construction. This action will provide 5 more operational submarines about nine months earlier than previously planned.

For fiscal year 1962, I recommend the construction of 10 more Polaris submarines, making a total of 29, plus one additional tender. These 10 submarines, together with the 10 programmed for fiscal year 1961, are scheduled to be delivered at the rate of one a month or twelve a year, beginning in June 1963, compared with the previous rate of 5 a year. Under this schedule, a force of 29 Polaris submarines can be completed and at sea two months before the present program which called for 19 boats, and two years earlier than would be possible under the old 5-a-year rate. These 29 submarines, each with a full complement of missiles, will be a formidable deterrent force. The sooner they are on station, the safer we will be. And our emphasis upon a weapon distinguished primarily for its invulnerability is another demonstration of the fact that our posture as a nation is defensive and not aggressive.

I also recommend that the development of the long-range Polaris A–3 be accelerated in order to become available a year earlier at an eventual savings in the procurement of the A–2 system.

This longer range missile with improved penetration capability will greatly enhance the operational flexibility of the Polaris force and reduce its exposure to shore-based antisubmarine warfare measures. Finally, we must increase the allowance of Polaris missiles for practice firing to provide systematic "proving ground" data for determining and improving operational reliability.

The increases in this program, including $15 million in new obligational authority for additional crews, constitute the bulk of the budget increases—$1.34 billion in new obligational authority on a full funded basis, over a 4-year period though only $270 million in expenditures in fiscal 1962. I consider this a wise investment in our future.

2. *Minuteman*—another strategic missile system which will play a major role in our deterrent force, with a high degree of survivability under ballistic missile attack, is the solid-fuel Minuteman. This system is planned to be deployed in well-dispersed, hardened sites and, eventually, in a mobile mode on railroad cars. On the basis of the success of tests conducted to date and the importance of this system to our overall strategy, I recommend the following steps:

(1) Certain design changes to improve the reliability, guidance accuracy, range and re-entry of this missile should be incorporated earlier than previously planned, by additional funding for research and development.

(2) A more generous allotment of missiles for practice firing should, as in the case of the Polaris, be provided to furnish more operational data sooner.

(3) The three mobile Minuteman squadrons funded in the January budget should be deferred for the time being and replaced by three more fixed-base squadrons (thus increasing the total number of missiles added by some two-thirds). Development work on the mobile version will continue.

(4) Minuteman capacity production should be doubled to enable us to move to still higher levels of strength more swiftly should future conditions warrant doubling our production. There are great uncertainties as to the future capabilities of others; as to the ultimate outcome of struggles now going on in many of the world's trouble spots; and as to future technological breakthroughs either by us or any other nation. In view of these major uncertainties, it is essential that,

here again, we adopt an insurance philosophy and hedge our risks by buying options on alternative courses of action. We can reduce lead-time by providing, *now*, additional standby production capacity that may never need to be used, or used only in part, and by constructing additional bases which events may prove could safely have been postponed to the next fiscal year. But that option is well worth the added cost.

Together, these recommendations for Minuteman will require the addition of $96 million in new obligational authority to the January budget estimate.

3. *Skybolt*—another type of missile less likely to be completely eliminated by enemy attack is the air-to-ground missile carried by a plane that can be off the ground before an attack commences. Skybolt is a long-range (1000 mile) air-launched, solid-fuel nuclear-warhead ballistic missile designed to be carried by the B–52 and the British V bombers. Its successful development and production may extend the useful life of our bombers into the missile age—and its range is far superior to the present Hound Dog missiles.

I recommend that an additional $50 million in new obligational authority be added to the 1962 budget to enable this program to go forward at an orderly rate.

B. *Protecting our bomber deterrent.* The considerably more rapid growth projected for our ballistic missile force does not eliminate the need for manned bombers—although no funds were included in the January budget for the further procurement of B–52 heavy bombers and B–58 medium bombers, and I do not propose any. Our existing bomber forces constitute our chief hope for deterring attack during this period prior to the completion of our missile expansion. However, only those planes that would not be destroyed on the ground in the event of a surprise attack striking their base can be considered sufficiently invulnerable to deter an aggressor.

I therefore recommend the following steps to protect our bomber deterrent:

1. *Airborne alert capacity.* That portion of our force which is constantly in the air is clearly the least vulnerable portion. I am asking for the funds to continue the present level of indoctrination training flights, and to complete the stand-by capacity and materials needed to place one-eighth of our entire heavy bomber force on airborne alert at any time. I also strongly urge the re-enactment of Section 512(b) of the Department of Defense Appropriation Act for 1961, which authorizes the Secretary of Defense, if the President determines it is necessary, to provide for the cost of a full airborne alert as a deficiency expense approved by the Congress.

2. *Increased ground alert force and bomb alarms.* Strategic bombers standing by on a ground alert of 15 minutes can also have a high degree of survivability provided adequate and timely warning is available. I therefore recommended that the proportion of our B–52 and B–47 forces on ground alert should be increased until about half of our total force is on alert. In addition, bomb alarm detectors and bomb alarm signals should be installed at key warning and communication points and all SAC bases, to make certain that a dependable notification of any surprise attack cannot be eliminated. $45 million in new obligational authority will pay for all of these measures.

C. *Improving our continental defense and warning systems.* Because of the speed and destructiveness of the intercontinental ballistic missile and the secrecy with which it can be launched, timely warning of any potential attack is of crucial importance not only for preserving our population but also for preserving a sufficient portion of our military forces—thus deterring such an attack before it is launched. For any attacker knows that every additional minute gained means that a larger part of our retaliatory force can be launched before it can be destroyed on the ground. We must assure ourselves, therefore, that every feasible action is being taken to provide such warning.

To supplement the Ballistic Missile Early Warning System (BMEWS), on which construction is now proceeding as fast as is practical, the satellite-borne Midas system, now under development, is designed to provide about 30 minutes of warning by detecting missiles immediately after launching. Together with BMEWS, Midas would greatly increase the assurance and reliability of timely warning. I recommend that an additional $60 million in new obligational authority be added to the 1962 budget to accelerate completion of the development phase of the Midas program, with the goal of achieving an operational system at an earlier date.

For the next several years at least, however, we shall have to continue to provide a defense against manned bomber attack. Such an attack is most likely to coincide with, or follow, a ballistic missile attack seeking to incapacitate our anti-bomber defense system. Measures must therefore be taken to enhance the ability of the air defense system to cope with a combined attack. I recommend $23 million in new obligational authority be added to the 1962 budget for this purpose.

D. *Improving the command and control of our strategic deterrent.* The basic policies stated at the beginning of this message lay new emphasis on improved command and control—more flexible, more selective, more deliberate, better protected and under ultimate

civilian authority at all times. This requires not only
the development and installation of new equipment
and facilities, but, even more importantly, increased
attention to all organizational and procedural arrange-
ments for the President and others. The invulnerable
and continuous command posts and communications
centers provided in these recommendations (requiring
an additional $16 million in new obligational author-
ity) are only the beginning of a major but absolutely
vital effort to achieve a truly unified, nationwide, indestructible system to insure high-level command, communication and control and a properly authorized
response under any conditions.

E. There are a number of other space and research
programs related to our strategic and continental air
defense forces which I find require additional support.
These include missile defense and penetration aids,
Dynasoar, Advent, Defender, Discoverer and certain
other programs. An additional $226 million in new
obligational authority is requested to finance them.

III. STRENGTHENING OUR ABILITY
TO DETER OR CONFINE LIMITED
WARS

The Free World's security can be endangered not
only by a nuclear attack, but also by being slowly nib-
bled away at the periphery, regardless of our strategic
power, by forces of subversion, infiltration, intimida-
tion, indirect or non-overt aggression, internal revolution, diplomatic blackmail, guerrilla warfare or a series
of limited wars.

In this area of local wars, we must inevitably count

on the cooperative efforts of other peoples and nations who share our concern. Indeed, their interests are more often directly engaged in such conflicts. The self-reliant are also those whom it is easiest to help—and for these reasons we must continue and reshape the Military Assistance Program which I have discussed earlier in my special message on foreign aid.

But to meet our own extensive commitments and needed improvements in conventional forces, I recommend the following:

A. *Strengthened capacity to meet limited and guerrilla warfare*—limited military adventures and threats to the security of the Free World that are not large enough to justify the label of "limited war." We need a greater ability to deal with guerrilla forces, insurrections, and subversion. Much of our effort to create guerrilla and antiguerrilla capabilities has in the past been aimed at general war. We must be ready now to deal with any size of force, including small externally supported bands of men; and we must help train local forces to be equally effective.

B. *Expanded research on non-nuclear weapons.* A few selected high priority areas—strategic systems, air defense and space—have received the overwhelming proportion of our defense research effort. Yet, technology promises great improvements in non-nuclear armaments as well; and it is important that we be in the forefront of these developments. What is needed are entirely new types of non-nuclear weapons and equipment—with increased fire-power, mobility and communications, and more suited to the kind of tasks our limited war forces will most likely be required to perform. I include here anti-submarine warfare as well as land and air operations. I recommend, therefore, an additional $122 million in new obligational authority to speed up current limited warfare research and development programs and to provide for the initiation of entirely new programs.

C. *Increased flexibility of conventional forces.* Our capacity to move forces in sizable numbers on short notice and to be able to support them in one or more crisis areas could avoid the need for a much larger commitment later. Following my earlier direction, the Secretary of Defense has taken steps both to accelerate and increase the production of airlift aircraft. A total of 129 new, longer range, modern airlift aircraft will be procured through fiscal year 1962, compared with the 50 previously programmed. An additional $172 million in new obligational authority will be required in the 1962 budget to finance this expanded program.

These additional aircraft will help to meet our airlift requirements until the new specially designed, long-range, jet powered C–141 transport becomes available. A contractor for this program has been selected and active development work will soon be started. Adequate funds are already included in the January budget to finance this program through the coming fiscal year.

I am also recommending in this message $40 million in new obligational authority for the construction of an additional amphibious transport of a new type, increasing both the speed and the capability of Marine Corps sealift capacity; and $84 million in new obligational authority for an increase in the Navy's ship rehabilitation and modernization program, making possible an increase in the number of ship overhauls (as well as a higher level of naval aircraft maintenance).

But additional transport is not enough for quick flexibility. I am recommending $230 million in new obligational authority for increased procurement of such items as helicopters, rifles, modern non-nuclear weapons, electronics and communications equipment, improved ammunition for artillery and infantry weapons, and torpedoes. Some important new advances in ammunition and bombs can make a sizeable qualitative jump in our limited war capabilities.

D. *Increased non-nuclear capacities of fighter aircraft.* Manned aircraft will be needed even during the 1965–75 missile era for various limited war missions. Target recognition, destruction of all types of targets when extreme accuracy is required, and the control of air space over enemy territory will all continue to be tasks best performed by manned aircraft.

Expected phase-out of Navy and Air Force fighters by 1965, together with reduced numbers and increasing obsolescence of the remaining aircraft, make necessary the development of an advanced tactical fighter emphasizing non-nuclear capabilities. I am requesting $45 million in new obligational authority for this purpose.

Meanwhile, I am recommending $25 million in new obligational authority for the modification of the F-105 tactical fighter to improve its capability to handle conventionally armed ordnance items, and to increase its suitability for airstrips of all types of areas.

E. *Increased personnel, training and readiness for conventional forces.* I am recommending $39 million in new obligational authority for increases in Army personnel strength to expand guerrilla warfare units and round out other existing units, and an increase in the Marine Corps to bring it up closer to authorized strength levels. (In addition, personnel is being added to the Navy for Polaris crews, and to the Air Force for the ground alert expansion.) The sum of these personnel additions is 13,000 men. I am also recommending $25 million additional in new obligational authority for pay of retired personnel of the military forces.

But more personnel alone is not enough. I am recommending an additional $65 million in new obligational authority for increased readiness training of Army and Air Force units. These funds will provide for additional field training and mobility exercises for the Army and test exercises for the composite air strike forces and MATS unit. We recognize the role of exercises and deployments in demonstrating to our friends and opponents our ability to deploy forces rapidly in a crisis.

IV. SAVINGS MADE POSSIBLE BY PROGRESS

The elimination of waste, duplication and outmoded or unjustifiable expenditure items from the Defense Budget is a long and arduous undertaking, resisted by special arguments and interests from economic, military, technical and other special groups. There are hundreds of ways, most of them with some merit, for spending billions of dollars on defense; and it is understandable that every critic of this Budget will have a strong preference for economy on some expenditures other than those that affect his branch of the service, or his plant, or his community.

But hard decisions must be made. Unneeded facilities or projects must be phased out. The defense establishment must be lean and fit, efficient and effective, always adjusting to new opportunities and advances, and planning for the future. The national interest must be weighed against special or local interests; and it is the national interest that calls upon us to cut our losses and cut back those programs in which a very dim promise no longer justifies a very large cost.

Specifically:

1. Our decision to acquire a very substantial increase in second-generation solid-fuel missiles of increased invulnerability (Polaris and Minuteman) enables us to eliminate safely the last two squadrons of Titan originally contemplated. These would not have become operational until 1964, and at a cost of $270 million—a cost several times that of the Minuteman missiles we are purchasing for the same period and could increase with our stand-by facility. $100 million in the 1962 budget can be saved by this adjustment.

2. The phase-out of a number of B-47 medium bomber wings already planned will be accelerated to provide promptly the trained crews required for the expanded round alert program. (Fiscal 1962 savings: $35 million.)

3. Additional personnel will also be made available by the immediate phase-out of the subsonic Snark air-breathing long-range missile, which is now considered obsolete and of marginal military value in view of ICBM developments, the Snark's low reliability and penetrability, the lack of positive control over its launchings, and the location of the entire wing at an unprotected site. (Fiscal 1962 savings: $7 million.)

4. The acquired missile capability programmed by this message also makes unnecessary and economically unjustifiable the development of the B-70 Mach 3 manned bomber as a full weapons system at this time. The B-70 would not become available in operational numbers until well beyond 1965. By that time we expect to have a large number of intercontinental ballistic missiles, fully tested and in place, as well as a substantial manned bomber force mostly equipped

with air-to-ground missiles. In view of the extremely high cost of the B-70 system, its lesser survivability as a ground-based system and its greater vulnerability in the air compared to missiles, its capabilities as a second strike system do not appear to have sufficient advantages over a much less expensive missile, or even a B-52 or successor bomber equipped with Skybolt, to justify a request in fiscal 1962 for $358 million.

We recognize, however, that there are still uncertainties with respect to the operational characteristics of our planned missile force. We also recognize that there are certain advantages inherent in a controlled force of manned bombers. To preserve the option of developing this manned bomber weapon system, if we should later determine such a system is required, I recommend that the B-70 program be carried forward essentially to explore the problems of flying at three times the speed of sound with an airframe potentially useful as a bomber, with the development of a small number of prototype aircraft and related bomb-navigation systems. We should also explore the possibility of developing a manned bomber system specifically designed to operate in an environment in which both sides have large ICBM forces.

Even on this more limited basis, the B-70 project will cost $1.3 billion before it is completed in 1967. Approximately $800 million has already been provided, $220 million is now requested for 1962—$138 million less than the amount included in the January budget—and the balance will be required in subsequent years. The total development program which I am recommending will cost $1.4 billion less than that previously planned.

5. Nearly fifteen years and about $1 billion have been devoted to the attempted development of a nuclear-powered aircraft; but the possibility of achiev-

ing a militarily useful aircraft in the foreseeable future is still very remote. The January budget already recommended a severe curtailment of this project, cutting the level of effort in half by limiting the scope to only one of the two different engines under development, although not indicating which one. We believe the time has come to reach a clean-cut decision in this matter. Transferring the entire subject matter to the Atomic Energy Commission budget where it belongs, as a non-defense research item, we propose to terminate development effort on both approaches on the nuclear powerplant, comprising reactor and engine, and on the airframe; but to carry forward scientific research and development in the fields of high temperature materials and high performance reactors, which is related to AEC's broad objectives in atomic reactor development including some work at the present plants, making use of their scientific teams. This will save an additional $35 million in the Defense budget for fiscal 1962 below the figure previously reduced in January, and will avoid a future expenditure of at least $1 billion, which would have been necessary to achieve first experimental flight.

6. The January budget did not include funds for the continued development of the Navy's "Missileer" fleet defense aircraft, but funds were included for the continued development of the Eagle missile—designed for use by the Missileer—in the hope that it could be adapted for use by some other aircraft. I am now advised that no such alternative use is in prospect; and I have directed the cancellation of that project, with a saving estimated at almost $57 million in 1961 and 1962.

7. The plan to install Polaris missiles on the Cruiser *Long Beach* has been canceled. For effectiveness in a nuclear war, the money would be better spent on the

far less vulnerable Polaris submarines. In a limited war, the cruiser's utility would be reduced by the presence of the missiles. (Savings in fiscal 1962: $58 million.)

8. Finally, technological progress causes obsolescence not only in military hardware but also in the facilities constructed for their deployment. We must continually review our nearly 7,000 military installations in the light of our needs now and in the event of emergency. Those bases and installations which are no longer required must be inactivated, and disposed of where feasible, and I have so directed the Secretary of Defense. He has already taken steps to have 73 domestic and foreign installations discontinued as excess to our needs now and at any time in the future; and studies are continuing now to identify additional facilities which are surplus to our requirements.

I am well aware that in many cases these actions will cause hardships to the communities and individuals involved. We cannot permit these actions to be deferred; but the Government will make every practicable effort to alleviate these hardships, and I have directed the Secretary of Defense to take every possible step to ease the difficulties for those displaced. But it is difficult, with so many defense and other budgetary demands, to justify support of military installations, with high operating and payroll costs and property values, which are no longer required for the defense of the nation. The closing of excess installations overseas will in many cases help alleviate our balance of payments deficit.

No net savings are expected to be realized in 1962 from these inactivations because of the added costs involved in closing, and no reductions in the 1962 budget are proposed on that account. Substantial savings, approximately $220 million per year, will be realized, however, in subsequent years.

(I am also proposing that $320 million of the obligational authority required be provided by transfer from the current balances of working capital funds in the Defense Department.)

CONCLUSION

Our military position today is strong. But positive action must be taken now if we are to have the kind of forces we will need for our security in the future. Our preparation against danger is our hope of safety. The changes in the Defense program which I have recommended will greatly enhance the security of this Nation in the perilous years which lie ahead. It is not pleasant to request additional funds at this time for national security. Our interest, as I have emphasized, lies in peaceful solutions, in reducing tension, in settling disputes at the conference table and not on the battlefield. I am hopeful that these policies will help secure these ends. I commend them to the Congress and to the Nation.

Biographies

Abigail Adams (1744–1818): With candid charm, her collections of lively letters paint a portrait of Colonial life as well as the political climate of the times. Adams was the wife of President John Adams and the mother of President John Quincy Adams.

Erma Bombeck (1927–96): An outstanding humorist of hearth and home, Bombeck was the author of twelve bestselling books and a syndicated column that appeared in more than nine hundred newspapers. She targeted marriage and family with delightful humorous accuracy.

Sandra Cisneros (1954–): Cisneros has been a teacher at every level, including visiting writer at universities throughout the country. Her fiction and poetry have won numerous awards and have been translated into over a dozen languages. Her books include *The House on Mango Street* and *Caramelo*.

Hillary Rodham Clinton (1947–): A graduate of Wellesley College and Yale Law School, Clinton is a U.S. Senator from New York. She is the author of *It*

Takes a Village (1996), which advocates children's rights, and *Living History* (2003). Clinton is the wife of former President Bill Clinton.

William Edward Burghardt (W.E.B.) Du Bois (1868–1963): Du Bois spent his life writing about and supporting the black struggle in the United States. He was the first black man to receive a Ph.D. from Harvard University. An educator and author, his writings include the classic *The Souls of Black Folk*.

Albert Einstein (1879–1955): Winner of the Nobel Prize for Physics, Einstein came to the United States from Germany in 1933 and joined the faculty of Princeton University. He garnered worldwide fame for his theory of relativity.

Dwight D. Eisenhower (1890–1969): A West Point graduate, Eisenhower rose in rank to become the supreme commander of allied forces in Europe during World War II. Following the war, he became president of Columbia University. In 1952, he was elected U.S. president on the Republican ticket and served two terms.

Ralph Waldo Emerson (1803–82): Poet, preacher, and essayist, Emerson was born and raised in Massachusetts. He gave up the ministry to devote himself to writing and gained worldwide fame as the central figure of the Transcendentalist Movement.

Leonard Everett Fisher (1924–   ): Fisher is a World War II veteran and graduate of Yale. He has written and illustrated more than four hundred award-winning books of fiction and nonfiction for children and young adults.

Benjamin Franklin (1706–90): American writer, states-man, scientist, and philosopher, Franklin is generally regarded as the first American literary humorist. His writings include letters, journals, satire, and essays.

Abraham Joshua Heschel (1907–72): One of the fore-most Jewish philosophers of the twentieth century, Heschel was born in Poland and came to the United States in 1940, eventually joining the faculty of the Jewish Theological Seminary—the center for Conser-vative Judaism—serving as professor of Ethics and Mysticism. A civil rights activist, he marched with Reverend Martin Luther King, Jr., in Selma, Alabama. Rabbi Heschel's writings have been described as elo-quent, poetic, and profound. His many books include *Man's Quest for God, God in Search of Man, The Sabbath,* and *Man Is Not Alone.*

John F. Kennedy (1917–63): Kennedy was born into a prominent political Massachusetts family. He served in the U.S. Congress and Senate and was elected presi-dent in 1960. In 1957 his book *Profiles in Courage* won the Pulitzer Prize for biography. He was assassinated in 1963.

Martin Luther King, Jr. (1929–68): King was a promi-nent minister and a leader of the civil rights move-ment. Through his preaching, writing, and action, he devoted his life to nonviolent civil disobedience. He was awarded the 1964 Nobel Peace Prize. King was assassinated in Memphis in 1968.

Judith Krug: Executive director of the Office for Intel-lectual Freedom of the American Library Association, Krug has been in the forefront of the fight against censorship in the United States.

Richard Lederer (1938–): Lederer has written more than three thousand articles and books about language and humor, and his syndicated column, "Looking at Language," appears in newspapers and magazines across the United States. He defines himself as a verbivore.

Abraham Lincoln (1809–65): Born in poverty in Kentucky, Lincoln struggled to educate himself, became a lawyer, and eventually was elected to two terms as U.S. president, never losing his common-man aura. His presidency was consumed by the Civil War. Five days after the war ended, Lincoln was assassinated.

Cotton Mather (1663–1728): Mather was a preacher and scholar who helped found Yale University. His extensive writings include *Magnalia Christi Americana,* a religious history of the Colonies, and the seven-volume *Diary*. He had a great interest in science, and was the first native-born American to be elected to the Royal Society of London.

Lance Morrow (1939–): Award-winning *Time* magazine essayist Lance Morrow graduated from Harvard University in 1963. He has authored seven books, including two essay collections, and is the winner of two National Magazine Awards.

Neal Osherow (1955–): Neal Osherow received his master's in social psychology from the University of California, Santa Cruz, and his law degree from Boalt Hall School of Law at the University of California, Berkeley. He has worked for more than a decade as a deputy public defender for Los Angeles County.

Katherine Paterson (1932–): Paterson is a prolific and highly regarded children's and young adult author. She has received virtually every prestigious award for her many books, including the Hans Christian Andersen Award presented by the International Board on Books for Youth.

Sam Pickering (1941–): Pickering has published numerous articles of literary criticism and is famous for his collections of humorous essays. He has taught at the University of Connecticut since 1978.

George Plimpton (1927–2003): Perhaps Plimpton's most notable contribution to the literary world is the highly regarded *Paris Review,* which he cofounded in 1953. Among his many books are accounts of his experiences as an amateur playing at various professions and collections of interviews with prominent authors.

Anna Quindlen (1953–): Quindlen has been a columnist for *Newsweek* and *The New York Times* and won the Pulitzer Prize for commentary in 1992. She is the author of four bestselling novels, including *Being Perfect,* and numerous works of nonfiction.

Franklin Delano Roosevelt (1882–1945): Roosevelt served two terms as governor of New York before being elected president in 1932. He served an unprecedented twelve years before dying early in his fourth term.

Gloria Steinem (1934–): A feminist writer and activist, Steinem founded the National Women's Political Caucus. In 1968 she was a cofounder of *New York* magazine, and in 1972, she launched *MS* magazine.

Steinem has also authored several books, including *Outrageous Acts and Everyday Rebellions* and *Revolution from Within*.

Henry David Thoreau (1817–62): Thoreau was a naturalist, writer, and philosopher whose most famous book, *Walden,* describes his two years living alone in a cabin at Walden Pond. He also wrote many travelogues and political pamphlets, including the widely influential "Civil Disobedience."

Mark Twain (Samuel Clemens) (1835–1910): Twain expertly employed American homespun humor to sophisticated effect in such novels as *Adventures of Huckleberry Finn*. He also wrote numerous short stories, travel reports, and essays, and was an accomplished journalist and lecturer.

Eudora Welty (1909–2001): A versatile writer, Welty created novels, essays, and literary criticism; but mostly she wrote short stories, many set in her native Mississippi. Her novel *The Optimist's Daughter* won the 1973 Pulitzer Prize.

AMERICAN CLASSICS

SPOON RIVER ANTHOLOGY *by Edgar Lee Masters*
with an Introduction by John Hollander
and a new Afterword by Ronald Primeau
A book of dramatic monologues written in free verse about a fictional town
called Spoon River, based on the Midwestern towns where Edgar Lee
Masters grew up.

SELECTED WRITINGS OF
RALPH WALDO EMERSON
with an Introduction by Charles Johnson
Fourteen essays and addresses including *The Oversoul, Politics, Thoreau,
Divinity School Address,* as well as poems *Threnody* and *Uriel,* and
selections from his letters and journals. Includes Chronology
and Bibliography.

EVANGELINE & Selected Tales and Poems
by Henry Wadsworth Longfellow
Edited by Horace Gregory, with a new introduction by Edward Cifelli
Includes *The Witnesses, The Courtship of Miles Standish,* and selections
from *Hiawatha,* with commentaries on Longfellow by Van Wyck Brooks,
Norman Holmes Pearson, and Lewis Carroll. Includes Introduction,
Bibliography, and Chronology.

WALDEN AND CIVIL DISOBEDIENCE
by Henry David Thoreau
150th Anniversary Edition
Two classic examinations of individuality in relation to nature,
society, and government. *Walden* conveys at once a naturalist's
wonder at the commonplace and a Transcendentalist's yearning for spiritual
truth. "Civil Disobedience," perhaps the most famous essay in American
literature, has inspired activists like Martin Luther King, Jr. and Gandhi.

**Available wherever books are sold or at
signetclassics.com**

SIGNET CLASSICS

WRITINGS FROM THE AMERICAN BODY POLITIC

THE FEDERALIST PAPERS
Alexander Hamilton, James Madison & John Jay

Edited by Clinton Rossiter, with an introduction and notes
by Charles R. Kesler

These are some of the most fundamental writings of the American political landscape. Here are the thoughts of the architects of the strong, united government that we have today. This collection contains all eighty-five papers from the edition first published in 1788. It also includes the complete *Constitution*, with marginal notes for relevant passages of the text.

THE ANTI-FEDERALIST PAPERS
& the Constitutional Convention Debates
Edited by Ralph Ketcham

While the Federalists supported a strong central government, the Anti-Federalists saw this as a threat to personal freedom and the liberties so hard-won from England. This split, between the desire for local control and the idea of a centralized power, is one of the major causes of the Civil War.

THE CONSTITUTION OF THE UNITED STATES
An Introduction
Floyd G. Cullop

The *Constitution* is among the world's most remarkable political documents. Yet, far too few Americans know anything about it. This book, which clearly explains our *Constitution*, is a "must" for every American.

Available wherever books are sold or at
signetclassics.com

READ THE TOP 20
SIGNET CLASSICS

1984 BY GEORGE ORWELL

ANIMAL FARM BY GEORGE ORWELL

FRANKENSTEIN BY MARY SHELLEY

THE INFERNO BY DANTE

BEOWULF (BURTON RAFFEL, TRANSLATOR)

HAMLET BY WILLIAM SHAKESPEARE

HEART OF DARKNESS & THE SECRET SHARER
BY JOSEPH CONRAD

NARRATIVE OF THE LIFE OF FREDERICK DOUGLASS
BY FREDERICK DOUGLASS

THE SCARLET LETTER BY NATHANIEL HAWTHORNE

NECTAR IN A SIEVE BY KAMALA MARKANDAYA

A TALE OF TWO CITIES BY CHARLES DICKENS

ALICE'S ADVENTURES IN WONDERLAND &
THROUGH THE LOOKING GLASS BY LEWIS CARROLL

ROMEO AND JULIET BY WILLIAM SHAKESPEARE

ETHAN FROME BY EDITH WHARTON

A MIDSUMMER NIGHT'S DREAM BY WILLIAM SHAKESPEARE

MACBETH BY WILLIAM SHAKESPEARE

OTHELLO BY WILLIAM SHAKESPEARE

THE ADVENTURES OF HUCKLEBERRY FINN BY MARK TWAIN

ONE DAY IN THE LIFE OF IVAN DENISOVICH
BY ALEXANDER SOLZHENITSYN

JANE EYRE BY CHARLOTTE BRONTË